MW01221927

Texada Tapestry
A History

Texada Tapestry
A History

Heather Harbord

Harbour Publishing

1 2 3 4 5 — 15 14 13 12 11

Harbour Publishing Co. Ltd.
P.O. Box 219, Madeira Park, BC, V0N 2H0
www.harbourpublishing.com

Edited by Betty Keller
Cover design by Teresa Karbashewski
Text design by Li Eng-Lodge, Electra Design Group
Map by Roger Handling, Terra Firma Digital Arts
Printed on Forest Stewardship Council-certified paper using soy-based ink
Printed and bound in Canada
Additional photo credits: Page 15, Davie Bay, Heather Harbord photo.
Page 137, James Raper's daughters and their families at Gillies Bay, courtesy Gary McLeod.

Harbour Publishing acknowledges financial support from the Government of Canada through the Canada Book Fund and the Canada Council for the Arts, and from the Province of British Columbia through the BC Arts Council and the Book Publishing Tax Credit.

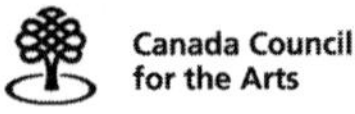

Library and Archives Canada Cataloguing in Publication

Harbord, Heather, 1939-
Texada tapestry : a history / Heather Harbord.

Includes bibliographical references and index.
ISBN 978-1-55017-537-0

1. Texada Island (B.C.)—History. I. Title.

FC3845.T54H37 2011 971.1'31 C2011-904620-2

Contents

Acknowledgements

This book is dedicated to archivist Doug Paton, Pete Stiles and the Texada Island Heritage Society, and also to the residents of Texada Island past and present, and their descendants. Without their considerable and willing help, it would not exist.

Thanks are also due to my editor, Betty Keller, who did a sterling job of refining the abundance of material, and to the staff at Harbour Publishing, who designed the layout and planned the marketing and distribution.

Thanks to Teedee Gentile at the Powell River Archives, staff at the BC Archives, UBC Special Collections, the Vancouver Public Library, Powell River Regional District, and Jean Barman, Jayne Mortenson and Laura Sisk. Unless otherwise noted, all illustrations are supplied by the Texada Island Heritage Society.

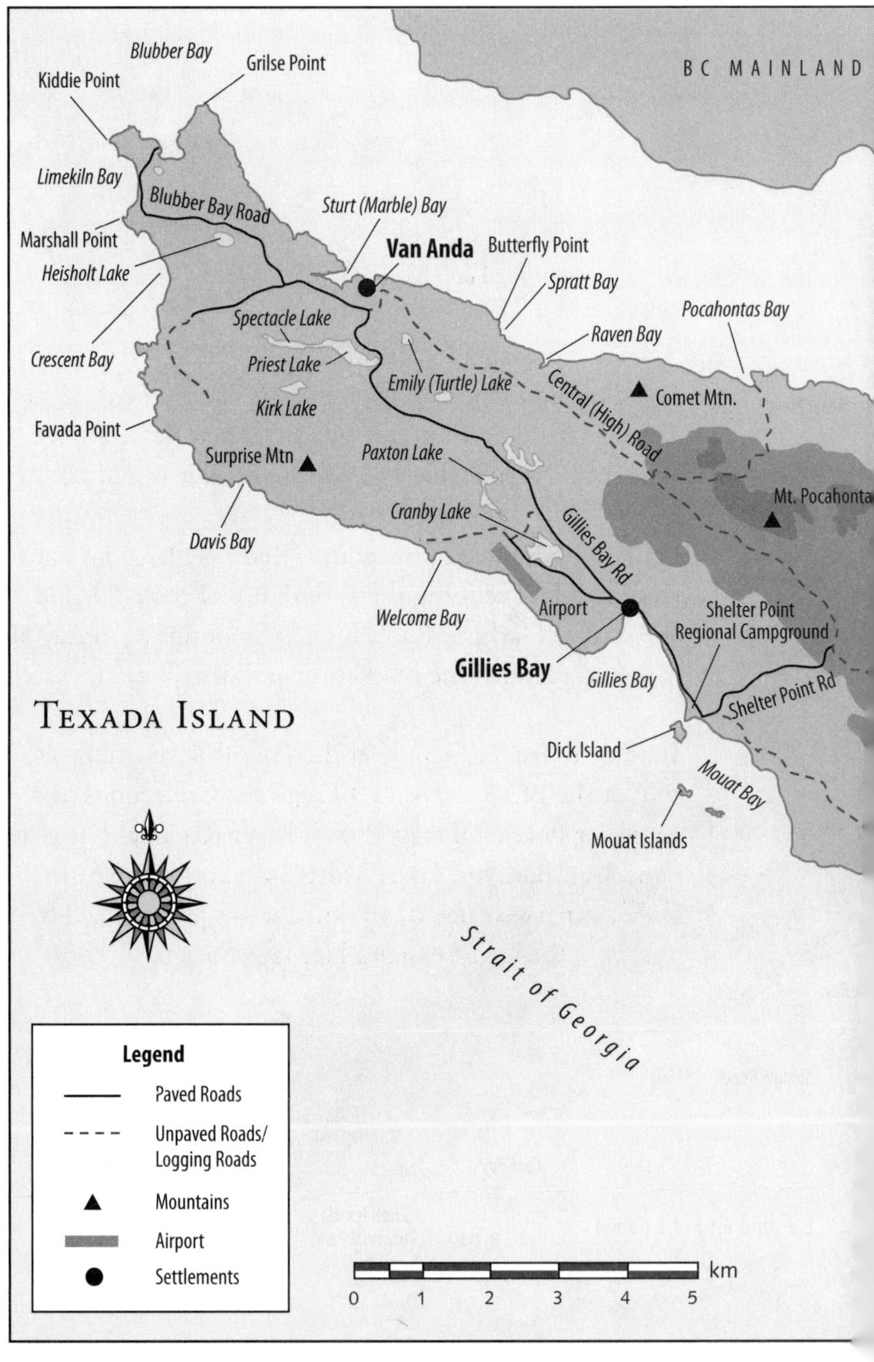
BC MAINLAND
Blubber Bay
Grilse Point
Kiddie Point
Limekiln Bay
Blubber Bay Road
Sturt (Marble) Bay
Marshall Point
Van Anda
Butterfly Point
Heisholt Lake
Spratt Bay
Pocahontas Bay
Spectacle Lake
Raven Bay
Crescent Bay
Priest Lake
Emily (Turtle) Lake
Central (High) Road
Comet Mtn.
Kirk Lake
Favada Point
Surprise Mtn
Paxton Lake
Mt. Pocahonta
Cranby Lake
Gillies Bay Rd
Davis Bay
Airport
Shelter Point
Regional Campground
Welcome Bay
Gillies Bay
Gillies Bay
Shelter Point Rd
Texada Island
Dick Island
Mouat Bay
Mouat Islands
Strait of Georgia
Legend
Paved Roads
Unpaved Roads/
Logging Roads
Mountains
Airport
Settlements
km
0
1
2
3
4
5

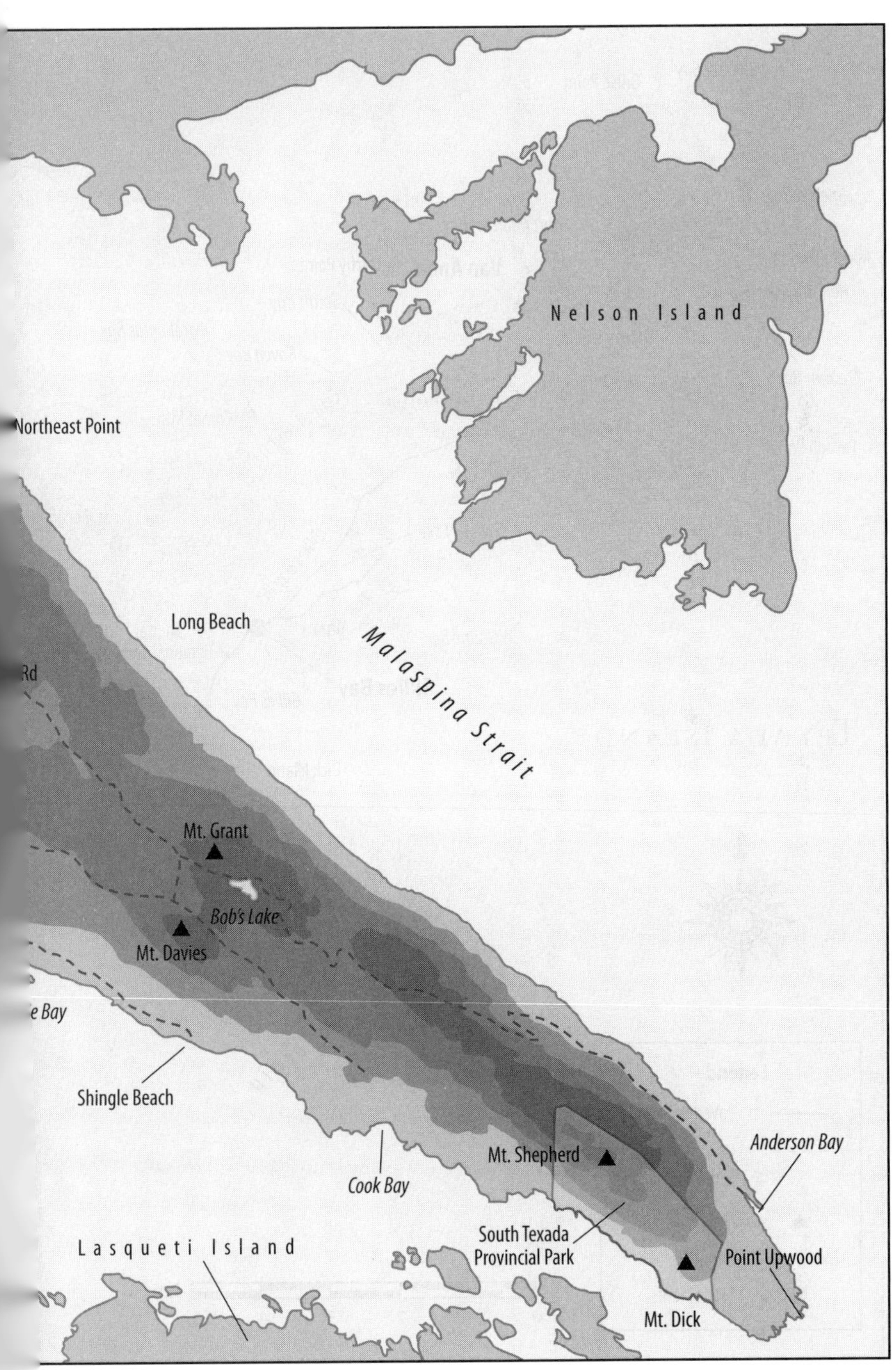

Nelson Island
Northeast Point
Long Beach
Malaspina Strait
Rd
Mt. Grant
Bob's Lake
Mt. Davies
e Bay
Shingle Beach
Mt. Shepherd
Anderson Bay
Cook Bay
South Texada
Provincial Park
Lasqueti Island
Point Upwood
Mt. Dick

Introduction

HAVING DEDICATED MY LAST BOOK, *Desolation Sound*, to Maria Zaikow, it seemed a logical progression to examine the history of the island where she spent most of her adult life. Although I have never lived on Texada, for the last twenty years I have seen it every day, as my Powell River house overlooks its rocky shores. I keep my forsythia bushes trimmed so that the neighbour behind me can glimpse the island of his childhood. Many former islanders live in Powell River.

In 2002 I spent a delightful week kayaking around Texada, photographing every headland and greeting every seal.

Having looked after the second-largest geological library in London, England, I was also interested in Texada's mining history, especially as I once wrote an article on the iron mines of nearby Lund on the mainland, which involve the same kind of granodiorite rocks.

One of the many sources of information for this book was R.G. McConnell's *Geological Survey Memoir*, researched in 1908, and this proved to be a treasure trove of information on the geology and mines of the island. Much of McConnell's information came from pioneer prospector James Raper, whose granddaughter, Violet Seaman, was one of the first people to record the history of Texada. She vacationed on the island as a child and returned to it when she was widowed in 1953. She interviewed her mother, her aunt and anyone else she thought useful and wrote a series of twenty articles, which were published in the *Powell River News* and the *Vancouver Province.*

All Texadans know about "the first book" written about the island, entitled simply *Texada*. Ostensibly this was prepared by the 1958 Texada

Centennial Committee, which was chaired by Cecil May and included his wife, Phyllis; Dave and Betty Webster; and Ben Nicholas, whose colourful phraseology marks much of the text. They were fortunate to be able to interview many of the old-timers and their children, whose combined memories stretched back to the arrival of the early prospectors in the mid-1870s. No doubt many of the discussions took place in Cec May's shop, around the warm portable stove known as a salamander. The original book had no index, but one was compiled later by Bill Thompson.

Thompson, a Powell River Museum volunteer, wrote the second book, *Texada Island*. He based it on the pre-1997 Texada information he found in the Powell River Archives and in old issues of the *Powell River News* and other local publications, but most of the interviews he drew on were done by others. He did not spend much time on the island, probably because he felt he had more than enough material. His index is very useful.

The online versions of the *British Colonist* and the *Globe and Mail* have been invaluable, though not infallible. The BC Archives Vital Statistics were also helpful, though some people lived and died here without being recorded. All of these sources are tools to which earlier writers did not have access.

The local magazine *Texada Island Lines*, indexed by Bill Thompson, has also provided a wealth of historical articles, obituaries and "Nature Notes," which have been of inestimable value.

I searched the complete set of online Department of Mines annual reports; those written by William Brewer in 1916 were particularly helpful. However, most of the reports in this collection leave something to be desired, especially when almost all of them used the same description of the Pacific Lime operation from 1909 to 1925:

> On Texada Island—in addition to the old plant at Marble Bay—a new and extensive plant is being erected at Blubber Bay. The limestone being used is of exceptional purity, but in some instances the limestone beds are cut by igneous dykes which have to be rejected and this somewhat increases the costs of quarrying.[1]

While this description may have applied in 1909, by 1925 the Blubber Bay operation was no longer new. A 1946 report talks about a sawmill burning down at the Little Billie Mine, but this was more likely the sawmill at Blubber Bay. The information on the Beale family's various quarries that is contained in the reports often conflicts with information supplied by the family. Sadly, the reports from 1969 onwards had so little detail as to be almost useless. Staff changes and telephone numbers took precedence over information about the mines the department was supposed to be monitoring; Texada was barely mentioned. MINFILE (a provincial government database containing geological, location and economic information on over 12,500 metallic, industrial, mineral and coal mines, deposits and occurrences in BC) was sometimes useful, but was certainly no substitute.

Over 110 Texada residents, former residents and their descendants generously shed new light on old stories and brought the material up to date. A striking number of their childhood memories spoke with unvarnished authority. Islanders are good storytellers.

Part One: The Land

CHAPTER I:

Natural History and First Nations

NATURAL HISTORY

GEOLOGY

THE STORY OF TEXADA ISLAND begins with the rocks because they are the foundation of the natural history that lies above them. Lava flows and other volcanic rocks similar to those found on Vancouver Island cover most of Texada Island's three hundred square kilometres, except in the three places where limestone is found: the Blubber Bay–Gillies Bay corridor and the areas adjacent to Davie Bay and Anderson Bay. About 80 million years ago, these three places were covered by calm, clear, warm Cretaceous seas. Tiny marine creatures living in these waters died and sank to the bottom, where their bodies, unadulterated by sand or gravel, compacted to form layers of Quatsino limestone rock. This process must have taken several million years, even after glaciation, as the deposit on the east side of the island is at least two thousand feet thick. As rain fell, it absorbed carbon dioxide from the atmosphere making it acidic enough to enlarge cracks in the limestone. These cracks or "grikes" resulted in a karst landscape in which creeks suddenly appear from small caves, only to disappear into sinkholes and re-emerge farther down the slope.

Although Texada's limestone deposit is the largest on the western seaboard of North America, correspondingly large cave systems do not occur here. No large rivers flow on the island, because Texada's groundwater lacks the necessary acidity to enlarge the few cracks in the deposit. Visitors wishing to see the stalactites and stalagmites in the small Davie Bay caves require special equipment, a love of muddy, claustrophobic spaces and a local guide. As these formations are brittle and easily damaged, and broken ones take thousands of years to regenerate, extreme care is necessary when investigating them.

Fossils are seldom found on Texada, but one vertebra of an *elasmosaur* or swan lizard was found at Mouat Creek. This is the same kind of long-necked marine reptile as the one whose fossil remains were discovered beside the Puntledge River on Vancouver Island and are now exhibited

Although Texada has only a few small caves, which are tough to access, they do have fragile stalactites and stalagmites. Mary MacLean

in the Courtenay and District Museum and Palaeontology Centre. These creatures, which grew to about twelve metres in length, lived in the same Cretaceous sea that formed Texada's limestone. Some fossil leaves have been found in the Gillies Bay area. These are often wet and very fragile, though they become more robust when dried. Some are pseudoctenis, a kind of sago palm or cycad; others are sycamore leaves or seed-fern fronds.

In long ago times, ultra-hot liquids seeped upwards from deep levels of the earth's crust, carrying the constituents that produced a variety of minerals nearer the surface, where temperatures and pressures were less. These minerals included a large mass of iron ore that covers several square kilometres on the northwest side of the island. Some of it lies on the surface but the largest mass is underground. Much smaller deposits of copper, gold and silver formed in association with the iron ore as well as elsewhere in the northern half of the island along the edges of the limestone. Texada's gold is found in veins as well as scattered on the surface where the rocks associated with it have been weathered away, a process that can concentrate the ore so that the surface deposits appear richer than the ore below. However, very little placer mining for gold has occurred on Texada; when done at all, it was used to search for outcrops of gold-bearing rocks that could then be staked and explored with shafts and adits. Gold found in veins associated with other minerals, such as silver and copper, usually has to be separated from them by smelting, and this is a more expensive process than most lone miners can attempt.

The ice ages, which started two million years ago, had a key effect on the formation of Texada's lakes. As the ice advanced and retreated, its weight on the land caused changes in sea level that may have cut off and restored ocean access to the island's lakes several times. It has been suggested that this may have caused the evolution of Texada's rare stickleback fish pairs.

CLIMATE

Texada is in the rain shadow of Vancouver Island, which brings warm, dry summers and mild, wet winters, but parts of the island are dry enough for desert plants to grow. The soils lying above the limestone are alkaline, while those on the volcanic basalts are acid. The island is part of the same Garry oak ecosystem that stretches from Victoria through the southern Gulf Islands up to Savary and Mitlenatch islands at the north end of the Strait of Georgia (now renamed the Salish Sea). About 70 percent of Texada's forests consist of Douglas fir and western hemlock. Half of the remainder is western red cedar, and the other half is a mixture of western white pine, grand fir, lodgepole pine and red alder. Only about 16 percent of the trees in the island's forests are more than 250 years old, and about 40 percent are 100 to 250 years old.

The special combination of geology and climate that exists on Texada explains some of its unique and unusual natural history occurrences, which include everything from desert plants to endangered fish species. Their continued existence is quite amazing, as early prospectors dynamited much of the island, processes at Pacific Lime and the Van Anda Smelter coated much of the vegetation with corrosive lime and smelter dust, and a 1967 forest fire destroyed about ten thousand acres of vegetation (about 13 percent of the island), though fortunately much of the forest has grown back.

Texada is part of the same Garry oak ecosystem that stretches from Victoria through the southern Gulf Islands up to Savary and Mitlenatch islands at the north end of the Strait of Georgia (now renamed the Salish Sea). Heather Harbord

FLORA

Many plants that are either rare or non-existent elsewhere grow on Texada. Retired geologist John Dove has found the adder's-tongue orchid, *Ophioglossom pusillum*, one of the rarest plants in Canada, to be abundant around Bob's Lake, while the island is also home to the fleshy jaumea, *Jaumea carnosa*, a salt marsh beauty with an orange flower, and Macoun's groundsel, *Packera (Senecio) macounii*, whose yellow flower ornaments the sandy gravel edges of logging roads. On Texada, the leaves of the foamflower, *Tiarella trifoliate,* are more finely divided than those of the same plant on the mainland.

The giant chain fern, *Woodwardia fimbriata*, is common on Texada and Lasqueti islands but rare elsewhere in the province. It grows on both acid and alkaline soils, wherever its roots can remain wet all year. As tall as a person or higher, it can live a hundred years or more. Other common ferns are the goldenback, *Pityrogramma triangularis*; maidenhair, *Adiantum pedatum*; and liquorice, *Polypodium glycyrrhiza*.

Evergreen huckleberry, *Vaccinium ovatum*, one of the commonest shrubs on Texada, is rare on the mainland, though it is also found on nearby Savary Island. A shrub elsewhere, on Texada the seaside juniper (formerly known as the Rocky Mountain juniper), *Juniperis maritima*, grows as a tree with a twenty-five-centimetre-thick trunk. Clubmosses such as *Lycopodium clavatum*, sometimes called staghorn clubmoss, are common. Pioneer prospector Walter Planta called it "monkey moss" and gathered it for Christmas decorations.

STICKLEBACK PAIRS

Texada's endangered stickleback species pairs are globally red-listed because their populations are so tiny. These small spiny fish, which occur in only a few low-elevation lakes on Texada, were identified in Paxton Lake in 1968 by University of British Columbia stickleback expert Don McPhail. He distinguished two kinds: small limnetics with long spines and armoured plates along their silvery sides, and darker benthics,

Tim Atwood at the helm of the Sticklechick, *explaining to delegates attending the Stickleback Species Pairs Conference how he collects water samples to monitor conditions.* Heather Harbord

twice the size of the limnetics but with only one or two spines and fewer lateral plates. The former feed on zooplankton in the central surface waters, while the latter bottom-feed on insects around the edges of the lakes. The two kinds were also discovered in Priest and Emily lakes but not in Kirk. For three summers, McPhail studied the ecology and distribution of the fish here. In 1974 his team looked for the same characteristics in sticklebacks on other islands and found them on Nelson and Vancouver islands. They were also found in Hadley Lake on Lasqueti Island. Since these discoveries, they became extinct in some lakes due to the introduction of catfish and crayfish, which compete with them for food. Scientific studies showed that both species are descendents of the marine three-spine stickleback, *Gasterosteus aculeatus*, but about thirteen thousand years ago, right after the last ice age, some began to inhabit fresh water as well. Those that adapted to fresh water are larger and have fewer armour plates than the marine stickleback. Genetic studies at the University of British Columbia revealed that a mutant gene, common in the freshwater variety and rare in the marine, is responsible. This evolutionary process is similar to that which created different finches on the Galapagos Islands and inspired Charles Darwin to write his famous *On the Origin of Species*. Unlike single species sticklebacks, which are relatively immune to changes in their environment, these stickleback pairs are sensitive to changes in aquatic weeds and the maintenance of water levels and quality, which can prevent mate recognition. However, despite their long period of reproductive isolation, the two species tend not to interbreed with each other.

In 2004 a stickleback workshop held at Van Anda resulted in the formation of the Texada Stickleback Group Association, made up of local volunteers who monitor the lakes and the fish and communicate their findings to the faculty and graduate students of the universities of British Columbia and Washington as well as some government departments. The significance of the research being done is of mind-boggling importance. By studying the genetics of the Texada sticklebacks, scientists hope to find out how species evolve—not just fish but humans as well. It is therefore crucial that no corrupting influences are introduced to these tiny lakes, either by kids or adults ignoring Fisheries Department regulations. Texada people know what is at stake; they vigilantly monitor the lakes, educate every school child, and hover over strangers wielding fishing rods.

ENDANGERED TURTLES

Texada's painted turtles, *Chrysemys picta belli*, are also on the endangered list. These turtles are not to be confused with the red-eared slider, *Trachemys scripta elegans*, an introduced species sold in pet shops, which looks very like the painted turtle and occurs in the same waters. However, painted turtles have red bellies and yellow neck stripes, whereas sliders have yellow bellies and usually a red stripe behind the eye in addition to yellow neck stripes. Painted turtles occur in four Texada lakes—Priest, Emily, Spragge and Cap Sheaf—and are visible from April to September, often basking on sloping logs. At present fewer than fifty adult turtles remain on the island, possibly a sign that the population has not recovered from local residents' predilection for turtle soup in the Hungry Thirties. As they can live up to fifty years, population recovery tends to take fifty

Endangered painted turtles in four Texada lakes are marked and monitored by researchers each year. Heather Harbord

to a hundred years. Preliminary research on recovery trends at Emily Lake suggest that adult turtles are being removed from the population at an unnaturally high rate, and anecdotal evidence suggests that the collection of painted turtles for pets or for food still occurs.

BIRDS

Gillies Bay is one of the few places on the eastern side of the Strait of Georgia that Brant geese visit regularly on their spring migration north. They start arriving in February and leave at the end of April. Smaller than Canada geese, with which they are often confused, they can be identified by their black necks and small white cheek markings. Since 1991 John Dove has been reading and recording the data on the leg bands attached by the US Fish and Wildlife Service at various breeding locations in Alaska and Siberia, where about one in ten birds is banded. Those with red bands come from Wrangel Island in Siberia, aquamarine from Prudhoe Bay, green from the Coleville River and Teshekpuk Lake areas, and yellow, orange, white and silver from the delta of the Yukon River. The repeated observation of individual birds is much easier here than on Vancouver Island, where much larger flocks are dispersed over a wider area. While the banding has revealed that some birds come back year after year, the majority do not, and in recent years flocks have only numbered between 175 and 200 birds compared to flocks of 400 seen in the mid-sixties. However, Dove thinks the reason for the decline in the flocks may lie in places where the birds winter, such as Baja California, because Gillies Bay provides plenty of eel grass as well as sea lettuce, the birds' favourite food. He sends his records to both the Canadian Wildlife Service and US Fish and Wildlife, and the latter sends him information on the birds he records. In this way he learns when the birds were banded and where and when they have been seen elsewhere; a number of birds have returned in later years, though not always in consecutive years.

Nesting boxes on the pilings at Van Anda are there to attract purple martins, which are breeding in similar boxes on pilings at Myrtle Point across Malaspina Strait, but so far the birds have not crossed over. These birds are an older species in the evolutionary tree than the eastern purple martins. They prefer single nesting boxes rather than the apartment blocks so much a hallmark of the easterners.

MAMMALS

Orca travelling up Malaspina Strait often cross from Grief Point over to Texada before continuing northwards, and lucky ferry passengers sometimes see them. However, in the 1890s and early 1900s, they were a common sight as they passed Van Anda, as were larger whales, including humpbacks. On a mid-August low tide in the 1930s, Margaret Devaney watched both grey and blue whales rubbing their bodies on the reef outside Davie Bay. Their puffing and blowing would wake her mother, and she would send Maggie out with a shotgun to scare them away. Maggie deliberately fired over them to avoid harming them. She remembered looking out toward Sisters' Light and hearing "a terrible loud crack" that meant the whales were present. Then she and her siblings would climb high up onto the cliffs to watch their mating dance. "The female lay on the surface while the male dove deep to come up by her face and jump sixty or seventy feet out of the water. Then both would dive and breach simultaneously with water flying everywhere."[1]

Harbour seals are to be seen in every cove on Texada's rocky coast, their silvery coats shining as they bask in the warm sun. From annual aerial surveys, scientists at the Pacific Biological Station in Nanaimo estimate the Strait of Georgia population to be around twenty thousand animals. The largest contingent of them in the Texada area breed on the Mouat Islands south of Gillies Bay, and for about ten years in the 1990s these seals had a bad reputation for attacking boats and biting people. These animals may have been shot at by fisher folk frustrated by having their catches eaten off their hooks. However, marine biologist Peter Olesiuk, visiting Gillies Bay to retrieve a time depth recorder that registers seal movements, said that salmon make up only 4 percent of a seal's diet.

Although Texada has a large deer population, there are no bear, cougar or wolves on the island, and no trace of them was found by the early prospectors or in archaeological digs. However, a number of animal species have been imported: bullfrogs in the 1940s, Pacific oysters in the 1950s and squirrels in the 1970s and 1990s.

PARKS

In 1997 the provincial government established the nine-hundred-hectare South Texada Island Provincial Park on the south end of Texada, extending from Point Upwood along the island's western shore to Cathedral Lake. It also encompasses the heights of Mount Shepherd and Mount Dick. Sheer rock faces rise nine hundred metres from the ocean, and it takes a four-wheel-drive vehicle to reach the head of a trail into the high forest. Although some of the area has been logged and replaced with natural regrowth, there is also some old growth here. Texada's only lizard, the northern alligator lizard, *Elgaria coerulea*, lives here at the northern limit of its range, but it moves so fast it is difficult to see, except at a distance when it is sunning on a warm rocky outcrop. The park is also home to the blue-listed herb *Anagallis minima*. Other plants occur here that are found nowhere else on the island; they include the mountain hemlock, *Tsuga mertensiana*; grape ferns, *Botrychium* sp.; and clubmoss, *Lycopodium* sp.

Anderson Bay Provincial Park was designated in 2000, and like South Texada Island Park, it is zoned "Natural Environment." Its thirty-five hectares are comprised of a strip of land on the eastern side of the bay and two islands. The two parks share the same management plan with the primary purpose of maintaining an example of the Strait of Georgia Ecosystem, including the CWFmm biogeoclimatic subzone.

FIRST NATIONS

There was a commonly held belief among the European pioneers that First Nations people never lived on Texada because they believed it was due to sink back into the ocean. No Sliammon stories support this. In fact, Texada beaches are strewn with immense clamshell middens that indicate hundreds of years of settlement in every nook and cranny of shoreline. All of these sites have Native names, though none appear on modern maps. An explanation for this misconception lies in the journals written by Captain George Vancouver on his 1792 expedition to this coast. Vancouver met people in Puget Sound who bore the scars of smallpox, and this information, coupled with other contemporary or slightly later accounts and First Nations' legends, points to an epidemic of smallpox that swept up the Pacific Coast of North America ten years earlier,[2] causing the death of 80 percent of a dense population.[3] In a matter of a few weeks, most of the elders died before they could pass their knowledge to the next generation. Survivors fled the villages on Texada and Lasqueti, leaving even the huge clam beds in Gillies Bay, to congregate in the Comox and Pender Harbour areas, which explains why First Nations from both these areas lay claim to Texada.

Once European traders arrived, they brought diseases like gonorrhoea and measles to which Native people had little or no resistance. Then in 1862 the well-documented second smallpox epidemic raced up the Strait from Victoria, once again reducing the population by 80 percent.

Thus, when European settlers began arriving in greater numbers, they found the indigenous people trying to recover from multiple disasters, which had reduced their populations to a mere 5 to 10 percent of their original levels. Extrapolations from the 1881 census[4] estimate the Native population in the Strait of Georgia to have been around fifty-four hundred at that time and therefore fifty thousand to one hundred thousand before the first smallpox outbreak.

Simon Fraser University archaeologist Dana Lepofsky, who studies this area, states that people lived all along the shores of Texada and points to the level terraces at Raven Bay as evidence. At the southern end of the Nature Trail at Shelter Point, at low tide trained eyes can see middens and fish traps or clam gardens. In the main campsite area, a skeleton belonging to a Native person was dug up in 1987. Archaeologists used tree-ring dating to establish that the death had occurred in antiquity.

First Nations people used scrapers such as these to prepare deer hides for clothing and other uses. Heather Harbord

Old-timers familiar with Blubber Bay before Pacific Lime altered the beach spoke of a large clamshell midden near the lime pit. Sometime between 1910 and 1914, when Frederick Dawson built the lime kilns there, he found a Native grave on the site of what became the quarry. The elaborateness of the paraphernalia in the grave led him to think it was that of a chief.

Native artifacts from arrowheads to scrapers and left-handed rasps have been found on farms all over the island. Often the farm children took them to school where they were lost; those that survived to be dated are about two thousand years old, though some may be as much as ten thousand years old. Dave Murphy, who finds a new artifact every spring when he rototills his bottom land, has a theory that women gathering clams in Maple Bay sent their men inland to hunt deer, but Lepofsky says the settlement on Murphy's land was probably permanent. Scientists can match the chemical compounds of obsidian scrapers to the volcano that produced them, and as a result, it has been established that many tools found on Texada likely came from either Kingcome Inlet to the north or Garibaldi, Squamish or Oregon to the south.

Following the directions of the late Norm Gallagher, traditional advisor to the Sliammon Treaty Society, BC Parks funded archaeological excavations in the summer of 2008 at three sites within South Texada Island Provincial Park. The team of four archaeologists, together with representatives of the Sliammon and Sechelt First Nations, excavated a metre of compressed shell layers in the shelter of a three-storey-high boulder. They uncovered long-buried bones, shells, stone implements, charcoal and ash fire remains, which they put through fine sieves to reveal almost two thousand years of forgotten secrets. Among the items found was a curved piece of mussel shell honed to the razor sharpness of a knife; juicy shellfish were the main items on the menu, along with deer. Exploring the steep hillside sixty metres above the beach, they found "a large oval stone, weighing about two kilograms, with a dime-sized hole ground clear through it." This was probably the counterweight of a deer snare, though a similar stone found fifty years earlier at sea level in Gillies Bay was deemed to be a net weight or an anchor.

With declining fish populations, the nests of Great Blue Herons are subject to eagle predation, but this youngster has survived to enjoy the sunshine of Emily Lake.
Heather Harbord

CHAPTER 2:

Exploration and Early Visitors

EARLY EXPLORERS

IN THE SUMMER OF 1790 a Spanish warship under the command of Manuel de Quimper (1757–1844) explored the entrance to the Strait of Juan de Fuca as far as the San Juan Islands. The following year the Spaniards penetrated farther into Puget Sound in three vessels: the seventy-two-foot *San Carlos*, the thirty-two-foot *Santa Saturnina* and the *San Carlos's* twenty-eight-foot longboat. The two smaller boats were better able to negotiate the fast currents in the shallow, narrow passages between the San Juan Islands. The expedition was commanded by Francisco de Eliza (1759–1825), the commandant of Spain's outpost at Nootka on the west coast of Vancouver Island. He was assisted by four navigation officers or pilots: Gonzalo Lopez de Haro (1785–1823), José María Narváez (1768–1840), Juan Carrasco (no dates available) and Juan Pantoja (no dates available). One of their duties was to draw maps of the areas they explored.

On June 14, 1791, Eliza sent Pantoja out in the *Santa Saturnina* to explore what we now call the southern Gulf Islands. Rounding the east end of Saturna on June 15, he looked north and saw a large body of water that he named El Gran Canal de Nuestra Senora del Rosario la Marinera. Today we call it the Strait of Georgia or the Salish Sea. In the distance he saw a round blue hill that we now know was Texada, but he did not

Modern sea cadets used this model of Vancouver's yawl to sail in his wake. John Treen

see the smaller, lower island just west of it. Turning east, he explored the San Juan Islands before returning to the *San Carlos* in Port Discovery.

On July 1, keeping Pantoja with him to write up his reports and create maps, Eliza sent the two smaller ships out again, this time under the command of Narváez. They sailed up Rosario Strait, past the present-day city of Vancouver and Bowen Island to anchor off Rio de la Aguada, a delta of land south of Sechelt formed by Wilson and Chapman creeks, where he filled his water tanks. He then anchored on the west side of the Thormanby islands. The next day, probably July 12, which was St. Felix's Day, he sailed up to the blue hill seen by Pantoja and named it Isla de Felis in honour of the saint. Then he sailed between it and the mainland until he reached the same latitude as Nootka. It was only when he turned south again that he discovered Lasqueti Island—which he named Texada. (Pantoja's map, which was completed after Narváez returned to the *San Carlos*, shows this configuration of names.) By this time food supplies were running low, and Narváez sailed west toward Hornby Island and Cape Lazo and then south along the east coast of Vancouver Island.

On their way back, Narváez and his crew saw many large whales, possibly humpbacks, and as they had only seen three or four since they left the San Juan Islands, they assumed the whales must have come there via another exit to the open ocean. There were also a great number of tuna fish. Unfortunately, the explorers could not remain to investigate further, and they returned to the mother ship on July 22.

A map drawn by Juan Carrasco and sometimes referred to as the "Narvaez Chart" summarizes Carrasco's own discoveries along with those made by Pantoja and Narváez during 1791, but on this map there are significant name changes. Instead of Isla de Felis, Texada is named Isla de Texada, and Lasqueti is called Isla de Lasquety. However, after the explorers returned to their main naval base at San Blas in Mexico, senior pilot Lopez de Haro consolidated the discoveries of 1790 and 1791 onto a third map on which he once again gives Texada the name Isla de Felis and Lasqueti is called Isla de Texada. A copyist's error reversed the names on the 1792 map used by Galiano and Valdés, and the error remained permanent.

Since running out of provisions had caused Narváez to return with his exploration work unfinished, the following year two ships were sent north to complete the mapping of the coast from San Francisco to 55°N. These were the *Sutil* under the command of Dionisio Alcalá Galiano (1762–1805) and the *Mexicana* under the command of Cayetano Valdés y Flores (1767–1835). Valdés had been at Nootka long enough to learn a little of the language spoken by the Native people there, and Galiano spoke English. At that same time, two British ships were on the same mission—the *Discovery* commanded by Captain George Vancouver (1757–1798) and the *Chatham* commanded by Captain William Robert Broughton (1762–1821). Both Spanish and British commanders had been instructed to cooperate with each other if they met, which they did in Birch Bay.

All four ships sailed past Texada in late June 1792. Vancouver had already named Point Upwood on June 21 when he saw it from afar. He now gave the name Marshall Point to the northwest point of Texada. (This was

When Vancouver sailed past Texada, he had already named Point Upwood at the south end of the island and now he named Marshall Point at the north end. Marshall Point's name was changed to Cohoe Point in 1913 and Kiddie Point in 1924. In 1952 the hydrographic service applied the old name of Marshall Point to another point two kilometres south of Kiddie Point at the end of Limekiln Bay.
Heather Harbord

renamed Cohoe Point in 1913 and Kiddie Point in 1924. In 1952 the hydrographic service resurrected the name Marshall Point and transferred it to a spot two kilometres south of Kiddie Point on the western side of the island.) Native legend has it that one of the British ships picked up a Native person from Texada to act as a guide; this story is not substantiated by any of the European records so far discovered.

MAP MAKERS

After these ships left, it appears that no Europeans visited the island for several decades. A British Admiralty chart based on additional surveys by Captain Henry Kellett in 1847 notes that Texada Island was inhabited, but it does not specify the sites. As most European settlers had taken up land much farther south, the people reported by Kellett were probably First Nations. News of their existence had likely been passed on to him by people such as Captain William McNeill of the *Beaver*, the first steamship to operate on the Pacific Coast. When Dr. J.S. Helmcken passed the island aboard the *Beaver* in 1849, he thought it uninhabited, but he may have been there at a different season than those who had given earlier reports.

With British Columbia acquiring provincial status in 1858 and the sudden influx of prospectors heading for the Fraser and Cariboo goldfields, Governor James Douglas set about having the land surveyed and mapped. Between 1857 and 1861, Captain George Henry Richards charted the coast in HMS *Plumper*, a bark-rigged steam sloop, which was armed with twelve guns and could travel at six knots. He returned to Britain in 1863, leaving Staff Commander Daniel Pender to carry on the charting using the *Beaver*, which had been leased to the government by the Hudson's Bay Company. One or both of these men travelled along the coast of Texada Island, poking into every cove and naming both the Mouat Islands and Gillies Bay.

According to G.P.V. Akrigg, author of *British Columbia Place Names*, Gillies Bay is named after a cruel captain who was thrown overboard into the bay, but his notes show no provenance for this incident. (Bruce Watson, who has made a twenty-year study of traders in the Pacific Northwest, has no Gillies or Gillis in his database.) The first time the name appears is on Captain Richards' 1859–64 chart. The first instance of the name Mouat Islands appears on the same chart. Captain William Alexander Mouat (1821–1871) was a somewhat irascible master mariner who became a trader for the Hudson's Bay Company in 1855 and captained the steamships *Otter, Enterprise* and *Labouchère.*

PASSERSBY

In February 1859, William Downie, a California gold miner, found himself "in a small cove at the south end of Texada Island with two Indians, a canoe, and nothing to eat." He was returning to Nanaimo after prospecting in Desolation Sound but had been delayed by a southeaster.

The Natives refused to go with him until he paid them with a blanket, but as he only had one, which he needed both for a canoe sail and to cover himself at night, he couldn't part with it. When he started rigging the sail in preparation for setting off alone, the Natives, seeing that he was wearing two shirts, said they would make do with one of them. "So I pulled off one and gave it to them, and their 'tum tum' was all right. Getting underway, we arrived at Nanaimo all safe."

Another man who passed by Texada Island was civil engineer Robert Homfray, who set out from Fort Victoria on "a fine day" in October 1861. The Hudson's Bay Company had hired him to explore the possibility of putting a road through to the Cariboo goldfields from Bute Inlet.

In 1859 prospector William Downie found himself in a small cove at the south end of Texada with two Indians, a canoe and nothing to eat. This cove, now the home of Jim Dougan, may have been the same one. It is also where George Edward Whittaker received his Crown grant in 1917. Heather Harbord

Homfray's equipment consisted of a dugout canoe, tents, muskets and ammunition, blankets, food and trade goods to smooth his way through Native territory. His travelling companions were the Bay's "three best French Canadian voyageurs: Coté, Balthazzar and Bouchier with Harry McNeill and two Indians."[1] Heavy sea encountered on the second day out caused the canoe to leak, and as a result, they had to go ashore and fix it after every gale, of which there were many. "Five days out from Victoria, we reached Texada Island at sunset. After we left next day we were almost lost in the heavy seas; when we landed to repair our canoe a deer passed us with a large wolf in full chase." It is not known whether this landing was on Texada or on the Powell River mainland, but there are no other recorded sightings of wolves on Texada. They continued through to Desolation Sound, where they were captured by hostile Natives but rescued by a friendly chief who escorted them to their Bute Inlet destination. Homfray Channel is named after this event.

WHALING

Starting in the 1860s, whalers called intermittently at the north end of the island. One of them was Captain Abel Douglass, who operated various whaling enterprises throughout the Strait of Georgia, basing himself on Pasley Island. In August 1872, his schooner *Emma* returned to Victoria from Marble Bay, having "killed six whales, but only managed to secure two of them, which yielded sixty-six barrels of oil."[2] Such losses were common. As late as the 1880s, whaler Elijah J. Fader[3] based himself in Blubber Bay. He used a small steam tug to tow his whaling boats to sites such as Rebecca Reef and even as far north as Mitlenatch Island. From April to October, the men in these boats speared whales with barbed harpoons attached to a line. Once the whale exhausted itself by dragging the boat around, the men lanced it to death and towed it back to Blubber Bay. Using a block and tackle to bring the whales ashore, they peeled off the blubber to boil in big metal "try pots." John Edwards (1847–1929), a homesteader who claimed to be the first European settler on Texada, remembered seeing "big black kettles" on the beach at Blubber Bay. The resultant oil was stored in fifty-five-gallon wooden casks. However, as the main focus of this venture was the humpback whale, which soon disappeared from the Strait of Georgia, Fader went broke and left the area to go prospecting in the Cariboo.

In 1910 six-year-old Ethel Dawson found traces of Fader's activities when she played around whale ribs and vertebrae on the beach, and as late as the 1930s, Jean Weisner (1925–2008) also saw these bones as well as a winch used by the whalers. She discovered the winch down by a big white rock that stood on the shore, but it is now at the back of the reclaimed land on which the quarry offices stand.

As Vancouver and the Spaniards sailed north on their way to Desolation Sound they would have seen this view as they approached distant Northeast Point. The long straight coast in between is euphemistically known as Long Beach but is cobble, not sand, and slippery to land on. Heather Harbord

CHAPTER 3:

The Iron Mines

THE FIRST IRON MINE

WHEN THE FIRST MINERAL CLAIMS were staked on Texada in 1873, the only mineral regulations in the province were for gold claims. During the 1859 gold rush to the Cariboo area of British Columbia, the government in Victoria had issued a Gold Fields Proclamation, which laid out rules for staking claims and included the appointment of two gold commissioners. A third was added for Vancouver Island in 1864. Other minerals were not considered of sufficient importance to warrant regulating.

This was the situation when Harry Trim discovered iron ore on Texada Island. Trim (1832–1922) was an Englishman who had earned a nest egg in the Cariboo gold mines, then in 1868 became a partner in Captain Abel Douglass's Howe Sound Whaling Company based on Pasley Island. For the next four years, he explored the Strait of Georgia, occasionally doing a bit of prospecting. During this period, he also married Susan Quiz from the Native village on False Creek and they started a family. In 1871, when mineral oil was beginning to supplant whale oil in popularity, causing prices to fall, Trim sold his share in the business to Douglass, loaded his family aboard his small sloop and sailed to an unnamed bay at the northern tip of Texada, which he referred to as Blubber Bay, perhaps because he had once beached a whale there. Being sheltered from the prevailing southeast and northwest winds, it provided a good anchorage, so he built a cabin there. No description remains of its exact location, but it seems to have been somewhere near the present ferry dock. It was also conveniently close to the excellent fishing hole off Kiddie Point. When Trim caught fish, Susan smoked and dried them. As his job took less time than hers, he was free to pursue his other passion of mineral prospecting.

Trim knew that compasses on ships sailing past the west side of Texada went crazy, so he investigated and found an iron ore deposit above Welcome Bay. Unlike gold, which is profitable enough for one man to mine, iron requires an expensive smelting process before it can be marketed, so it was some time before Trim took a sample of his ore to an assayer, but the man "neglected it." However, the Trims periodically sailed down to Burrard Inlet to sell their fish, buy supplies and visit Susan's relatives on the False Creek Reserve. While on these expeditions, Trim got to know Sewell P. Moody (c. 1835–1875), owner of the Moodyville Sawmill Company in North Vancouver, and discovered that Moody had an assay office. In April 1873 he brought Moody an ore sample.

Moody was a swashbuckling businessman and savvy promoter, and when he saw the results of Trim's assay, he began enlisting investors to develop the deposit, iron ore being the key ingredient in the manufacture of the steel rails required for the railways then being built across the country. On June 10, 1873, Moody sailed his sidewheeler, *Cariboo Fly*, to Victoria to meet with his partner, Hugh Nelson, who was returning from a business trip back east. Nelson was enthusiastic about the possibilities of the find, as was another friend named A. Watson, and they wanted to see it for themselves. The *Cariboo Fly* recrossed the Strait of Georgia to North Vancouver, where the ship took on more wood to fuel its steam engines, before proceeding to Texada. The wind was "blowing pretty fresh," so they anchored overnight in Blubber Bay. Next day they proceeded to the west side of the island, where they drilled a hole and blasted out some ore. The surface deposit looked very promising, as it stretched for several miles.

They were not sure how best to stake their claim. Trim was familiar with the rules for placer gold mining, but as a different mineral was involved, they wondered if the recently enacted homestead laws would better suit their purpose. Although the rules kept changing, basically, any British subject or anyone prepared to swear allegiance to the Crown could pre-empt 160 acres of land by paying a fee and registering the pre-emption's coordinates with the Lands Office. The land was then surveyed, and after making improvements such as clearing several acres and building a dwelling, pre-emptors could apply for a Crown grant or certificate of indefeasible title. Initially, these pre-emptions included other rights such as mineral or timber rights.

Trim gave Nelson verbal power of attorney to stake a pre-emption for him, and on June 20, 1873, Moody, who could not register one himself because he was an American citizen, directed the registering of the pre-emptions with Robert Beaven, chief commissioner of Lands and Works in Victoria. Then, to make sure everything was done correctly, he arranged for a man named John Hall to take the papers to Texada, where Hall and Trim sank the stakes in the ground for four pre-emptions, including one for Trim. On July 1, when Trim was back in Vancouver, Moody explained that the multiple pre-emptions were necessary so that several people could perform the necessary improvements on the land in order to qualify for Crown grants. Once these were in place, they would form a mining company and sell the whole package.

Moody then organized a second trip to Texada, this time taking his brother-in-law, William Dalby, who was the mayor of Victoria; J.C. Hughes, a member of the legislature; Amor De Cosmos, the premier of the province; and a number of other interested parties. At the last minute on July 29, Attorney General George Walkem begged to come along, saying he wanted to see the logging operations on Burrard Inlet. This time the weather was better, so the *Cariboo Fly* anchored in Gillies Bay. Harry Trim had not been alerted that they were coming, but he accompanied them as they toured the deposit. On the way back, Moody and De Cosmos talked of building a steel mill in Vancouver to supply the Canadian Pacific Railway. De Cosmos told Dalby that he would like the job of selling the company when the time came, and Dalby told him to talk to Moody about it. On their return on July 3, J.C. Hughes also filed a pre-emption. The group then contacted the Geological Survey of Canada, who sent geologist James Richardson to confirm the discovery. Richardson reported that the deposit was of "incalculable value," as the rock assayed at 80 percent pure iron of the best quality.

Around August 10 or 11, prospector and promoter C.T. Dupont of Nanaimo approached Richardson to confirm the quality of the find and was told that not all the land covering the deposit had been pre-empted. On August 14 Dupont and a friend named Thomas A. Bulkley loaded a dugout canoe onto the steamer *Douglas*, which took them across the Strait and dropped them a couple of miles off the coast of Texada. Once ashore, Dupont and his party found five posts that seemed to be claiming more than the regulation 160 acres, but at that point Harry Trim arrived in his sloop with a load of lumber and accused Dupont of staking on top of the existing claims. Dupont replied that he "did not expect to get more than [they] were entitled to."[1] (Trim's lumber was probably for the cabin he built on the iron mine site. His son Edward was born on the island on October 6, 1876, likely in this cabin. The Texada Archives have a picture of W.H. Lee in front of the cabin, taken long after Trim left it.) Dupont would later report that "Mr. De Cosmos expressed great indignation when he learned that I and others had gone to Texada Island to pre-empt."

Back in Victoria on August 20, 1873, Dupont made a personal application to Robert Beaven, chief commissioner for Lands and Works, for permission to purchase land adjacent to those of the Moody/De Cosmos group, only to be told that the government was revising the rules regulating the sale of lands, and until the revision was complete, nothing could be done. Later, Dupont reported that when he asked whether he "could pre-empt land without prejudice to the right of purchase when the [new] regulations were [finalized]," Beaven showed him the other pre-emption applications on Texada. To Dupont's surprise, the Moody/De Cosmos group had described their pre-emptions as three and a half miles *north* of Gillies Bay, when by Dupont's reckoning the iron deposit was actually three and a half miles *east* of the bay. (The iron deposit is actually northwest of Gillies Bay.) Dupont asked whether the application forms or the claim posts on the island "ought to govern" in this situation, and Beaven replied that "the practice was uncertain but that he wished to do equity or justice" and told Dupont to go to New Westminster to apply for leave to pre-empt. In the Lands Office in New Westminster, Dupont's agent learned that a number of applications had been received on August 18 that covered much of the same ground, but Dupont was granted leave to apply with the proviso that his pre-emptions did not interfere with the previous applications.

That fall, when De Cosmos left for Ottawa to discuss federal–provincial relations, rumours began flying that he had actually gone there to sell the Texada iron deposits to Prime Minister Sir John A. Macdonald as the price of his support for Macdonald's government. And in London, someone associated with the Nanaimo coal mines saw a notice labelled "Iron Ore" on the green baize board in the office of the provincial agent, G.M. Sproat, and assumed Sproat was trying to sell the new iron mine property in England. Then on February 8, 1874, the headline on the *Daily Colonist* newspaper read "Taxhada Island Ore Grab," followed by the subheading "Local government deeply involved!" The story described how Beaven had allowed Moody's group to pre-empt while Dupont had been rebuffed, and how De Cosmos had attempted to sell the mine to Macdonald, then offered stock in the mine on the London Exchange. The ensuing uproar in the legislature caused De Cosmos to resign as premier the next day, and on February 20, BC's first Royal Commission was appointed to enquire into land acquisitions on Texada Island. Judges Begbie, Crease and Gray held hearings between March and October, in the end absolving De Cosmos of all wrongdoing. It was, however, too late and he did not return to office.

Newspaper headlines about the "Taxhada Ore Grab" created a ruckus in the Provincial Legislature, causing Premier Amor De Cosmos to resign. British Columbia's first Royal Commission was immediately appointed to investigate the scandal.

W.H. Lee, the Alabama furnace man who was sent to examine the iron deposit before the Puget Sound Iron Company purchased it. He stands in front of the second cabin that Harry Trim, who discovered the iron mine, built.

All this publicity attracted other entrepreneurs, and a trio of San Francisco shipping men hired an Alabama furnace man, Captain William H. Lee (1847–1922), to examine the minerals on the Texada property. Harry Trim, now living in the cabin he had built on the property, showed him around. The following year, after Lee turned in a favourable report, Amor De Cosmos, still acting as agent for the original pre-emptors, sold their claims to the Puget Sound Iron Company of San Francisco. The principals behind Puget Sound Iron included some of the wealthiest men on the West Coast, among them Charles Miner Goodall and Senator George Clement Perkins of the Pacific Coast Steamship Company, which ran ships from San Francisco to Alaska, and J.E. Prescott, D. Merrill and H.O. Howard of the Union Iron Works of San Francisco, which built steam locomotives and steel-hulled ships. The new owners staked mineral claims over the original Crown grants to secure the precious metals beneath them.

Meanwhile, Trim continued to live on the property for another year before moving to Westham Island, where he went towboating. Sewell Moody had little time to benefit from his share of the money from the sale, as he drowned in November 1875 while on his way to San Francisco aboard the SS *Pacific*. Ironically, this ship, which sank after colliding with another ship with the loss of 250 passengers, was owned by Charles Miner Goodall and Senator Perkins of Pacific Coast Steamships.

THE PUGET SOUND IRON COMPANY

It was September 1880 before Puget Sound's iron mine was ready to send its first five hundred tons of ore to the company's new smelter at Irondale near Port Townsend, the first iron-producing blast furnace in the state. They chartered the Vancouver Coal Company's schooner *Mary Parker* from Nanaimo for the job. However, the mine did not get going seriously until 1883, when the company sent the "genial and enthusiastic" Captain William H. Lee back to Texada as their agent. By this time the company had opened three mines there—the Prescott, Paxton and Lake claims—and they became the Irondale Smelter's sole supplier, as the Washington State iron mines, which the smelter had been built to service, had remained undeveloped. The pig iron produced there from the Texada ore proved to be of high quality and was sent on to the car-wheel works at Edison. The Irondale Smelter, however, closed permanently in 1889, forcing the iron mine to close as well, and it was July 1893 before the company's new smelter was completed at Everett, Washington. But 1893 was also the year that the company's plant, rolling stock and tramway on Texada burned, forcing operations to be scaled back temporarily, although the facilities were soon replaced. Pioneer prospector James Raper landed the job of watchman till the mine was rebuilt. Another slowdown in 1897 resulted in the ore being lowered to the sea in an endless chain of buckets.

Australian "Black Jack" McLeod, who may have met Captain Lee at the Irondale Smelter, came to work at the iron mine around this time, but when the work palled, he used his sailboat to ferry supplies for the mine to and from Vancouver Island. To avoid the storms that lashed the coast below the mine, McLeod anchored in Gillies Bay, which he dubbed "the coldest spot on the Island at night."[2]

William H. Lee, who became affectionately known as "Pop" Lee, was one of Texada's least flamboyant promoters. From the interviews he gave to the *British Colonist* between 1899 and 1901, it is apparent that his forecasts never reached the enthusiastic heights displayed by other Texada promoters. In June 1899 he told the *Colonist* that there were ten million tons of ore in the deposit that was conveniently close to the two wharves. At that time he estimated that eighty tons of ore could be shipped each day to Port Townsend. Thirty-five workmen would be required, and this number was expected to quadruple later. Hopes went higher on May 1, 1900, when the *Colonist* stated that "the Union Iron Works, San Francisco, are to put 400 men to work on their Texada Island iron mines right away." However, although a new large body of ore had been found—larger than any before—Gold Commissioner Marshall Bray reported only twelve men were at work there that year.

The Puget Sound Company's fortunes had rebounded by 1901 when Lee announced plans to build a railway to accommodate a locomotive drawing ten cars to transport the Texada ore to nearby Gillies Bay, where wind and tide would not interfere with loading. Later that year a three-quarter-mile-long tramline was constructed from the Prescott Mine, which was 450 feet above sea level, to what would later be known as Cox's Lagoon, a cove northwest of Gillies Bay. The Paxton, which was at the 290-foot level, also used this tramline. But it was horses and not a locomotive that drew the loaded cars to the head of the tramway, where a large wheel or "head sheave" lowered the cars to the wharf and drew back the empties. The Lake claim, which was nearly at sea level some 1,300 feet east of the Paxton, had a longer tramline, but it was not on an incline.

Lee subsequently met with representatives of Andrew Carnegie, the Pittsburgh steel magnate, and this meeting resulted in the Pacific Steel Company leasing the mine from Puget Sound Iron, but the lease reverted to the company a year later. In 1907 Puget Sound leased it to Cox and Moore of Seattle, which extended the tramway another half mile and constructed a four-hundred-foot wharf and two large bunkers at Cox's

This 1901 picture of the Prescott Mine shows the tramline down which loaded ore cars ran 450 feet over three-quarters of a mile to the water. The big wheel, or head sheave, then pulled the empties back up.

Lagoon. Shipments from there ceased in 1908, by which time 26,213 tons of ore had been shipped over the twenty-eight years of the mine's operations.

"Pop" Lee stayed on the island after Cox and Moore leased the mines, prospecting with various partners, including George McLeod on the Highland claim and William McDonald on the Retriever claim on Surprise Mountain, and the Nancy Bell group, which included the Silver Tip claim originally developed in 1897 by James Findlay for a Saint John, New Brunswick, syndicate. Fire destroyed the remaining iron mine buildings in 1922, and Lee died in Vancouver on December 18 of the same year. Lee's two sons, William and Alexander (Alec), known for their quiet courtesy, lived out their lives on the island in a spotless cabin near the Gem Mine beside Kirk Lake. In the 1950s Alec Lee, by then in his seventies, was a familiar figure on Texada, roaming the island with a pack on his back.

All was quiet at the Puget Sound Iron Company's mine until 1929, when the company brought in a couple of diamond drillers to re-explore the Prescott, Paxton and Lake ore bodies with a view to redeveloping them in combination with Vancouver Island coal. Nothing came of this. That same year H. McMillan bought out the estates of his two partners, W.H. Lee and William MacDonald, to become sole owner of the Nancy Bell claims, which he was still working. However, the shafts and adits of these workings were subject to cave-ins, which made it difficult for Department of Mines inspectors to assess them.

MORE IRON MINES

The Puget Sound Company's iron mine was only one of four attempts to exploit the iron deposits on Texada. On October 8, 1879, the *Nanaimo Free Press* made mention of Spratt's iron mine at Spratt Bay, now called Butterfly Bay, just south of Van Anda. Joseph Spratt (1834–1888) was the owner of the steamers *Maude* and *Cariboo Fly*, which he must have purchased from the estate of Sewell Moody (1835–1875), and for a time he held the mail contract between Victoria and Nanaimo. In August 1888 the *Nanaimo Free Press* announced the discovery of yet another iron deposit just north of Harry Trim's discovery. By February of the following year, the owners of this new mine had formed the Texada Iron Company, with $70,000 in capital stock divided into 750 shares valued at $100 each. The company controlled twenty-five claims including the Golden Slipper. Neither of these mines was ever developed to the production stage.

The fourth iron deposit lay northeast of Surprise Mountain. While mine owners were usually men from big cities like New York, San Francisco or Victoria, in the case of the Surprise claims, the owners were eight Comox men who had combined their resources and their manpower. The 1897 Department of Mines annual report states that they sank a 258-foot shaft and equipped it with a horse-whim, this being a set of gears and a wheel that a horse pulls in a circle around a shaft to raise a bucket of ore to the surface. "In places for several feet it is barren, then will succeed a mineralized body, from which assays from $4 to $34 in gold, silver and copper have been obtained, one such body 18 inches wide carrying, Mr. Jell states, $20 in value."[3]

THE SECOND COMING OF THE IRON MINE

In June 1951, local prospector Jim Brennan got a call from his old friend Ted Mason, a well-known mining consultant, to say that Utah Mines, the new owner of the Puget Sound Company's iron mine, had decided to reopen it. They had hired Mason to recommend a site for a shipping dock, and he wanted Brennan to show him around.[4] Jim Brennan (1909–1984) had come west from Quebec in 1927 to work in the mines at Barkerville. He moved to Texada in 1942 to get away from underground mining, left for three years, but returned to work at the Little Billie Mine until it closed in 1952. He then worked for Ideal Cement as a limestone quarry driller till he retired in 1974. In his spare time he served long hours on the water board and the school board. His vehicle licence plate was "AURUM," but it was the thrill of discovery, not the possession of gold, that was important to him and to his wife, who was also a prospector.

On that June day in 1951, Brennan and Mason drove as far as they could in Brennan's battered pickup truck before bushwhacking to the old Prescott Mine, where Mason just shook his head. Then they drove up a logging road to reach a height of land. Looking over the coastline from that vantage point, Mason decided to recommend a site close to the original Prescott Mine wharf, northwest of Gillies Bay, where Cox and Moore had built their loading dock in 1908, because despite its shallow depth and lack of shelter from the prevailing southeast and northwest winds, he deemed it to be the only possibility.

In addition to being a keen prospector, Jim Brennan served on the Texada School Board for many years. In 1982, he also helped prevent Vancouver from dumping its garbage on Texada.

It was not difficult to restart the mine; Ben Nicholas and Stan Beale took a compressor over to the property and were able to produce ore almost immediately from the old workings, which outcropped about five hundred feet above the western shore of the island. Soon diamond drillers were re-exploring the magnetite deposits on the Prescott, Paxton and Lake properties. Meanwhile, the president of Utah Mines, Allen D. Christensen of San Francisco, had registered the operation in BC as Texada Mines Ltd., leading some islanders to think that Utah Mines was a small company. It was not. Utah Mines was part of the Utah Construction Company, a multinational with worldwide interests. Texada was only a very small part of its operations.

The new mine manager was tobacco-chewing Bruce Alexander, a Toronto graduate engineer with experience in Ontario, Saskatchewan and BC. Within six months he had overseen the building of gravel roads to the three main deposits: Prescott, Paxton and Lake. He installed a crusher and magnetic separation unit as well as a dock to accommodate freighters. Milling at the open-pit mine began on May 21, 1952, using ore from the Prescott deposit, which had provided most of the mine's first phase of operation from 1885 to 1903 and again in 1908.

With the reopening of the iron mine in 1952, the island's population doubled as over a hundred high-income jobs became available. At the same time, the island's logging industry was doing poorly, so loggers and anyone else who had been barely scraping a living were glad to get work there. Hardrock miners from off-island moved in to work, for a while renting cottages from the summer people, and then moving into tents when the owners arrived. However, it wasn't long before the company provided better accommodation in two bunkhouses, a staff house and a commissary at the head of Gillies Bay. Unfortunately, as the subsoil is clay, all the septic fields drained into the bay, and for the first time green algae appeared on what had been a silver beach. It has never left. The company also built houses for some executives on Pine Street, which intersected with the main highway across the island.

In 1956 Ted Mason's qualms about the suitability of the site he had chosen for a dock were borne out when a sixty-mile-an-hour gale hit the wharf. The dock's pilings were embedded in clay overlain with fine tailings, and overnight five hundred feet of the dock disappeared into the Strait of Georgia as the clay liquefied and shifted, taking the tailings and all the pilings that supported the wharf with it. Afterwards the company moved the tailings discharge to the south and rebuilt the dock on the same site. While the old dock had only one conveyor on a boom to feed the ship being loaded, the new one had twice the berthing capacity and two retractable loading towers, eighty feet apart, with attached loading booms. These could be raised or lowered or swung from side to side. This dock was mainly used to load the frequent shipments of iron concentrate going to the Far East, but it also accommodated the twice-yearly shipments of copper concentrate to refineries.

The next attempt at new development at the old mine came in 1959, when geophysicists bounced radio waves off the layers of rock under the surface. Different types of rock reflect the waves back differently, and they also have different magnetic, electrical and gravitational properties. The scientists found two new bodies of ore on the Yellow Kid and the Le Roi Crown grants that had been staked at the time the original iron mine was staked, and from then until 1962, employment rose from 170 to more than 200 men, who systematically stripped all the waste away from the top of the Yellow Kid and Paxton pits.

Texada's second boom started in 1962, when Texada Mines Ltd. contracted with the Quebec company Temiskaming to develop the underground portion of the newly discovered Yellow Kid ore body. After the company went underground the following year, surface mining continued at a significantly reduced pace until 1976. Hardrock miners from eastern Canada poured in to work there, and Canus Services was contracted to run the camp and provide a home-away-from-home atmosphere.

By the end of that year, the shaft was down 736 feet. Two Koepe friction hoists, the first in the province, were installed, because their counterweights reduced the amount of power needed to bring ore to the surface. Down below, a network of railways transported supplies, heavy equipment and ore to and from rock faces. Above ground, a collection of buildings contained compressors, welding and electrical equipment, a heavy-duty machine shop and warehouse/change/lamp room facilities, as well as an 89,000 gallon freshwater supply tank. Keith Hughes surveyed an airstrip on company land, but it remained in a rudimentary condition.

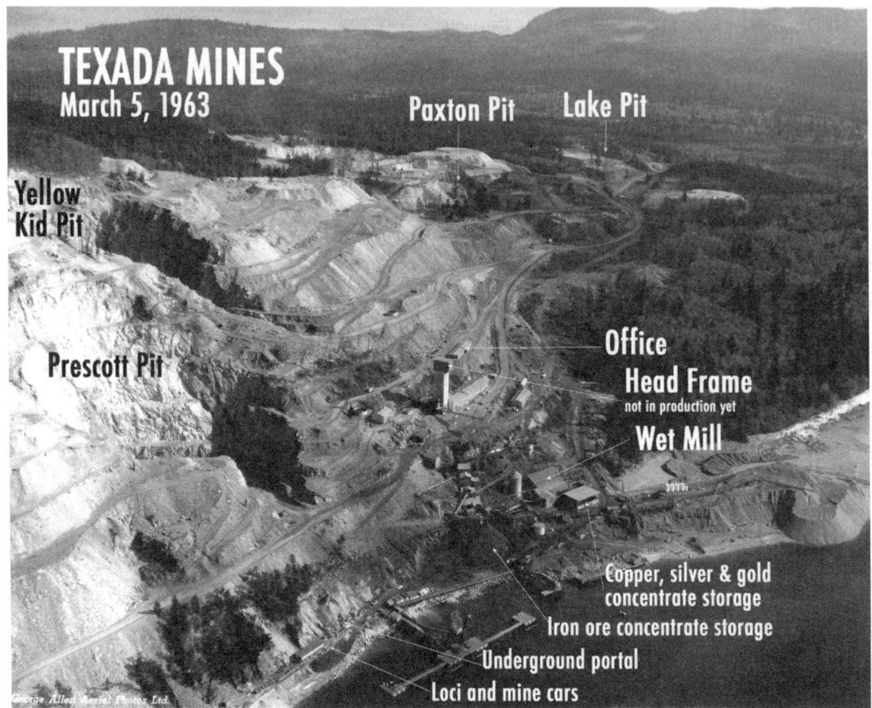

The Prescott, Paxton and Lake pits were dug by the first iron mine, but geophysical prospecting revealed the greater underground treasure of the Yellow Kid. Texada Mines went underground to access it.

In the camp area, new bunkhouses were built, as well as an addition to the staff house, and the cookhouse was doubled in size.

In 1964 Arnold Walker replaced Bruce Alexander as general manager, and when the production of ore from underground began that April, the number of men employed rose to 245, with 107 of them working underground. Many of them had trouble finding homes to rent, but a partial solution was found at Blubber Bay. Domtar, having closed its lime kilns there to concentrate on crushing limestone, had downsized its workforce and was willing to rent the empty houses for thirty-five dollars per month, although this was double the rate the company charged its own employees.

The deeper the iron mine's workings went, the more copper appeared. The crushed ore that was subsequently produced was upgraded by magnetic pulleys and exported to Japan. But when it was discounted there due to its impurities, to avoid further penalties, the company installed its own wet mill with a dry magnetic circuit followed by wet fine crushing, grinding and flotation circuits to produce copper and iron concentrates. The latter was further upgraded by wet magnetic drum separators, and both concentrates were then dewatered. The copper concentrate contained small quantities of silver and gold. Waste rock from the dry magnetic separators was carried by a long conveyor to a waste pile on the beach, which gradually grew until it extended out into the ocean; this was nicknamed Mount Shuttleworth after the underground superintendent. The magnetite concentrates were shipped to Japan while the copper concentrates were sent to Tacoma.

The ships loading ore for Japan hosted opulent dinners for the local managers and their friends. There were four glasses at each place for water, beer, rye and saki, and none were ever allowed to become empty; as soon as the guest took a sip, a crew member topped up the glass. Meanwhile, the men loading the ships—who were never invited to these fancy dinners—would turn their backs when they saw unauthorized people going

A gourmet dinner aboard ship is enjoyed by (L to R) Elmer Paton, crew member, Captain Fred Millwright, Noreen Paton.

One of these Panamax-sized vessels, which carried ore to Japan, was the specially built MV Texada Maru.

aboard to barter for Japanese cameras and other desirable goods. Even Vancouver prostitutes found their way aboard. However, all this came to an end when Texada Mines Ltd. ordered the construction of the 815-foot ore carrier *Texada Maru* to make monthly trips between Texada and the Mitsubishi Corporation in Japan. Its first load of 68,500 tons was the largest cargo loaded at a BC port up to that time.

Men were still migrating from Ontario to work for Texada Mines Ltd. Typical of this breed were the two Plante brothers, who came from Ontario in 1966. The following year, a third brother sold his eighty-acre farm and, along with several other relatives, formed a cavalcade of fourteen people in a Volkswagen bus, a car and a U-Haul. Every day as they drove across the country, they bought enough food to make sandwiches for themselves, and in the evening all fourteen shoehorned themselves into one motel room. It was apparently worth the discomfort, because after they reached Texada, they made double the money in the mines than they had on the farm.

In 1967 the Kaiser Aluminum Chemical Corporation of California bought the iron mine. Most of the ore was coming from underground by this time. Over the following year, Kaiser drove tunnels sixteen feet in diameter down into the iron mine and replaced the rail access and associated equipment with new trackless equipment with Load Haul Dump (LHD) capabilities (where one machine does all three actions) to feed the ore passes on each level leading to the crusher at the deepest level of the mine.

Kaiser shut down the mine in December 1976, and the last shipment of ore left in January 1977. A number of factors caused the final shutdown, but the main reason was that the ore was ceasing to be economically viable. Although there were ore reserves below the level of the crusher at the bottom of the mine, prices had dropped so that the returns did not warrant the expense of driving a new shaft and installing new hoists. Japanese customers could buy iron ore for less elsewhere, as iron ore deposits had been discovered in Labrador, Quebec and Australia that were easily accessible as open-pit mines with cheaper operating costs and potentially longer lives.

Maintenance Superintendent Kurt Prime talks to the operator of the first of two jumbo drills to be built in Texada Mines' shop around 1970. This one was built on the chassis of a haul truck for use when the mine went trackless. Although the drills were pneumatic, the other mechanisms were hydraulic so that one person could drill three ten-foot holes simultaneously. A drift round of 24 holes could be drilled in 2-3 hours. This took out a chunk 12 feet wide, 10 feet high and 10 feet deep.

CHAPTER 4:

Gold Fever

THE TEXADA EXCITEMENT

ALL THE PUBLICITY AND SCANDAL surrounding Texada's iron deposits during the 1870s caught the attention of prospectors near and far, and they developed even greater interest in the island after 1876, when a man named Alfred Gill (1836–1889), a Cornish prospector living in Nanaimo, found gold on his Copper Queen claim.[1] By November 1879 another prospector by the name of Howse also had good gold showings on a Texada copper claim, probably in the vicinity of Raven Bay on the island's east coast. Among the other new prospectors to come to Texada were cousins Alfred and James Raper. Although perhaps not the first to arrive, it is known that they made short prospecting trips to the north end of the island at this time, probably arriving by dugout canoe. They and Alfred's father, Ben, had come from England in 1862, and by the 1870s they were operating the Nanaimo branch of A.B. Gray's dry goods store. Alfred married Sarah Flewett from DeCourcy Island in 1875 and set up a home on Gabriola Island, from which he commuted to work. In 1880 a court case involving charges of embezzlement severed the Rapers' connection with A.B. Gray. James left for the US and did not return for thirteen years, but Alfred opened his own store, Raper, Raper Co., in Nanaimo, where he was very active in the business community for many years. He was greatly assisted by the arrival of James's brother Thomas and his wife, Polly, who subsequently ran the store, releasing him to spend so much time

Alfred and Sarah Raper. While still living in Nanaimo, where he was active in the Chamber of Commerce, Alfred was a pioneer prospector on Texada from the 1870s onwards. He lived on the island from 1893 to 1908, during which time he served as Justice of the Peace for twelve years. Although he later moved to Vancouver, he returned to die on Texada in 1913.

prospecting that the *British Colonist* dubbed him "the pioneer of the Texada mines." Thomas and Polly later moved to Texada, where they lived the rest of their lives.

Island legend says that it was either the Rapers or fishermen who found the Little Billie (or Billy or Billee) claim in 1880. It lay just above the high tide line a half-mile southeast of Van Anda Cove and was originally worked from a tent on the beach. Then in October 1882, Alfred Raper and J.W. Sutherland discovered a two-foot-wide seam of gold within a wide belt of porphyries near Spectacle and Kirk lakes. They called their new claim the Nutcracker.

Another of the early prospectors to arrive on Texada was Calvin R. Miller (1842–?), who brought his family to the island in 1887, though they had entered Canada from the US two years earlier. He crushed and panned "considerable gold" from his Golden Slipper claim, which was the first on the island to be Crown-granted. Working alone, he pounded five thousand dollars from a small calcite vein that varied from one to four inches wide and about nine feet long until it ran out at a depth of seventy feet. According to Ed Raper, one of the twin sons of Alfred Raper, it was Miller's wife, Caroline, who had found the vein.[2]

Disputed claims were common. In October 1880 the court in Nanaimo heard that Alfred S. Gill had threatened to throw rocks down on W.F. Tolmie (1812–1886), a retired MLA, as he worked down a shaft for the "Malispina *[sic]* Straits Prospecting Company." Tolmie had twenty-five claims on Comet Mountain near Raven Bay, and it appears that the ownership of at least one of these was in dispute. The case was dismissed after Gill assured the court that he'd had no intention of harming Tolmie.[3]

Between September 1888 and January 26, 1889, Nanaimo's government agent, Marshall Bray, issued ninety-three mining licences for Texada Island before learning that the island was not within his jurisdiction. Thereafter, Texada claims had to be recorded in New Westminster. This surge of activity, which the *Nanaimo Free Press* called the "Texada Excitement," was blamed on the news of the activity at Calvin Miller's Golden Slipper claim.

Prospectors began flocking from Nanaimo aboard steamers like the *Rustler*, the *Muriel*, the *Isabel* and the *Spitfire*. Men even tried to sneak aboard the *Ferndale*, which carried ore from the iron mine and was not supposed to take passengers. After some miners were misled by reports of

Some early claims had shafts well below where daylight penetrated. Before the days of carbide lamps, prospectors and miners used candles to light their way.

a boarding house on the island, parties going there were urged to bring their own food and tents. Full of hope they came, packs a-jangle with tin plates, hammers, chisels, axes and gold pans, their moleskin pants held up by sturdy leather braces over warm, long-wearing, Stanfield's woollen underwear. Their feet were encased in sturdy rubber boots and their heads shaded from the sun by battered felt hats. Those with prospecting experience had gained competence in rowing little boats in all weathers, and the savvy ones understood that the island's big iron deposits would distort their compass readings, so they used the North Star to navigate instead. They knew how to build fires, erect shelters, and fish and hunt game in order to sustain themselves. Many had heard of, if not participated in, the recent gold rushes in California, Australia and the Cariboo. They knew how to search the edges of white quartz veins for glints of precious metals. Many of them carried free miner's certificates entitling them to stake a claim anywhere that the government would recognize and perhaps grubstake them to develop it. Wealthy individuals also grubstaked miners with promising claims.

However, many of these licence holders were totally inexperienced and thought that anything that even looked like quartz must contain gold, and in April 1889, when mining engineer and assayer Dr. W. Bredemeyer[4] examined over fifty claims on the island, he found that many specimens had been salted with ore from the Golden Slipper. Claim jumping was also rampant, and owners had to be continually alert to protect their property.

Throughout 1889 new gold discoveries were reported almost daily. On January 19, a specimen "as large as a goose egg" was discovered and estimated to assay at ten thousand dollars to the ton. Hugh Kirk, a coal miner from Nanaimo who had arrived on the island in 1880,[5] finally struck it rich in March 1889. Then, afraid that another prospector would try to steal his find, he covered it over with earth and ferns until he was able to get to Nanaimo and properly register it as the Gladstone claim. On his return, he wrote to government agent Marshall Bray: "I have struck a very rich gold ledge. The old gold miners say it is the richest they ever saw. You can see the gold standing out plain. If you think proper you can come up and see for yourself. It would take five million to buy me out.

Early prospectors brought their own tents and fodder and looked out for themselves.

I am the discoverer of this ledge and therefore entitled to full credit of the find."[6] Neil Campbell, a miner from the Cariboo who arrived on the Texada scene in April 1889, reported that, although the island "has a lovely climate, it is a rough place to travel in,"[7] and "it is not easy for a man to get away from here," as steamboat service was lacking. On the plus side, food was no problem, as there were "plenty of fine deer and beautiful lake trout, the best I ever saw." He also noted, "Great activity prevails all over the island. Every hour of the day you hear the boom of dynamite in all directions. Ledge matter [surface outcrops of minerals] is as good as at any camp I have ever been in."

While Campbell was on the island, two rich strikes were made. One was on the Nutcracker claim, where men grabbed "fully $200 worth of specimens." Some pieces of quartz as large as a man's hand were literally studded with gold nuggets. "The company who own the claim had finally to fill the cavity with loose rock to prevent further depredations." Although the Nutcracker had been discovered by Raper and Sutherland in 1882, they had apparently not maintained it, because on March 18, 1889, it was registered to a man named R. Dugdale. Then, probably as

These two prospectors planned on staying for some time in their snug cabin.

the result of this new find, Dugdale was quickly bought out, and by June 10 of that same year it was owned by Mrs. Elizabeth Gough and Robert Evans of the Nanaimo Hotel and J.W. Stirtan, who was the manager of the Nanaimo Water Works, along with Hugh James and Lewis Griffiths, also of Nanaimo. That year it was deemed to be the richest claim on the island, and Griffiths brought rich samples to Nanaimo every time he returned from the island. These new owners hired Hugh Kirk and William Alfred Fowler to do development work on the claim in 1890. The claim lapsed but was restaked in 1895. Between 1896 and 1898, two thousand dollars was taken out of it. Again the claim lapsed, but it was reopened in 1924, this time as the Gem Mine. It was worked under this name in 1933, 1938–41, 1981, and even into the twenty-first century.

The second strike while Campbell was there was on the Caledonian or Surprise claim. As they cleared the post-blast debris, they found several nuggets in a single slab of rock. Campbell reported, "In less than ten minutes, men who knew the value of the discovery had gathered on the spot, and a scene of wild excitement ensued. One man took a sledgehammer and broke a portion of the detached rock. The pieces fell apart, and there in the centre shone out the nuggets. In a porous cavity about six inches long lay a magnificent nugget shaped like a winding serpent, while others were of all shapes and sizes." Campbell noted that the property, "like all good things, is in dispute between a Vancouver syndicate and the present company." In fact, Alfred Raper and Elijah Priest of Nanaimo, who were working the claim, called it the Surprise; the Texada Mining Company, which disputed their ownership, referred to it as the Caledonian. The issue landed in the courts in December 1889.

As prospectors working on their own didn't have the resources for full-scale mining operations, in January 1889, after extracting all the easily mined gold in the Golden Slipper, Calvin Miller acquired some partners and formed the Blue Bell Mining Company, which then claimed ownership of the Golden Slipper. The company's trustees were A.R. Johnson, W. Wilson and J.M. Rudd; Thomas Bell sometimes spoke on behalf of this company. However, on February 8, Elijah Priest announced that he was about to "open the Blue Bell Ledge." (Prospectors of that era called surface outcrops of minerals ledges.) This announcement was followed by a story in the February 17, 1889, issue of the *British Colonist* that stated that C.R. Miller, along with J.E. Jenkins, Richard Prouse, Alexander Easson, William Tree and George Tippet, had registered themselves as the Texada Mining Company, with headquarters in Nanaimo. The company had capital stock of $75,000 in 750 shares of $100 each and controlled twenty-five claims on Texada, including the Golden Slipper, Dalkeith, Devon Great Consul, Blue Bird, Old Flag, John Pawson, British Queen and Prince of Wales.[8] Within weeks, a group of Vancouver businessmen tried to buy the company for fifty thousand dollars, but only if the claims proved profitable. Miller and his associates turned the offer down. (Why Miller would form two companies both claiming ownership of the Golden Slipper is a mystery, as they seem to have operated simultaneously.)

A March 4, 1889, article in the *Nanaimo Free Press* quotes Alfred Raper as saying, "Oh, Texada is all right, by jiminy, there's gold there and plenty of it, too." The paper reported that nine men from the Texada Gold and Silver Company, with which Raper was associated, and from Miller's Blue Bell Mining Company had come over from Nanaimo for the day aboard the *Muriel.* They went ashore at the iron mine wharf and proceeded to their claims, later meeting at Calvin Miller's cabin. When Miller invited the men to sample his Golden Slipper claim, two panfuls of dirt were washed in the presence of J.A. Strong, Thomas Bell, J.M. Rudd, P. Gables, A. Raper, J.W. Stirtan, W. Scoville, and Nanaimo aldermen James Abrams and W.E. Webb. They then posed for a photograph with Calvin and Caroline Miller. One man in the photo appears to be using a magnifying glass to examine an ore sample.

Miners from other gold rushes also followed the news and soon arrived on Texada. One of these was William Williams, who had discovered the famous "welcome" nugget at Red Hill Ballarat, Australia, in 1857. On May 23, 1889, the *Nanaimo Free Press* reported that on Texada, Williams staked the Welcome claim within twelve hundred feet of the Nutcracker.

No claim maps have survived from 1889. The earliest is A.S. Going's map of 1899, which, while it shows the location of the Golden Slipper, the Nutcracker and a Hugh Kirk Fraction, gives no indication where the Gladstone, Welcome and Blue Bell claims were. This was probably because they were all overstaked by that time.

Meanwhile, on January 19 and February 6, 1889, Elijah Priest, Ezra Cook, T.D. Jones, Alfred Raper, T. Morgan and J.W. Stillman applied to BC's chief commissioner of Lands and Works to purchase parcels of pastoral land, ranging from 160 to 480 acres, on the south side of Texada. According to Cook's granddaughter, he had no intention of farming there and was only interested in the mineral rights, and this was undoubtedly true of all the men in this group, especially Raper, who had been prospecting on the island since the 1870s. News of these land purchases probably reached the ears of local miners and prospectors very quickly, because in February 1889 a meeting of Texada miners in Vancouver urged the provincial government that "no grants of land for pastoral purposes be made on Texada Island, as such grants would interfere with mining operations."[9]

On March 4, 1889, a group of nine investors from Alfred Raper's Texada Gold and Silver Company and Calvin Miller's Blue Bell Mining Company came over from Nanaimo on a day trip aboard the Muriel. *After inspecting their claims, they met at Miller's cabin, where this picture was taken. The group includes Calvin Miller and his wife, Caroline, along with Alfred Raper and investors J.A. Strong, Thomas Bell, J.M. Rudd, P. Gables, A. Raper, J.W. Stirtan, W. Scoville and Nanaimo aldermen James Abrams and W.E. Webb. One man in the photo appears to be using a magnifying glass to examine an ore sample.* City of Vancouver Archives

The government did not act on their advice. However, when Priest sold his Lot 15 to John E. Glover on March 25, 1889, he had to sign an affidavit that the land was "unfit for cultivation, does not include meadow or swamp land, and is valueless for lumbering purposes." Ezra Cook, who had received a Crown grant for his Lot 19, signed a similar affidavit when he sold it on April 6, 1889. In the ensuing years, Alfred Raper concentrated his efforts on the northern part of the island, so these southern properties must have shown little promise of mineral wealth. Cook Bay on the southwest side of Texada is named for Ezra Stephens Cook (1854–1912).

GOLD FEVER ABATES

In 1890 and 1891 Alfred Raper obtained crown grants to five quarter-sections of land east of the iron mine. His original quarter section, which became BC Crown Grant No. 1, is now District Lot 25. Alfred's father, Ben Raper, obtained a Crown grant for an adjoining quarter-section in 1892. All three parcels were probably chosen for their mineral rights, which at that time came with the land, but Alfred did build a large log home on Crown Grant No. 1. It was also reported that he staked out five claims around Kirk Lake and had a gold mine called the "Victoria" at the east end of the lake, which he dammed to allow the water to run down a flume to an eight-foot waterwheel that powered his rock crusher. However, he did not spend all of his time on Texada; he commuted back and forth between the island and Nanaimo, where he worked enthusiastically on the city's exhibit for the 1893 Chicago World's Fair, an exhibit that included samples of ore and Texada clay, which he had found suitable for the manufacture of firebricks.

By this time J.W. Sutherland, the prospector with whom Alfred Raper had found the Nutcracker in 1882, had become a successful mining broker in Fairhaven, Washington. According to the *Nanaimo Free Press*, after Raper invited Sutherland back to visit, he arranged for several island companies to bond their claims to "American capitalists" for development. These companies included the Texada Gold and Silver Mining Company, the Minerva Mining Company and the Georgian Mining Company.

In December 1892, the *Colonist* reported that Hugh Kirk had been lost in the bush for three days and arrived home in bad shape, with swollen legs and feet. This escapade did not prevent him going back, but the following spring, he disappeared again. "Old Felix" tried to visit him in late January 1893, but though he found a little fire in the cabin, Kirk was not there. Since interest in Texada's minerals had waned by this time, most prospectors did not overwinter on the island, and only C.R. Miller and James Raper, recently returned from a thirteen-year absence, were available to search for Kirk. All they found was a note on Kirk's cabin door: "Gone for deer. Back soon." It was not until March 29, 1894, that W. Fowler, "a comparative stranger on the island" and not related to Kirk's former partner, William Alfred Fowler, found his rifle and then his skeleton near his cabin. Death records in the BC Archives reveal that Hugh Kirk was only forty when he died.

Alfred Raper's cousin James returned to Canada in 1893, having spent his thirteen years of exile working in the coal mines of Montana, Utah and Washington. In March 1893, Alfred's Texada Gold and Silver Mining Company was pleased to contract James Raper to sink a shaft, and he returned to the island in "a little sloop," bringing his family with him, and they enjoyed a prolonged stay in the log cabin he built for them. At the same time, the nearby iron mine, which had suffered a fire, hired him as watchman.

About this time gold was discovered on the Lorindale claim. "Fifteen dollars in free gold was picked out of one of the corners of a chunk with a penknife. It is the richest ore ever seen here," said the *British Colonist* newspaper on October 14, 1896. Unfortunately, it was only a small surface deposit.

This was also the year in which the New Westminster office of the Ministry of Mines transferred one hundred Texada Island records to the Nanaimo District office. A year later the Ministry, noting the prospectors' disregard for settlers' rights, issued a notice advising that the locaters of mineral claims "may be required to put up a bond to indemnify the owner of the pre-emption for any damage that may be done in prospecting and mining, and only the precious metals can be taken by the owner of the mineral claim." A Ministry representative who visited Texada from November 10 to 16, 1897, reported six areas of activity: the Victoria, Raven, Silver Tip, Lorindale and Nutcracker claims and an unnamed company in Van Anda that had shipped ore to Tacoma to determine its value. Several of these claims had shafts sunk as deep as sixty feet. Interest in Texada was still sufficiently high by the following year for James Dunsmuir to lend his ship *City of Nanaimo* to take the newly appointed provincial mineralogist, William F. Robertson, on a hurried official visit to Texada. In 1899 over 30 percent of the 493 mineral claims staked in the Nanaimo Mining Division were located on Texada.

Laid-back Walter Planta always dressed nicely, even while prospecting. The lucky fellow discovered the Marjorie claim while eating lunch one day and used the proceeds to get married and then invest in a series of businesses on the island, ranging from logging to lime production and land speculation.
Courtesy Maurice Liebich

In the late 1890s, a laid-back, happy-go-lucky prospector arrived on the island. Born in Australia, Walter Planta (1871–1948) had grown up in Nanaimo, where his parents were teachers. On Texada he staked several claims and worked with James Raper in the Victoria Mine. Like many of the prospectors and miners of this period, he didn't have separate work clothes: all his prospecting was done in a suit and bowler hat. One day in 1901[10] while eating lunch about two miles west of Van Anda, he rolled back the moss from a rock and discovered a pocket of free gold seven feet long and six feet deep. Quickly he staked the Marjorie claim, which brought him sixty-five hundred dollars. On his next trip to Seattle, he married a pretty young woman and brought her back to Texada, though eventually he set her up in a house in Vancouver, where their two daughters were educated. Planta himself returned to Texada, where he became involved in everything from land speculation to logging. His Marjorie claim became part of the Planta Group of claims operated by the Texada Gold Mining Company Ltd.

CHAPTER 5:

Gold and Copper Mines

THE VAN ANDA COPPER AND GOLD COMPANY

APART FROM RICH CLAIMS, what the gold mining industry on Texada really needed at this time was an experienced mining promoter who could persuade people to invest in ventures there. Although a group of Victoria investors had sunk a twenty-foot shaft into the Copper Queen claim, which was discovered in 1876 by Alfred Gill, they had abandoned it in 1890 when they hit granite. Similarly, the Little Billie Mine, discovered in 1880, and the Cornell Mine, which was discovered in 1893–94 by either Alfred[1] or James Raper just inland from the Little Billie, remained undeveloped for want of investors.

Fortunately, Texada's gold came to the attention of mining promoter Edward Blewett (1848–1929). Blewett came from a Cornish mining family, but in 1867 he had settled in Fremont, Nebraska, because, although he loved prospecting, he also loved cattle drives. Sometimes he was able to accomplish both on the same trip, but he always came back to his beloved wife, Carrie Van Anda, who remained in the handsome Fremont house he built for her and their six children. Livestock and railways made him rich before real estate and mining made him richer, and by the time he crossed the border into the Revelstoke area of BC's Southern Interior in 1894, he was an experienced mining promoter, looking for more prospects.

It was some peacock-coloured bornite ore displayed in the window of a Victoria store that caught Blewett's eye soon after he landed on

Blewett named Van Anda and many of his mining properties throughout the Pacific Northwest after his wife, Carrie Van Anda.
Courtesy Rob Wellington

Vancouver Island, and it was not long after this that he met prospector Alfred Raper. It seems likely that he purchased Raper's claims to the Cornell on the spot, then acquired the Saunders Syndicate's Copper Queen and Little Billie claims, as the three mines lay in line running almost due south from a point on the beach just east of Van Anda Cove. The Cornell and Copper Queen mines, where the metals were found in two copper sulphides, bornite and chalcopyrite, were destined to become the two biggest producers of copper, gold and silver on the island during the next stage of Texada's gold boom.

At the land office in New Westminster, Blewett transferred his purchases to the company he had formed in Washington State to receive them: the Van Anda Copper and Gold Company Ltd. In Vancouver he bought hand drills, a steam boiler and a compressor to run the Cameron pumps used to keep mines dry, a hoist to haul the ore to the surface, horses and wagons. By January 1896, Blewett had all the equipment in place to blast and dig out the ore, hoist it to the surface and prepare it for shipping. He imported his eldest son, Ralph, to be mine superintendent, and they shipped three hundred tons of ore to Swansea, England, as the cost of smeltering there was cheap and the ore could go as ballast in sailing ships. That ore "averaged .34 ozs in gold, 6 ozs in silver and 6.2% of copper."[2] Thirty tons of ore from the Little Billie Mine went to a smelter in Everett and yielded "18 ozs silver, $4–5 in gold and 12% copper." These adventures with distant smelters convinced Blewett that it would be cheaper to build a smelter on Van Anda Cove above the company's new wharf, which extended out into the water for four hundred feet, and work began on its construction. At the same time, three miles south of Van Anda on Spratt's Bay, the Blewetts, along with Joseph Spratt's son, C.J., and other investors, employed eight men to work on the Raven claim, but the findings there were disappointing.

One of Blewett's biggest successes was his recruitment of his successor. In 1896, with his pockets full of coloured ores, probably bornite, he met a honeymooning couple on a train and enthused about his finds. The newly married couple were Harry Whitney Treat (1865–1922) and his bride, Olive Graef (1869–1945), a New York beauty. The enthusiastic Blewett, who was quoted in the *Colonist* of August 31, 1897, as saying that he preferred the glittering prospects of Texada to those of the Klondike, talked Treat into several mining ventures, one of which was on Texada. Treat, who became secretary–treasurer of the Van Anda Copper and Gold Company, was a wealthy man with business connections in both Chicago and New York. A graduate of Cornell University and Harvard Law School, he maintained his own office at 65 Wall Street. He was "a slim figured, dapper and bouncy blond, replete with wavy hair and a grand manner . . . a great lover of horses and women, not necessarily in the order named." He was also "a man about town with a flare for getting the right kind of attention—and, incidentally, having the money to maintain a perpetual place in the spotlight."[3] Treat's wife, Olive Marion Graef, was the daughter of the US importer of Mumm's Extra Dry Champagne. Both Treats moved in the same social circles as the Vanderbilts and the Rockefellers,[4] and the family scrapbook has a picture of Olive Treat with John D. Rockefeller Jr., who may also have encouraged Treat to invest in Seattle's future. Blewett had already been active on that scene and may have influenced him as well.

Although rich "float boulders" had been discovered by Alfred Raper on the Cornell claim some years earlier, it was only when he and the Treats were examining the property in October 1898 that Mrs. Treat stumbled over a rich ledge. When interviewed for an article that appeared in the November 25, 1898, *New York Times*, Olive Treat said that she and her husband had been deer hunting when, "We noticed a piece of green pyrites stained with copper suspended in the roots of a large dead tree, which had

Harry and Olive Treat, Edward Blewett and a group of miners at the Cornell Mine.

fallen over . . . I saw at once that it was rich in copper, and upon examining it closely we were amazed to find it dotted with specks of free gold. There was at least $1,000 worth of ore in sight, scattered about just as if nature had been at play there."

With the renewed activity on Texada, investors living in Victoria and Nanaimo were eager to visit the island, and from time to time Henry Saunders of Victoria organized trips for them. The first of these was aboard the *City of Nanaimo*, "a very comfortable passenger boat," on Sunday, December 4, 1898.[5] Among the passengers from Victoria were fifteen businessmen, four mining engineers and brokers and two newspapermen, along with "bluff and jolly" Harry Helmcken, member of the BC legislature from 1894 to 1903. From Nanaimo came government agent Marshall Bray, mining broker Thomas Kitchin and M. Morton, a hardware merchant who owned shares in Texada's west coast mines and several others. En route, two musicians played stringed instruments to entertain the party. Despite the strong winds and heavy seas, "a better meal was served than any steamer running out of Victoria" before the ship tied up at the wharf belonging to the Marble Bay Company at 11:30 a.m. The visitors were met by Edward and Ralph Blewett, Harry W. Treat, J. Kitty, who was the assayer for the Van Anda mines, and F.W. McCrady, manager of the Marble Bay Company. Also there to greet them were Alfred Raper, Dr. Alex Allen Forbes and his brother, Robert Forbes, a Minnesota mining engineer.

On this crisp, sunny morning, as they made their way up a well-built wagon road to the Copper Queen Mine, the visitors were treated to a grand view of new snow on the distant mainland peaks above Jervis Inlet. As the miners were at dinner, they continued past the Copper Queen along a trail to the Cornell Mine, where two of the visitors took photographs of the others. Returning to the Copper Queen, they learned that forty miners had been hired, and a portion of the land owned by the Van Anda Copper and Gold Mining Company had been designated as a townsite and subdivided into lots. A school was also being built and a hotel was planned. They were also informed that the Blewetts' Raven Mine, south of the Van Anda property, had recently contracted to supply fluxing ore for the Everett smelter.

In adjacent Texada City, McCrady showed the group the Marble Bay Mine, where the shaft had been recently collared to exploit the copper–gold surface showings. This operation was the main holding of J.J. Palmer and William Christie, whose Marble Bay Company had reopened a marble quarry that Palmer had purchased and operated some years earlier. In August 1898 they had constructed a lime kiln there that still stands.

While the visitors explored the mines belonging to the Van Anda and Marble Bay companies, Bray and Morton hiked farther along the wagon road and over to the west coast of the island to the wave-battered wharf at the Victoria–Texada Mine. Their purpose was to see the Surprise Mine, which "has had a larger amount of development work than any other mine on the island." Nearby was Calvin R. Miller's original claim. Later at the Treat residence, the visitors admired the view over the Strait and the sitting room fireplace ornamented with "cleverly arranged pieces of the varicoloured Van Anda ore." They heard that the island's total population was now about three hundred, of which half were miners, mostly living around Van Anda, and that eight of the mines on the island had steam hoisting plants. The return trip to Victoria was made much faster on calm seas, and they arrived at 6:30 p.m.

Blewett ended his active involvement in Texada in March 1899. He resigned as president and manager of the Van Anda Copper and Gold Company, explaining that his business interests in Nebraska required his attention, and he sold his shares to Treat.

The four-hundred-foot-long Van Anda wharf collapsed in a south-easterly gale on March 11, 1899, with a team of horses and their driver narrowly escaping injury. Work began on a replacement immediately, and by the end of the year, the steamer *Clayoquot* was already tying up there again. Meanwhile, the company's smelter on Van Anda Cove finally began operating on July 15, 1899. This was actually the company's second furnace, as the first one, installed the previous year, had blown up shortly after it began operating. The second was a used furnace that had been imported from Vancouver, and with it came master mechanic and blacksmith Alex McKelvie (the father of BC historian Bruce McKelvie), who had previously installed the furnace in Vancouver. However, because the Texada ore was roasted in the open air before it was put into the kiln to be smelted, very soon the sulphur from the process had denuded every tree in the surrounding area.

At this point, Treat brought in Thomas Kiddie, a metallurgist from New Jersey, to be his superintendent of mining and smelting operations, and this proved to be a good move. Mining engineer William M. Brewer reported after a February visit to the island that:

> I think it is to be regretted that previous managements neglected to thoroughly and systematically exploit the various levels of the mine . . . Under the superintendence of Mr. Kiddie, a more systematic method of carrying on the work both in the Copper Queen and the Cornell Mines has been adopted . . . he is working to block out ore in sight while previous managements apparently merely worked to gouge out any ore that was exposed, regardless of future development.[6]

Tramways and trestles now connected the Copper Queen, the smelter and the lime quarry so that "all material received by water (coke, ore etc.) can be at once hoisted, weighed, sampled and either dumped into the bins or run back onto the roast piles."[7] Fuel for the boiler came by trestle from the company's sawmill, beside which shops had been constructed for carpenters and blacksmiths alongside an oil room, storerooms and a new assay office. The company also installed a telephone system between the various properties, which must have been extremely well used, especially after 1899, when Blewett's Raven properties, which were some distance away, were added to the Van Anda Company's holdings.

The smelter was the main object of interest for the second tour of investors who arrived aboard the *City of Nanaimo* in August 1899.[8] Treat and Thomas Kiddie, the new smelter superintendent, showed them the "white molten metal pouring forth from the smelter." After lunching aboard the steamer, the party visited the Copper Queen and Cornell mines, but operations there had suffered during a recent strike. However, the mine superintendent, a Mr. Lawrence, reassured them that "the places of the striking miners would very soon be filled up."[9]

Dr. John Sebastian Helmcken, who had come to BC in 1850 as a surgeon for the Hudson's Bay Company and stayed to become prominent in the province's political life, was on this trip, and he added a fulsome letter to the report printed in the *British Colonist* on August 8.[10] He likened Treat to a magician showing off "numerous Aladdin's caves, their guards and governors, a bewildering scene of disciplined labour, the pride, the glory, the loved child of the multi-talented, enthusiastic, over-active magician" who had converted the ores into copper, gold and silver. Of his walk up to the mines, Helmcken reported that "the roads are rather rough and a trifle hilly, rather trying to those who have corns, but really nothing to the industrious, healthy, who laugh at dust, a little climbing and sweating faces." In describing his visit to the Copper Queen Mine, where the shaft had reached a depth of three hundred feet, he noted that Mrs. Treat, "although holding a high social position in New York, had, I was told without hesitation, explored this shaft." Between the Copper Queen and the Cornell mines, he saw "fat cattle penned in" and "large stables sheltering a dozen magnificent draught horses and Mr. Treat's riding one—for he is indefatigable and ubiquitous."[11]

Several other skilled smelter men arrived from the east; they included Joe Thompson, Paddy O'Neill (who had to quietly leave town after he threw his wife through a window at the New Year), William Gilchrist,

For the second time, a group of investors from Victoria chartered the City of Nanaimo *to bring them for a visit in August 1899. This time they came to see the smelter.*

Charlie Jessop, Bill Dwyer, assayer Jens Marstrand and the Treats' friend Al Eschweger, son of a New York Supreme Court judge.[12] Despite his Harvard degree, Eschweger was prepared to turn his hand to any project. He started out as wharfinger and later worked in the mine.

LABOUR UNREST

The company's management style was paternalistic, providing the workers with ground on which to pitch their tents, piped water, and the occasional picnic and Christmas party. The Treats always funded a generous picnic when they came to the island. Annie McLeod, who lived on Texada most of her life, reported that the island "was a very happy place with no labour troubles until the Blubber Bay Strike,"[13] but she must have been looking through rose-coloured glasses. Strikes did occur on the island and received the typical treatment of the day. Often they involved the Chinese workers: some miners didn't want to work with them, while others were outraged at their treatment. In the Vancouver Island coal mines, independent miners were sending Chinese workers underground as assistants and sometimes left them there to do the work by themselves.[14] Questions were raised in the legislature and in the press. On Texada, Chinese were at first only employed to sort ore and cut firewood, but this soon changed, and in February 1898, Elisha Read, "manager of the Van Anda metalliferous mine on Texada Island," pleaded guilty to employing Chinese underground in contravention of the Mines Inspection Act. He was fined $49.90. (Treat, who was usually described as the manager, must have been conveniently out of town.) Then there was the question of importing strike breakers. Helmcken's letter in the August 8 issue of the *Colonist* says the strike breakers were brought in as a result of the new "eight-hour law" and the "unwilling but compulsory employment of a few Japanese or Chinese to replace [the striking miners] in all rough work." In August 1899 the *Salt Lake Herald* reported that Treat had reduced the workers' pay from $3.50 for an eight-hour shift to $3, and 130 men went on strike. Treat's reaction was to say that he had enough ore on hand to run the smelter for at least three and a half months.

In February 1901 several newly hired engineers arrived at the Cornell Mine and learned that they were expected to lower sixty Japanese muckers underground. When they refused, the Japanese used ladders to reach the worksite; the mine was 260 feet deep at the time. One engineer quit and the others met with Superintendent Kiddie, who, after considering the matter, paid them off. Although the company considered the matter resolved, the miners' union did not. However, further developments seem to have been overtaken by the leasing of the mines to various other companies, although government agent Marshall Bray noted that "the strike had a somewhat depressing influence"[15] and "has had an effect on the development work done." Treat had difficulty selling the Van Anda Company. His first attempt was in December 1900, but the deal fell through. While waiting to sell, he leased the mines to various companies, who each did a little work and then vanished.

THE MARBLE BAY MINE

Palmer was more fortunate. When he sold his Marble Bay Mine to Tacoma Steel in 1902, things went very well for them, as they struck a new copper ore body just below the point where Palmer had left off, and this financed the company's debt. In fact, the bornite ore the experts despised went down to the 1,750-foot level, producing copper all the way. The company also made a good choice of manager in Alexander Grant. He stayed with them for over a decade, oversaw the installation of well-chosen equipment and maintained good public relations with the press. Grant was also well regarded by his peers, who inducted him into the Canadian Mining Institute in October 1908.

Tacoma Steel consisted of five partners from Washington State with backgrounds in mining, forestry and land speculation. None of them had any experience in steel, but they were hungry to cash in on the profits to be made supplying steel rails to the railway companies. As they couldn't afford to build their own smelter immediately, they speculated that their Texada mining properties would profit them in the short term while providing them with an exclusive long-term supply of limestone from the other property they had bought on Limekiln Bay.

THE MARBLE BAY MINE STRIKE

In 1906 "one of the richest bodies of ore ever uncovered" in the Marble Bay Mine was discovered. By coincidence, this find was followed by a significant rise in copper prices early the following year, and not surprisingly, the workers at the mine, who were all members of Texada Lodge No. 113 of the Western Federation of Miners Union, requested a wage increase. However, at almost the same time this was happening on Texada, the smelter workers at Tacoma Steel went on strike, and manager Grant was told to stop shipping ore from Texada. When he responded to his bosses' order by laying off some of the miners, they assumed this was his answer to their demands for higher wages, and on March 25, 1907, fifty of the white men working in the shafts and on the winze laid down their tools.

Once Tacoma Steel bought the Marble Bay Mine from J.J. Palmer, they were delighted to discover a whole new ore body, which paid for their purchase and produced more copper than all the other mines on the island at that time.

(Some Chinese also struck, but their numbers were not counted.) The miners at the Cornell Mine also went on strike. William Lyon Mackenzie King, then deputy minister of Labour, was called on to mediate between the strikers and the mine owners, though pressure of work in Ottawa prevented him from actually visiting Texada. The Marble Bay Mine management then invoked the new Industrial Disputes Investigation Act, which had only been passed into law on March 22, 1907. By its terms, strikers taking action without first going through a mediation process were liable to a fine of ten to fifty dollars per day.

As this was the first prosecution under the act, which had been proclaimed just three days before the miners went out on strike, neither side really knew how it was supposed to work. However, on the afternoon of Saturday, May 18, Magistrate H.C. Alexander heard from manager Alexander Grant and Mr. C.B. McNeil, KC, counsel for the Tacoma Steel Company. The Western Federation of Miners Union, which was headquartered in the US, was scheduled to testify that same evening, but the Van Anda courthouse was not available due to the yells of a mentally ill person incarcerated in the cell adjoining the courtroom. The hearing was therefore switched to the Miners' Hall, a little room on the second floor of a small frame building on the main street.[16] As the place was filthy, some of the miners swept the floor just before the hearing began at 7 p.m., stirring up "a cloud of dust which would have done credit to a sandstorm on the Sahara."[17] A dozen coal oil lamps were lit to penetrate the gloom. Representing the union were Matt Halliday, vice-president, and T.T. Rutherford, secretary, backed up by Marble Bay employees Harry DeGreek and J.H. Jess, both of whom were union members. (Harry DeGreek [1861–1914] had worked for the Marble Bay Mine for six years. A New Yorker who was born Harry Greek, he had immigrated to Canada in 1893 via Nebraska and Qualicum, where he changed his name to DeGreek. Three of his thirteen children were born in Nebraska, two in Qualicum and the remaining eight on Texada, where his wife, Anna, practised as a midwife.)

Speaking on behalf of the union, Matt Halliday called for an adjournment of sixty days, but Magistrate Alexander said they could only have eight days. He then offered his services as a mediator. Halliday replied that no mediation was wanted and told him to proceed with the charges. After further discussion, the two sides agreed to adjourn for a week. The court reconvened at 10 a.m. on May 30, with C.B. McNeil again representing the company and lawyer J. Edward Bird representing the miners. By 10:30 p.m. of the same day, the case was settled, with a new wage scale established for all categories of employees. No one was fined. The men went back to work on June 8.

Another strike occurred in 1908 when paycheques were late, and the company sent fourteen New Zealand miners to take the places of the strikers. Then eleven surface workers served notice that they would have to quit work at the end of April, as they did not approve of the methods used by the Western Federation of Miners, which was threatening to blacklist them. "The men below ground who went out on strike were all replaced [by the New Zealand miners], and the new men are remaining loyal to the company," they said. "A number of the men are married and have [had] their homes at Van Anda for years . . . Management intends to replace the union workers with non-union ones."[18] However, this dispute must have been settled, because everyone went back to work and the union versus management scene remained calm for another twenty-five years.

THE CORNELL AND LOYAL MINES

In 1902 the lessee of the Cornell Mine started work on a tramway between it, the Copper Queen and the smelter. (The remains of this tramway, with one of its crosspieces still visible, now form a pleasant walk along the shores of Emily Lake.[19]) However, later that year the smelter was closed down and shipped to Ladysmith, along with the McKelvie family, and by 1903 the Van Anda Copper and Gold Company properties were shipping ore to the smelter in its new location.

Treat had other mining interests on Texada, notably the Loyal claim. Although it had been discovered in 1897 on Crown grant land close to Grilse Point, its finders gained little, because they were unable to buy the land on which it was located from its owner, Francis L. Carter-Cotton, a member of the BC legislature and co-owner and editor of the *Vancouver Daily News–Advertiser*. Treat, however, bought the land from Carter-Cotton in 1900, and three years later, he leased it to a Tacoma company, which opened it up. In September 1904, Treat wrote his wife that he was negotiating to lease it to a Colorado syndicate. However, he must have valued this claim, because when their second daughter was born in 1906, he named her Loyal. At the time of his death in 1922, he was still leasing out Texada mining property, and as a result, his estate took several years to dispose of all of it.

COPPER MINES AFTER 1920

In the early 1900s, copper prices fell, and as a result the mines suffered from periodic shutdowns. Then in 1919 the price of copper plummeted, resulting in the closure of the Marble Bay Mine, though not before it had produced more valuable ore than all three of the mines belonging to Van Anda Copper and Gold Ltd. In April 1928, when Fred Beale (1885–1965) paid a visit in his yacht to Marble Bay, he wrote to his son that "all the old mines were intact." The Marble Bay Hotel still stood on the hill above where the Texada Boat Club marina is now, and Beale wandered through the empty rooms, which looked as if the occupants had just left the day before. Two years later, having resettled his family in Vancouver, he came back to Marble Bay, but by then "everything had been removed piecemeal by Texada residents . . . mostly by the farmers."[20]

Prospecting for minerals, however, remained an ongoing activity on Texada. During the 1920s and 1930s, prospectors poked around, but no development was significant enough to generate jobs until Lester Prosser, a silver-tongued American mining promoter, arrived in 1943 and bought the claim to the Little Billie Mine, which had been exploited for its gold since 1880. After it closed and the rights lapsed in 1919, it had been re-staked by George McLeod. "Prosser was a likeable sort of guy from the US," said Ben Nicholas, "not very tall but loaded with energy. He was good at gaining people's trust. He had the whole top floor of the Devonshire Hotel in Vancouver for a year, but something had happened in the US and he couldn't even go back there for his wife's funeral in New York. When he left, he had everybody in the country as his creditors, and his death in the Cariboo may have been suicide."

At the time Prosser arrived on Texada, he was president of Industrial Metals Mining Ltd., and within a short time he had hired twenty-seven workers, a great boost for the island's workforce. He dewatered the Little Billie Mine, which was basically a zinc mine at this time, and cleaned up down to the 280-foot level. He then acquired the Copper Queen, Cornell and the Marble Bay mines, previously developed mainly for their gold, which he said would now "become one of the biggest copper and gold mines on the Pacific."[21] Just a year after he arrived, he hired Victor Dolmage,[22] a geologist and mining engineer, who found a whole new ore body, but unfortunately, he was unable to dewater the Marble Bay Mine below the seven-hundred-foot level.[23] In January 1945, Prosser sold out to the Vananda Mining Company Ltd. (NPL), a consortium of Pioneer Gold Mines Ltd. and Sheep Creek Mines. The new owners concentrated their efforts on the Little Billie,[24] where they put in a new power plant. However, lack of funds was a continuing problem, and even reconstituting the company as Van Anda Mines (1948) Ltd. only enabled them to continue operating until June 1952.

In the ensuing years and on into the twenty-first century, prospectors like Bob Duker, Ed Johanson, Joe Christensen, Stanley Beale Jr., and many others continue to search for the elusive motherlode they believe is just waiting to be found.

Modern prospector Bob Duker, on the right, shows Texada Island Heritage Society's Pete Kenney the mill he uses to reprocess ore from his various claims. Heather Harbord

Steam hoists like this were used to haul ore to the surface at several Texada mines. Pete Palm's city clothes are indicative of what some Texada men wore to work at that time. Although he is not in the 1901 census, he is listed in that of 1911 and there were other Palms in the Gillies Bay area.

CHAPTER 6:

Marble and Lime

MARBLE QUARRYING

CAPTAIN HENRY EVELYN STURT (1841–1885) was the officer in charge of taking the British troops home after the Pig War on San Juan Island, but during the first four months of 1873, as he waited for a ship home, he travelled the West Coast investigating money-making opportunities and even had some cattle landed on Lasqueti. He returned to the province in 1876 to continue his search and found a marble outcropping at what is now known as Sturt Bay (or sometimes Marble Bay), on the north end of the island, just northwest of Van Anda Cove. He dashed off to San Francisco to reconnect with some of the wealthy people he had met there three years earlier, but was back on Texada in April 1877 to make "arrangements to work and develop the extensive marble beds"[1] on claims he had located "some months since." He obtained crown grants for them in 1878 and 1879.

In June 1878, his wife and child came from San Francisco to join him. They were accompanied by "a posse of mechanics and others necessary for the successful operation of the marble quarry."[2] Among them was D. Sharkey, a member of a San Francisco family who imported fine marble from Italy and Vermont to adorn wealthy homes. The family was so interested in finding a closer source of marble that they sent him to Texada to examine the deposit. The marble was to be shipped to San Francisco, where Sturt expected it would find a ready sale. In August stonemasons

Mortimer and Reid in Victoria began advertising headstones made from Texada marble, and by September the quarry was producing well.

Then on December 9, 1878, Daniel Buck, secretary to the Texada Marble and Commercial Company of San Francisco, paid for an advertisement in San Francisco newspapers to announce "that H. Evelyn Sturt is no longer in our employ, and that we will not pay any debts of his contracting on account of the . . . Company." This ad also appeared in the *British Colonist* in January 1879. Then on March 8, the newspapers reported, "The marble of the Texada quarry has been condemned. The San Francisco company who undertook to open the quarry have closed their works and withdrawn their men. Judges say the marble is too much broken up to be of any value."

This turn of events may be partially explained by a pair of lawsuits that were heard in the Nanaimo courthouse a short time later. J. Hirst, a Nanaimo merchant, brought the first suit against Sturt in April 1879. According to evidence presented in court, Sturt, as agent for the Texada Marble Company, had ordered supplies from Hirst. Instead of paying for them immediately, though, he had shown Hirst a Wells Fargo draft that he'd received from the Texada Marble Company, but said he wanted to use that money for other purposes. Although he gave Hirst drafts drawn on the San Francisco company, they refused to pay them, because they said they had issued Sturt with funds for this purpose and had no intention of paying twice. The judge ruled that Sturt must pay Hirst. This suit was followed by one that was heard on October 2, 1880, in which the judge ruled that Sturt must pay C.L. Sharkey the thirty-five dollars owed to him. Meanwhile, others in San Francisco had heard about Texada's iron and marble. John Jackson Palmer (1851–1928), a Canadian who was a partner with Valentine Rey in the Palmer and Rey Type Foundry of San Francisco, joined forces with "bluff, honest and outspoken" Joseph Britton (1820–1901), a prominent San Francisco lithographer, to send an agent to Texada with six thousand dollars and instructions to buy claims for both marble and iron. The agent bought several thousand acres on the east side of the island, including land along the waterfront between Sturt Bay and Marshall Point. This purchase was made directly from the provincial government, which retained the rights to precious metals but transferred all other mineral rights to the purchasers. Unfortunately, before the agent staked any iron ore claims, he went on a bender and blabbed about his intentions, and the claims were staked by others before he sobered up.

John Jackson Palmer is a shadowy figure in early Texada life. He owned property from Marble Bay to Blubber Bay and platted Texada City, but sold all his island holdings in February 1902. Although he had investments as far afield as Australia, latterly he was based in Toronto, where he was president of the Toronto Type Foundry.

In 1879, when Palmer came to see the place for himself, he bought up Sturt's original Crown grant in order to reopen Sturt's marble quarry. He and Britton then invested another twenty-five thousand dollars to hire a crew to work it, build derricks, lay tracks for tram cars and construct a stone wharf. In October 1879, one of the Sharkey family—perhaps C.L. Sharkey—arrived to manage it. There was a brief flurry of excitement in July 1880 when the partners received word that one of their claims was being jumped. Valentine Rey, Palmer's partner (he was also Britton's nephew), and Sharkey chartered the mail steamer *Pilot* for a special trip to Texada to check this out but returned three weeks later to report that all was well. Soon thousands of tons of marble were ready for shipment. Unfortunately, when it arrived in San Francisco, customs officers there rated the Sturt Bay marble as limestone and charged a higher tariff on it. Palmer returned briefly in 1882 to monitor his investment, but in 1884 he saw a better investment opportunity elsewhere, perhaps in cable cars, as Britton was busy establishing the Clay Street cable car line, the first of its kind in the world. The partners then closed their Texada operation, though they continued to pay the taxes. After ten years, Britton tired of this and gave his share to Palmer.

THE LIME KILNS IN LIMEKILN BAY

In 1885, in the hope of finding coal to assist in smelting the Puget Sound Company's iron ore deposit, the legendary George M. Dawson of the Geological Survey of Canada surveyed Texada's coastline. Although rocks at both Cook and Gillies bays looked promising, he found no coal, but he did delineate the huge limestone deposit that would later become the largest limestone mine in Canada. At that time and during the early twentieth century, limestone was in great demand on the West Coast as a flux for purifying steel, while quicklime (calcium oxide), which is made from limestone (calcium carbonate), found a ready market in the manufacture of cements and mortars for the construction industry. To make quicklime, quarry workers broke the limestone into uniform-sized chunks that were fed into kilns and heated to temperatures above 825°C. But quicklime is an unstable powder that will recombine with air to become lime again or combine with water to become slaked lime, so it had to be stored in wooden barrels, usually made in onsite cooperages. The secret to the successful processing of lime was the kilnsman, who had to know precisely how long *his* particular kiln would take to cook the lime, turning the blue rock to white powder.

The first Texada lime kiln was built in 1887 on Blubber Bay, on the northern tip of the island, by W.H. Lee, manager of the iron mine. The owner was Francis L. Carter-Cotton, newspaperman and MLA, who probably put in a manager, but the kiln was only in operation for less than a year. During the late 1880s, some quarrying was also done at Limekiln Bay, on the west side of the island, about half a mile to the southwest of Blubber Bay, but it is not known if a kiln was built there at that time. However, the history of Texada that was produced by the Centennial Committee in 1960 says that a couple of wood-fired kilns were built there in 1894–95, and these might have been the work of Donald Menzies, who bought a crown grant for Lot 23 in that bay for $220 in 1894.[3] In July of the following year, Menzies mortgaged his crown grant to Hugh Archibald Urquhart for $571.10.[4]

In March 1897, William Mellis Christie (1829–1900), the wealthy owner of Christie's Biscuits and father-in-law of John Jackson Palmer, who had invested in the marble operation on Sturt Bay thirteen years earlier, visited Texada to inspect his investment in the Victoria–Texada Gold Mining Company. Like many Scots, he was a man of strong principles. Nicknamed "the General," he was "obsequious to no man's opinions, having plenty of his own, ready to take up any gauntlet and hold his own with the best of them; a dour *carle* to thwart, but a big man [in] every way, with a warm heart and an open hand."[5] Christie quickly became so enthusiastic about Texada's mining prospects that he persuaded his son-in-law to go into partnership with him for a second round of quarrying, even though all the equipment Palmer had left on the island in 1884 had disappeared. By this time, Palmer was no longer associated with Palmer and Rey of San Francisco, having moved back to Toronto to become the president of the Toronto Type Foundry, a large wholesaler of printing equipment.

In May 1897, Palmer dutifully returned to Texada, where he hired Frank W. McCrady to manage a renewed operation on Sturt Bay. This time he opened a new quarry on the southwest side of the bay, where he had McCrady build a thirty-foot lime kiln close to the wharf and began burning lime in August 1898. A sawmill and cooperage produced barrels in which to store the finished product. Most of the workers who sorted the rock were Chinese who lived in a bunkhouse on the west side of Emily Lake. Unfortunately, the Sturt Bay lime contained silica kernels that left holes in finished plaster surfaces, so production soon ceased, and Palmer stopped quarrying there entirely in 1900, shortly after the death of his father-in-law and partner, W.M. Christie. Then, having bought Menzies' Lot 23 on Limekiln Bay on the west side of the island, he had four kilns constructed at the north end of the lot, obliterating the 1894–95 kilns. Rather than make a big investment here, Palmer had his kilns constructed from the surrounding limestone, lined with firebricks and protected with metal doors to prevent the outside walls from burning. Since water access to this location required a combination of calm weather, a high tide and shallow-draft boats, he continued to operate his sawmill and cooperage on Sturt Bay to service his new operation. However, although the lime from the

All but one of these kilns in Limekiln Bay, dating back to 1900, were obliterated when the road was rerouted in 1985.

new site was of a better quality than that at Marble Bay, it did have magnesium impurities, so he never constructed the expensive power plant and harbour facilities that would have been needed for further development.

Meanwhile, on Sturt Bay, Palmer had noticed outcrops of bornite, the mineral associated with gold in the Copper Queen Mine, so he sank a shaft and found copper, which he proceeded to extract. He called it the Marble Bay Mine. However, in those days geologists believed that bornite only occurred near the surface and that when it came to an end, the associated copper, gold and silver also ended, so when Palmer was advised that the bornite in the Marble Bay was petering out, he decided to sell all his Texada properties. Tacoma Steel, which purchased Palmer's properties in February 1902, only learned of the impurities in the Limekiln Bay stone after the deal was signed. While they discovered that the magnesium occurred in some rock layers and not others, hand sorting to remove the affected limestone, even with cheap Chinese labour, cut too deeply into profits to make it worthwhile to quarry it. However, they couldn't sell off the property, because they needed it for their long-term plans. The company's next move was to hire Walter Planta as their sales agent, but he sold the product so cheaply that he triggered a price war with lime producers in Washington State. Tacoma Steel closed their Limekiln Bay operation in 1912 but continued to operate the Marble Bay copper mine at Sturt Bay, where they also sold eight acres to the Powell River paper mill, giving that mill a cheap nearby source of lime for bleaching pulp.

THE BLUBBER BAY LIME KILNS

In 1907 a group of Vancouver men calling themselves the Blubber Bay Syndicate began burning lime in a kiln built in Blubber Bay. In February 1910, when they needed more funds, they formed the Vancouver–Texada Lime Company. Five months later, realizing they needed still more funding, they wound up the company and formed a new one, Pacific Lime Co. Ltd. whose purpose was to acquire land containing limestone, marble and sandstone deposits, and to market the products so obtained.

By 1913 Pacific Lime had "extensive storehouses and wharves"[6] and was using a steam drill to drill blast holes. One round of holes produced enough rock to feed the kilns for several weeks. The rock was hand-dug by Chinese workers, who descended a series of ladders that were ultimately over 320 feet to reach the bottom of the pit; they preferred this to going down in the bucket operated by white workers whom they did not trust. Using shovels, forks and pickaxes, they dug out the lime, filled metal wheelbarrows and dumped them into a one-ton iron bucket. A steam hoist raised the bucket to the edge of the pit, where it connected to a "bicycle" that guided it up to the head of an A-frame above a bunker. As it reached the bunker, a chain hanging from the bucket caught on a pin and tipped the contents into the bunker. Gravity then sent the "bicycle" and the empty bucket down, before separating them at the edge of the pit so that the bucket could descend for another load. These Chinese workers also sorted the limestone before it went into the kilns.

The kilns spewed out ten tons of quicklime dust per day, coating the trees with white as far away as the old iron mine. Every spring green shoots would poke out of these whitened trees and the process began again. Protective clothing was a thing of the future, so all the workers became covered in quicklime dust, too. It burned exposed skin on contact, especially on men who sweated heavily, and as a result, even small flesh cuts could be excruciatingly painful. The men wore handkerchiefs over their faces to protect their lungs and wooden clogs on their feet, as the dust ate leather. But apart from unavoidable injuries from the dust, the workers were very safety conscious, as the only way out of the Glory Hole, as Pit No. 1 was called, was for the injured person to lie on a stretcher that was placed across the ore bucket.

The company had its own sawmill. Although built to machine-cut cordwood into four-foot slabs for the kilns, it also turned out lumber, much of which was used to build the Stillwater dam and houses in nearby Powell River. The man in charge of the mill, Ben Buholtz, "created special solutions for special functions . . . with a junk pile that could produce the answer to any problem."[7] The mill's accumulated sawdust was used to feed the boilers of a steam plant and steam turbine

No. 1 pit, the Glory Hole, was hand dug by Chinese workers, who climbed down ladders rather than trust non-Chinese to lower them over two hundred feet to the bottom.

powerhouse. Young Robert Maylor's[8] grade four school assignment, written about 1926, notes that two of the five kilns had by that time been converted to running on sawdust from the sawmill as well, instead of slab wood, which had to be brought from too far away. The company's barrel factory used local fir for heads and staves, but the iron for hoops was imported from Oregon and the east.

Although the company changed hands in 1916, the majority of its shares now being owned by the Niagara Alkali Company of New York, it retained the Pacific Lime name for another forty years. By 1916 its kilns were burning 150 barrels of lime a day, and its hydrating plant was treating another sixty barrels of lump lime daily, while every month the Blubber Bay plant shipped three thousand tons of limestone up the coast to the smelter at Anyox, where it was used for fluxing purposes. Every two weeks Pacific Lime's subsidiary company, Kingsley Navigation, which was formed in 1918 and named after the company's president at that time,

By 1916 Pacific Lime's kilns at Blubber Bay were burning enough rock to produce 150 barrels of lime a day. Heather Harbord

In 1918, Pacific Lime set up a subsidiary shipping company to transport its products but in 1942, the ships, including the E.D. Kingsley *seen here, were taken over by the navy and after the war the company operated independently.*

shipped barrels of quicklime to San Francisco, leaving the lower grades of limestone to be sorted and sent up the coast to the Anyox smelter. The ships employed on these runs, the *E.D. Kingsley, Queen City* and *Rochelie,* were soon familiar sights in Blubber Bay.

Andrew Williamson (1887–1964) arrived in 1917[9] to become the plant foreman, joining fellow Scot Jonathan Ross, who had been hired earlier as chief engineer for Pacific Lime's steam plant; they had previously worked together in Kimberley. Williamson stayed with Pacific Lime for the next twenty-five years. His daughter Jean recalled watching as the bay was dredged to deepen it, with divers in huge helmets and suits laying dynamite charges that her father detonated.

In 1924 the Chinese began complaining to the company about their wages, which were only a fraction of what Caucasian workers earned. They got nowhere,[10] but company officials were shocked by this confrontation, and when it was time to dig a second pit, they brought in machines to do the work. Unfortunately, the limestone in Pit No. 2 was not up to standard. They dug Pit No. 3, but the result was the same, so they ended up using the hole for coal storage.

These were the days when Chinese women were not allowed to immigrate to Canada, so the workers were all single men who lived in three bunkhouses, some of which were built on stilts over the water just east of the pits. They paid one dollar a month for their accommodation, light, fuel and water, but there were no showers and only rudimentary latrines. Many of them raised ducks, chickens and pigs and grew vegetables to supplement the food available in the company store. Married white workers were accommodated in company cottages on the west side of the harbour, while single white workers lived in small houses at Limekiln Bay. Despite the wage disparity between the Caucasian and Chinese workers, relations between the two were friendly enough that everyone stood together when the big strike came a few years later.

OTHER LIME OPERATIONS

Drawn by the success of Pacific Lime, the Fogh family erected a cylindrical kiln and other facilities on their property in the centre of Blubber Bay, but for some unknown reason they operated it for only a short time. Then in 1926, the Western Lime Company tried to operate on the same property, but the limestone there was not as pure as that on Pacific Lime's property, so the operation folded after just eighteen months. In 1929 George and Lorne McLeod cut a trail from their house on Wall Street in Van Anda east to Lot 499, just past the Little Billie Mine, where they started their own limestone quarry. At the same time a Bamberton company, BC Cement, opened a quarry near Grilse Point, on the northernmost tip of the island, to ship lime to their Bamberton plant for processing. (This company's Tod Inlet quarry had closed in 1921; the site is now occupied by Butchart Gardens.) On Texada they installed a modern diesel-powered plant complete with conveyor belts that could load two 450-ton scows a day and approximately three miles of narrow gauge railway tracks on which their four gas locomotives hauled six- to nine-ton ore cars. Among

The remains of the BC Cement operation still stand in Blubber Bay opposite the ferry dock. It was never as big as Pacific Lime. Heather Harbord

Henry Liebich at BC Cement, where he followed his father's calling and became a driller. When the Blubber Bay strike began, he refused to cross the picket line to go to work and obtained a transfer to work at BC Cement's Bamberton plant near Victoria. His son, Maurice, was born after this move.

the people who worked on the startup was Bill Bushby, an Englishman who married Bertha Liebich and played a prominent role in the ensuing strike.

Fred Beale settled his wife, Mary, and family in Vancouver before returning to found Beale Quarries, which brought much-needed work to Van Anda at the height of the Great Depression. Courtesy Stanley Beale

Although the stock market crash of 1929 crippled economies around the world, the impact was not felt on the BC coast until 1931. This was the year that saw the return of Francis Joseph "Fred" Beale (1885–1965), who had visited Sturt Bay briefly in April 1928. Like Blewett, Treat and Palmer before him, Beale had business interests in other places. Although born and raised in Auckland, New Zealand, he was now operating a limestone quarry at Ocean Falls, three hundred miles north of Texada. Beale liked the look of the McLeod quarry but didn't immediately buy it. Instead, he took over the Powell River Company's Sturt Bay operation, as he realized that he could do the work cheaper than the pulp and paper company was doing it. The limestone they were using was inferior, but the harbour was good and their mill was close to it. He was able to reduce their costs from $2.15 to $1 per ton, and he later told his son that at that time "Van Anda had nothing except government relief of 20¢ per day. It was understood that anything was better than nothing, so that if I could get orders for limestone, even at a very low price, the local people would work at a very low rate. For a time it was 17¢ per hour [and] 35¢ for the driller, and it gradually rose." He brought in a one-and-a-half-ton dump truck to move the rock and was the first to load four-hundred-ton barges in open water.

In 1933 Beale finally purchased George McLeod's quarry on Lot 499 for two thousand dollars[11] and opened a second quarry on the same property. The limestone in this new quarry was better quality than that in the Sturt Bay operation, which he then closed. With anywhere from thirteen to twenty-two men depending on him for work, Beale began supplying the pulp mills at Woodfibre and Port Alice as well as the Powell River Company. Next he set up a stucco mill in the old smelter building beside the Sturt Bay dock. He also bought a little seiner called the *Neekis* for three hundred dollars and used it to tow scows to Lot 499, where he built a wooden ramp on the shore as his first loading dock. Here his men loaded the scows with jute bags each holding a hundred pounds of agricultural-quality limestone fines. (Although fines are the consistency of flour, handling them in the jute bags tore the men's hands to shreds.) Once loaded, the scows were towed to Vancouver Island, where the cargo was sold.

George McLeod stayed on to work for Beale for five years after the buyout, and as a result, stories about Beale abound in the McLeod family. One of these stories involved Beale's self-propelled steam shovel, a machine that took two men to run, an engineer with a steam ticket and a fireman. When he sold the shovel to a Vancouver buyer, his men built a ramp down to the barge that was to take it away. They planned to fasten a cable to a tree to brake the shovel's trip down onto the barge, but when the tug was late in arriving and the tide was falling, Beale, who tended to be a little impatient, decided to use an old rope to secure the shovel. The fireman and engineer started it down the ramp, but as the steam shovel started to roll, the rope broke and the shovel picked up speed. The fireman bailed out right away, but the engineer rode it down and stepped neatly off onto the scow, which was, unfortunately, slowly moving away from the ramp. The steam shovel fell into the gap between the barge and the shore, and there was a big puff of steam as it disappeared into the ocean. A couple of days later, a crew of divers and a steam cherry picker arrived to put it back on the scow.

THE BLUBBER BAY STRIKE

Although the economics of the Depression caused Pacific Lime to close down its Blubber Bay operations for two months in 1934, the company continued to provide jobs for the community. Over the years, however, there had been steady rumblings of unrest among the Chinese workers because of the disparity between their wages and those of white workers. Young people had also been subject to discrimination, being paid less than older workers even when doing the same jobs. Finally, in 1937 the discontent erupted into a series of strikes and altercations that culminated in the bitter 1938 strike, the echoes of which reverberate on the island even today.

It began on July 23, 1937, when 175 men from all three island quarries joined Local 2775 of the Lumber and Sawmills Union, a precursor to the International Woodworkers of America (IWA), and organized a protest strike against recent pay cuts. BC Cement and Beale's company, which between them employed twenty-five of the men, settled, but after six weeks Pacific Lime finally conceded a small wage increase, then began firing workers for taking part in union activities. When the union protested, the provincial government sent an arbitration board chaired by Judge J. Charles McIntosh to Blubber Bay. The board, acting under the terms of the government's new Industrial Conciliation and Arbitration Act (ICAA), was designed to stave off the growth of militant international unions and promote "company unions" instead. At the end of the hearings, the judge ordered Pacific Lime to reinstate workers fired for union activity and awarded the workers a modest increase, but the company still refused to recognize the union.

Then in May 1938, at a meeting in the Blubber Bay schoolhouse, the men, now under threat of another pay cut, again voted to strike. The company retaliated by firing twenty-three of the men whom they claimed had organized the union, and on June 2, 1938, 102 of Pacific Lime's 156 employees walked off the job, demanding the reinstatement of the fired men. Pacific Lime retaliated by evicting its Chinese workers and threatening to evict some white workers. When the Chinese refused to leave, Pacific Lime's management called in the BC Provincial Police to escort the Chinese to the wharf to await the next Union Steamship, then ordered that all company buildings—including the post office, police station, school, medical, telephone and telegraph facilities—were off limits to the strikers. The workers responded by setting up a picket camp in a meadow about half a mile from Pacific Lime's property. On June 21, the *Lady Cecilia* brought in the first twenty-five scabs. It was soon after this that someone tampered with the company's waterline. On July 20 Union Steamships' *Capilano* arrived with more scabs, and about forty strikers and their supporters were on the wharf to meet them. The ensuing melee resulted in the arrest and conviction of fifteen unionists and supporters.

By August the strikers' families were getting desperate. The Chinese strikers, who were in the majority, were living in tents on a lot the union had leased in Limekiln Bay, while the rest of the workers squatted on the Fogh property adjacent to the quarry. The IWA's *Laur Wayne* brought in food and cash from the Lower Mainland, while Annie Liebich and a friend named Olga collected donations from the Chinese sawmill workers in Powell River. The provincial police tipped over the Woodhead brothers' truck as they delivered milk and vegetables to the strikers.

On September 17, as the Union Steamships' *Chelohsin* tried to dock at Blubber Bay, the provincial police guarding the replacement workers on the ship warned their passengers to stay aboard, because "there was going to be a showdown."[12] When the police finally tried to bring the workers ashore, there was a solid line of picketers waiting for them on the dock, and a riot broke out. As the police tried to clear a way through them using clubs and rocks, they found themselves not only striking picketers but innocent bystanders as well. Within the crowd waiting on the dock that day were five members of the extended Liebich family. Walt Liebich was picking up supplies for his employer, logger Charlie Klein. Bill Bushby, who had worked on the startup of BC Cement's operations on Texada and now worked at Pacific Lime, was there with his wife, Bertha, Walt Liebich's sister, because they were expecting to pick up supplies for themselves. Bob Gardner, who worked at BC Cement and was married to Walt's sister, Mary, had come in his rowboat for the same reason.

In the ensuing scuffle, Bertha (Liebich) Bushby fell off the dock and had to swim to shore. Walt Liebich then knocked a policeman into the water. Mary Gardner arrived in time to see a policeman attempting to snap her husband's leg. Her screams made him stop, but Bob was taken into custody, where later that night he was taken from his cell and assaulted by Constable A. Williamson. He sustained four broken ribs and suffered numerous lacerations.[13] Gardner may have been targeted because, since he spoke Chinese, he had often interpreted for the Chinese workers and continued to do so throughout the resulting trials. Joe Eng was also jailed for assaulting an officer.[14] Eventually, the riot involved 140 people and the police used tear gas to break it up.

Although Bob Gardner did not work for Pacific Lime, he was caught up in the riot, arrested and charged, probably because he spoke Chinese and interpreted for the Chinese workers throughout the proceedings.

Afterwards, Bill Bushby went home and packed a bag, expecting the police to arrive to arrest him. Two police arrived at Charlie Klein's logging camp to arrest Walt Liebich, but when he asked if he could drive his car home, they agreed. He took them on a wild ride over the back roads, and as they went down a hill, he yelled, "Hang on, it has no brakes!"[15] By the time they reached Blubber Bay, both policemen were carsick. In all, twenty-three union members were charged with unlawful assembly and rioting; of these, fifteen were tried and twelve, including Bob Gardner, convicted and sentenced to six months in Oakalla jail at hard labour. But Williamson, the policeman who had assaulted Gardner, was also tried, convicted and sentenced to six months at hard labour. Bob Gardner caught pneumonia while in prison and never recovered his health; he died at age forty-nine in 1945.

That fall, with all the union leadership in jail, Pacific Lime went back to business by using replacement workers. The union's strike and relief committee nominated a new bargaining team, but the company would only agree to reinstate seventeen of the striking workers. By the end of April 1939, the company was operating with a full or substantially normal workforce, and the following month, as the last picketers gave up, the union officially called off the strike. The only concrete gain for workers in general was an amendment to the ICA Act that allowed working people to choose an international union to bargain on their behalf, but there was still nothing in the Act to compel employers to negotiate with such a union.

THE EVOLUTION OF PACIFIC LIME

Business did not pick up again for Pacific Lime until 1941, by which time fifty men were working in the quarries. However, a year later, with many men away at war, there were only twenty-two employed, though there was work for more. In 1944 six kilns were operating. After fire destroyed the company's sawmill on December 30, 1944, the company's New York owners, not recognizing that the mill was a profit-making enterprise, did not rebuild it, and instead ordered the kilns to be converted to run on gas. However, the steam plant did survive the fire and was used to power the winches that unloaded rail cars onto the scows, as well as load the kilns and heat several buildings, including the company offices, the townsite bunkhouse, the guild hall and Dr. Schwalm's house.

Pacific Lime's pits No. 4 and No. 5 at Blubber Bay were quarried from 1948 to 1966, when they were abandoned due to quality problems. The complex of workings around these pits became the popular swimming place known as Heisholt Lake.[16] Pit No. 6, which was nearly a mile in length, 650 feet wide, and 275 feet deep, continues to operate into the twenty-first century. (Pit No. 7, a dolomite lime quarry, opened in 2002.)

In 1955 Gypsum, Lime and Alabastine Canada Ltd. took over the assets of the Pacific Lime Company, and the following year, when nineteen-year-old Alex Fielkowich arrived from Rosthern, Saskatchewan, to work at the quarry, the company had 135 workers. These included about thirty Chinese, some now in their seventies, although many were much younger, having been recruited directly from China by Yip Sang of Vancouver, whose sons also worked in the quarries. Although few of the Chinese workers spoke English, Fielkowich found them good to work with, though he noted that they were poorly paid at a mere thirty-five to thirty-eight cents per hour. Safety apparatus for breathing was still limited to a rag to cover the nose, and long sleeves were the only protection from dust. Hard hats did not become compulsory until about 1966.

The Blubber Bay quarries changed hands again in 1959, when Dominion Tar and Chemicals Ltd. (later renamed Domtar) bought Gypsum, Lime and Alabastine. When natural gas came to Tacoma, Washington, in 1957, Gypsum, Lime and Alabastine began shutting down the Blubber Bay kilns and shipping the limestone to Tacoma for processing in the kilns there. This changeover was complete by 1961. Blubber Bay then began supplying crushed limestone to the cement and chemical lime markets and diverted its product to new markets. Since the early 1950s, research began to reveal many new uses for limestones of different chemical structures as well as a variety of physical sizes; these uses included everything from toothpaste to reinforced concrete that was designed to be easily malleable and either fast or slow to harden under fresh or salt water. Techniques were also developed to reprocess waste piles from long ago to produce fillers for wallboard and plastics, extenders for paint, and flux for steelmaking.

In the 1970s, with the demise of the company town, there was no longer a need for a bull gang to maintain services such as the aging and complicated septic fields at the quarry site. As the kilns there had ceased to operate in 1961, the company offices were moved to reclaimed land near the present ferry terminal, making more room for storage.

In 1983 the Blubber Bay operation was sold to Oregon Portland Cement (OPC), which was 25 percent owned by Ash Grove. The following year Ash Grove took over operations from OPC.

THE BEALE QUARRIES

Fred Beale's son, W. Stan Beale (1918–2008), had worked during school holidays hand-loading in his father's quarry. He also went to university for two years, but he later told his son Stanley (1946–) that "everyone else [at university] was smarter than I was, but I decided I could hire them if I needed them." Once he left university, he opened his own quarry on District Lot 423, three miles down the road from his father's quarry and closer to Gillies Bay, and trucked the white limestone from it to his father's stucco mill. This arrangement came to an end in 1940 when he was drafted into the army, and he and his wife, Phyllis Hume, left for Petawawa.

As limestone was a key component in goods manufactured for the war effort, Fred Beale had not expected his son would be drafted. Just after Stan left, Fred, without consulting him, accepted an offer from Balfour Guthrie & Company for Beale Quarries on Lot 499 and used the money to start an unsuccessful cement plant in Vancouver. He kept some Texada property,

For over forty years, Fred Beale's son, Stan, held management positions in island quarries and used his vast store of knowledge to mentor men like Pete Stiles and Harold Diggon. Courtesy Stanley Beale

notably the manager's house, later known as the guest house, where Stan's family had been living, and the old Marble Bay Quarry, which he gave to Stan after the war.

Balfour Guthrie kept the name of Beale Quarries Ltd. and hired W.D. (Dave) Webster as superintendent. As Webster's wife, Betty, had a flare for numbers, she did the bookkeeping and basically ran the quarry while her husband harrumphed his approval; on the other hand, he was always willing to lend a hand with local problems, and he fixed the community waterline several times. The couple lived in the Treat house, which had changed hands along with the quarry. In 1943 Balfour Guthrie employed about thirty men to install a new crushing plant for the production of agricultural lime. Beale Quarries was sold to Lafarge in 1956, an acquisition that provided that company's cement plant in Richmond with a guaranteed supply of raw material. Lafarge installed a new crushing, screening, conveying and stockpiling facility, a new dock and a barge loader.

When Stan Beale returned to Texada after the war, he re-opened the old Marble Bay Quarry (which his father had originally acquired from the Powell River Company) on Sturt Bay and incorporated himself as W.S. (Stan) Beale (1946) Ltd. He then bid aggressively on contracts up and down the coast, while at the same time purchasing land and mineral rights on land adjacent to his core properties whenever they became available. He also opened a gypsum quarry at Invermere in the interior of BC, though he subsequently sold this to a larger company.

In August 1949, Beale bought Lot 25 on the west coast of Texada adjacent to the old iron mine. As Lot 25 is several hundred feet above a very rocky shoreline, he trucked the limestone that he quarried there down to Sturt Bay on the east coast of the island, where he processed and shipped it. In 1951 the old Marble Bay Quarry became W.S. Beale Limited.

In 1954 the Ideal Cement Company of Denver, Colorado, undertook an extensive drilling program and geological survey of Stan Beale's property. Finding it suitable for their purposes, they purchased it three years later. Ideal's newly acquired Texada properties played only a small part in a big company that had land and processing plants in Spokane, Seattle and Richmond, but Beale, who had been retained as manager when Ideal bought his company, was at last working in the kind of multi-armed business he had dreamed of as a young man. His new job gave him the scope to go out and find more contracts with which to expand the operation. Limestone, of course, has never been a particularly valuable product—in fact, taking inflation into account, it may be cheaper at the present time than it was in the Great Depression—but Beale knew that the trick was always to find value-added uses. One of his clever moves was that, whenever they were blasting and broke out a Volkswagen-sized cap rock, instead of blasting it into smaller pieces, he stored it. Thus, when the government required large boulders for the Iona jetty in Vancouver, he had a mass of large boulders on hand, and he charged the marine contractor extra for "big rock," saying it had to be specially quarried.

In 1973 Ideal Cement installed a new facility for handling limestone on the west side of Texada adjacent to Texada Mines; this plant included crushing, screening, conveying, stockpiling, reclaiming and barge loading capabilities. Beale then made use of the services of his brother-in-law, Ron Margetts, a partner in Chapman Industries, to develop the loading system on the west side of the island at Beale Cove.[17] As this had to be strong enough to withstand ships smashing into it in bad weather, three large re-inforced concrete caissons were cemented to the sea floor and a 90-foot pivoting gantry was constructed firmly on shore. Three years later, Texada Mines ceased operations, and Beale tried to convince Ideal's management to buy the industrial part of the mine site, complete with its ship loader, two crushers and shop buildings. They were reluctant to do so, until he told them he would buy it himself and could be in competition with them within ninety days; as a result, on July 1, 1977, they bought it, thereby closing the door for any other limestone operator to enter the picture. The German company Alm Forest bought the rest of the Texada Mines' land.

In 1978 the company erected another screening, stockpiling and reclaiming system for handling chemical grade limestone. Beale continued to make improvements at the former Texada Mines' site, and during the early 1980s, shiploads of limestone began going to the sugar refineries in California. By the time Beale retired in 1983, he had seen the evolution from breaking rock by hand to sending out two thousand tons of rock per hour on a conveyor belt.

Beale's successor as manager at Ideal was Pete Stiles, whom he had mentored. The son of a mining engineer, Stiles had grown up in Trail and then followed in his father's footsteps, taking engineering jobs in Zeballos and Port McNeil. When he moved his family to the visitor's house on Texada in 1966, it was the first time he had brought his wife to a real community where, he recalled, "she could enjoy a social life and she dug right in." Stiles began work at Ideal as a quarry engineer, but he became superintendent when Keith Johnson retired and then manager when Beale retired.

Unfortunately, during Stiles' years at Ideal, the parent company made a decision to diversify and expand. All this cost a lot of money at a time of high interest rates. The construction of a huge cement plan in Mobile, Alabama forced them into bankruptcy protection. The company's assets were bought out in 1989 by Holnam, which is an acronym for Holderbank of North America, owned by the Swiss-based cement company Holderbank. To Stiles, the Texada operation was "a lost orphan in this foreign-owned company, and since Canada was a long way from the head office," the quarry's survival depended on innovative thinking. The company had a plan for a cement processing plant on Texada, but in the end, the power sources proved to be

Pete Stiles fell in love with Texada when he arrived in 1966, and he returned to retire in the Haddon Burditt House. His encyclopedic knowledge of the quarries and the old mining claims is much prized by the Texada Heritage Society.
Heather Harbord

too expensive. However, there was one positive development during this period; before he retired, Beale had begun negotiations with Quinsam in Campbell River to tranship their coal to the Far East, and in 1990 the first ships—some of them as much as one hundred thousand tonnes—were loaded for ports in Japan. Stiles made sure that Stan Beale was on hand for the loading of the first ship.

Meanwhile, another takeover of Stan Beale's old company was in the works. By the late nineties Holnam's interests had become focussed on the Mississippi River system, while Lafarge, which owned Fred Beale's old quarries, was in expansion mode. As a result, in 1998, a year after Stiles retired, Lafarge took over Holnam's Texada operation, including its mineral claims, and began operating the quarry as a joint venture with Steve Bregolis's Kamloops Plateau Construction. This combined operation used the name Texada Quarries Ltd., though it is usually referred to as TQL.

When the senior Lafarge people came to see the operation, Stiles' successor, Harold Diggon, showed them the deep-sea dock, the quarry and all the lands. They asked him, "What do you need here to make it better?" Lafarge and their chequebooks provided a new dock and loading system, which will last another fifty years. Before Stan Beale died in 2008 at the age of ninety, he saw a ship at that brand new dock loading aggregates that were destined for Hawaii, while Panamax-sized vessels, 950 feet long and just narrow enough to squeeze through the locks of the Panama Canal, had begun calling at the island, too.

Islander Harold Diggon started as a summer student at Texada Mines and worked his way up to Quarry Manager. Heather Harbord

Harold Diggon, a native son of Texada, had been just a small child when the Blubber Bay store hired his father as a butcher. The first summer after he began university was spent working at Texada Mines, which fascinated him so much that he abandoned his studies to stay on at the mine and become a surveyor.

TQL's head tower overlooks the storage piles and Lafarge's new dock, which is built to withstand the Strait of Georgia storms that have plagued both the quarries and the iron mines in the past.

He was involved in planning a number of stopes, and he participated in the open-pit mining of the Lake and Paxton claims. While he was working there, geophysical prospecting uncovered the larger treasure of the Yellow Kid claim, which only showed minimally on the surface. As the mine went underground, tunnels connected the various workings. Diggon left Texada Mines six months before it closed in 1976 and was hired by

Ideal Cement when they began mining the limestone deposit adjacent to his former employer. Since then, Diggon has been manager or director for a string of owners: Ideal Cement, Holnam, Lafarge and Texada Quarrying Ltd. (TQL). He has also seen several major upgrades on his watch, including one of $34 million in 1999.

At the heart of TQL's present operations is an immense crusher, several stories high, which crushes limestone for the cement industry and secondarily for lime manufacturers. Although this setup is designed to run automatically, cameras are focussed on one or two gates, their signals appearing on television screens in a control hut overlooking the operation. This equipment, especially the software, needs to be updated at least every ten years.

Texada Quarrying Ltd. is the largest limestone quarrying company on the West Coast, and it also surpasses the output of Ontario's Manitoulin Island, which only turns out limestone, whereas Texada has multiple products. Today TQL tranships coal and ships cement rock, chemical rock and aggregate. It is almost impossible for any other company to compete with its two-dock systems in Beale Cove and at the former Texada Mines site, where four or five thousand tons can be loaded every hour. In fact, Lafarge products can be shipped from Texada to China and then, depending on economic conditions, reverse that process.

It is now recognized that the "waste" from one operation can often be the treasure of a future one, and TQL has capitalized on this fact by reprocessing some of Texada Mines' "waste" piles that accumulated after a magnetic process extracted the iron ore, leaving behind marketable limestone. Had Sturt's 1877 product with its silica impurities and J.J. Palmer's product with its magnesium impurities found the right buyers, they would not have given up on Texada's limestones. Knowing this, TQL keeps material from its various outcrops separate, as only the future will decide how it can be used. Not all aggregates are the same.

In 1986 Lafarge shut down the former Beale Quarries on the east side of Texada. The empty terraces remain unrecovered and the machinery on site is now obsolete.

Several stories high, this crusher is the heart of TQL's operations. One man in a control hut overlooking the operation monitors closed circuit camera screens and tweaks them by computer. Heather Harbord

IMPERIAL LIMESTONE

Back in 1942, Stan Beale's departure for the army had opened up an opportunity for Don McKay, who had inherited his father Alex's quarry (founded 1934–35) on Lot 500 just south of Van Anda. He had previously pulverized and sacked his product in the old smelter building there, but Fred Beale's larger stucco plant operation almost put him out of business. However, with Stan Beale gone, McKay took over supplying Beale's stucco plant, allowing him to continue in business until Imperial Limestone bought his operation and leased his quarry in 1959. When Imperial tore the old Beale smelter building down in 1974, they built a new steel building at Butterfly Bay, and this new stucco mill continued to operate until sometime in the 1980s.

In 1979, when Ed Liebich went to work for Imperial Limestone, the company was employing twenty-three men to produce 160 thousand tons of lime a year. As he rose to be manager over the next thirty-one years, Liebich watched production increase to 250 thousand tons a year, while attrition decreased the workforce to eight people. Whenever there were gaps, he filled them with islanders, but he has only hired three new people since he came to Imperial in 1979. Each member of his well-trained staff holds down at least three different jobs, and they have tickets for every one of them.

Most of this quarry's output goes to Imperial's Seattle operation, where it is used in the manufacture of glass, fertilizer, paint whitener, car filler or toothpaste, while Adams Concrete in Powell River takes about three thousand tons a year for decorative landscaping purposes. Despite the recessions of recent years, business has been fairly steady, probably because so much of the output goes into glassmaking, and increasing numbers of people are drinking wine and beer. However, rising extraction and transportation costs are ongoing problems that are compounded whenever the Canadian and US dollars are at par.

Until recently, Imperial Limestone got their white limestone from a deposit close to Van Anda, but geophysical prospecting does not always give advance warning of changes, and this white limestone suddenly ran out. When Liebich phoned Harold Diggon at TQL to see if they had any, TQL decided to supply them instead of getting into the business themselves.

RECENT QUARRY DEVELOPMENTS

In 1985 the Kansas-based cement and lime company Ash Grove Cement bought the Blubber Bay operation that had begun as Pacific Lime.[18] Ted Thompson became a superintendent there in 1990 and rose to the manager's job in 1995. Having spent his early years in Bralorne, he was familiar with mining towns. When he arrived at Blubber Bay, the company had forty-four employees, including eight in the office, and by 2004 they were producing 2.2 million tons of product annually. But that was also the year that Ash Grove decided it was cheaper to get limestone from TQL than to produce it themselves. In a major layoff, staff numbers went from sixty to fourteen, and the company then became a supplier of aggregate and dolomitic limestone. In 2008 another layoff reduced the staff to four, with Thompson one of those to go. Two years later, the quarry at Blubber Bay sent two years' supply of dolomitic limestone to Ash Grove's processing plant in Portland; the facilities at Blubber Bay now operate only when the company has contracts for aggregates.

BC Cement had continued operations at Grilse Point on the northern tip of Texada throughout the war years, but in 1956 the company decided to concentrate operations on Vancouver Island, and they closed their Grilse Point quarry; the remains of the concrete foundations of the plant and some of the dock pilings are still visible today. However, they continued to hold onto their Texada property at Davie Bay, seven miles south of Gillies Bay, and in 2009 Lehigh Hanson, a company that had previously been part of BC Cement, considered developing a small limestone operation there to replace the aggregate that had been produced by their recently closed quarry at Metchosin. Although the infrastructure would take much money at a time of falling demand, they made plans to put in a conveyor belt to a barge terminal. Lehigh Hanson remains ready to proceed with this project when market conditions pick up, thereby going into competition with Lafarge, which holds a near monopoly on the coast.[19] Some Texada people are opposing these plans, arguing that the ecosystem at Davie Bay should remain undisturbed.

CHAPTER 7:

Logging

EARLY LOGGING OPERATIONS

IN TEXADA'S DRY CLIMATE, TREES GROW SLOWLY. Whereas on Vancouver Island forests are ready to be logged again in eighty years, on Texada, before climate change, it took 120 years for a new crop of trees to be ready for cutting. Now timber grows more rapidly. Since there were no replanting projects in the early days of logging in this province, there have been no shortcuts in this regeneration time. Fortunately, the Ministry of Forests initiated tree planting programs in the 1960s, and twenty years later wrote a replanting clause into all logging company contracts.

Most of the trees harvested on Texada in the early days were Douglas fir and later spruce and cedar, while hemlock and alder were ignored because there was no market for them. In those days the steep slopes along the southern coasts of the island were a handlogger's dream, because by the terms of their cutting licences, handloggers were limited to the use of axes and saws to harvest their trees and Gilchrist jacks and gravity to herd them down to the water. There is only a smattering of information available on the early Texada Island handloggers. It is known, for example, that W.L. Tait took out a series of Texada handlogging licences between 1899 and 1904,[1] but where he logged remains a mystery. However, more is known about later handlogging operations. In 1921 Joe Pillat handlogged for Malcolm Galbraith between Raven and Pocahontas bays, near the point where the short-lived Malaspina Mine had been located. His tools were a crosscut saw or "hand-fiddle" and a Gilchrist jack, and because Texada wood is full of pitch that gums up saws, he also carried kerosene in a Heinz ketchup bottle to clean his saw. Galbraith had a habit of taking his profits and blowing them on blackjack games with the Chinese quarry workers at Blubber Bay, but he was always careful to keep back enough to pay Pillat's wages.

From the 1890s on, most logging operations on Texada used oxen or horses to haul their logs to water; it is known, for instance, that Parker Belyea, who was living at Mouat Bay just after the turn of the century, logged there with oxen. Charlie and Bill Klein were still using Clydesdale horses in 1923 to log Terrace Bay, the next bay to the south of Mount Pocahontas on the east side of the island. Though born in the US, the Klein brothers came from a German family that had settled in Pender Harbour. (Charlie Klein, a very large, tall man of immense strength, was renowned for being capable of lifting a full gas drum.)[2]

Texada's earliest sawmill was slightly used, having been in operation for twenty years at a Cumberland coal mine. In July 1899, George McLeod arrived to help set it up for two brothers, John and Henry Carter. They located it at the mouth of Van Anda Creek and catered to island needs for many years. Henry, who was also an accountant, became a Justice of the Peace, leaving John to run the mill. Much of the lumber he produced was used in local mining operations, particularly for tunnel supports.

MECHANIZED LOGGING

While many loggers on the island continued to use horses and oxen to haul their logs well into the 1920s, by the beginning of World War I, most loggers were replacing their animals with donkey engines and other mechanized equipment. The five Little brothers—Robert, Matt, Ike, Steve and Joe—had begun handlogging on Texada in the early 1900s,[3] probably in the Long Beach area. Later, when they acquired oxen, they used them to pull the logs out over greased skid roads. But by 1917, when their camp was running an account at Deighton's Store under the name N.E. Point Logging,[4] they had acquired a steam donkey, a state-of-the-art

This relaxed quartet of Little brothers saw logging change from the days of Gilchrist jacks and lots of patience to the innovations of oxen, donkey engines and even trucks.

piece of equipment that made it possible to extract logs that were farther from the water. The roads they built both here and over toward Davie Bay were noted in the 1919 Department of Mines Annual Report as being of possible assistance to prospectors. They were still logging at Northeast Point in 1921 when Steve Little brought his adopted son Joe to live in their camp there.

Between 1910 and 1912, Walter Planta and Jack Abercrombie logged the Van Anda Lagoon area, probably with oxen, though it seems likely that Planta, who had a job in Limekiln Bay, supplied the funds and Abercrombie performed the work. In 1927 they bought out the Little brothers, built a tote road, and brought in a steam donkey and hard-rubber-wheeled wagons for their logging venture. Bob Shields purchased similar equipment about this time, but also introduced the first Cletrack crawler tractor to Texada.

The Alberta Logging Company, which dates back to at least 1907, logged around Gillies Bay, where they built a skid road over three thousand feet long. In 1920 they tried to use a single drum steam winch and a steam tractor, but the tractor frequently got stuck, as it was too heavy for the

The Little brothers were the first on Texada to buy a logging truck, probably in the early 1920s.

terrain. By this time, Alberta was the largest logging show on the island, but the company lost its licence later that year when an "authorized" burn in Gillies Bay got out of control.

In 1937–38, the Tom Green Logging Company, which had six or eight Chinese fallers in its crew, built a breakwater of pilings on Long Beach, where the BC Hydro lines now cross the island, in order to boom logs behind it. Then late one afternoon, when the company just happened to be two months behind in paying wages, a west wind blew a mysterious fire out of control very close to where the loggers were working about half a mile inland on the side of a steep mountain. The men used axes to chop the mainline leading to the company's one and only donkey engine, hooked the machine onto a log on the beach below and tried to pull it to safety over old logging slash. Halfway down, the donkey engine got hung up on a stump and they couldn't move it either forward or backward. As darkness fell, the wind began to gust, tearing the roof right off the machine. When the wind began blowing "the tops off the second-growth fir, breaking them off and wheeling them through the air,"[5] the men abandoned the donkey engine and ran, stumbling down the hill and along the beach in the pitch-black night for more than two hours to reach their camp, which luckily was not in the path of the fire. The Pender Harbour fire boat was summoned to the rescue, but it was unable to quell the fire, because its pump became plugged with sand. Insurance paid 60 percent of the men's wages, but the company went bankrupt. A year or so later, Green's son-in-law started the show up again with a new machine. But in August 1940, another fire raged unchecked over this area and then moved farther south where the Long Beach Company was working. With so many men off to war, there was no one available to fight the fire and it had to be left to burn itself out.

As steam donkey engines were replaced by gas-fuelled engines, some logging outfits on Texada began using one or more to gather the logs to a central point from which another engine hauled them to the water, where they were stored in booms until sold. This is how "Cap" Harrison and Bill Horth logged in Raven Bay in 1938. Captain Horace William Gillespie Harrison (1894–1978) was born in Victoria, and during World War I, he served in the British Navy. When he returned to Vancouver after the war, he and a partner, Ben Butler, built the tug *Pacific Foam*; by 1925 Harrison had his master mariner's papers, and in October of that year he and the *Pacific Foam* went to work for Pacific Coyle Navigation. The partners sold the tug to Pacific Coyle in November 1927, but Harrison continued to work for the company at the wheel of the tug right into the Depression years. Then one day his boss, E.J. Coyle, came in to the office to say that there was no work and all the tugs were tied up. "One of us has to go," Coyle said. Harrison was the one to go.

Harrison began running a tugboat on Comox Lake, where he met his wife, Winifred. However, he had always been interested in logging, and soon he and Bill Horth formed HWG Logging and moved to Raven Bay on Texada, but as that bay was totally exposed to the winds, they boomed their logs in nearby Pocahontas Bay. Horth had only one hand, but "he could swing an axe like mad with it."[6] In the early 1940s, they incorporated as H&H Logging and moved their operation to Shelter Point on the west side of the island, just south of Gillies Bay. After the war, Harrison bought out Horth and moved the operation back to Pocahontas Bay, where he employed about ten people, including his daughter, who acted as whistlepunk.

Harrison spent thirty years in the logging business. He was a heavy-set man and a gruff character who didn't stand for much nonsense. He never lived at Pocahontas Bay, preferring to build a big house overlooking the water in Van Anda. He drove around in a big Chrysler[7] car with a large steel plate bolted to the bottom of it to protect its engine from logging road hazards. His crummy was an elderly Plymouth station wagon. In later life, he was sometimes referred to as the "mayor of Texada" because of his active participation in sports and community affairs.

THE WOODHEAD FAMILY LOGGING OPERATION

As a child, Kirby Woodhead (1909–1986) had watched the Little brothers logging and swore that no matter what happened to him, he would never go logging because the work was too hard. Instead, he tried farming but found it even harder, so he changed his mind, began logging and never regretted his decision. After starting out with a horse, in 1939 he and his brother, Cecil (1919–1982), scraped together enough cash to buy a little Caterpillar tractor.

Margaret Shairp (1919–) and her sister, Vida (1916–1987), would walk the five miles through the forest from Van Anda to Crescent Bay, where the two young men were working. "They'd be high up in the air on springboards," Margaret said in an interview in September 2010, "one on either end of a long saw. They were stripped to the waist and sweaty." Kirby was ambidextrous, so if he and Cec were working together, Cec used his right hand and Kirby his left. As Cec had lost an eye in a quarry accident, he had a little pension, which enabled him to marry Vida in 1940; Margaret and Kirby had to wait two more years till they had saved up enough money. The foursome then made a team,

Margaret Shairp and her sister Vida married Kirby Woodhead and his brother Cecil. As a family logging company, they worked hard and eventually did well.
Heather Harbord

with Margaret working out in the bush with the men and Vida, who was pregnant with her first child, doing the cooking for everyone.

While other logging companies on the island borrowed money to get started, the Woodhead brothers never went into debt, because this was a basic principle instilled into them by their parents. "The men would have [borrowed the money] if the women had pushed them," said Margaret, "but our upbringing was even stricter than theirs. You didn't buy anything if you didn't have the money." However, by 1942 the Woodheads had saved enough to buy a big Cat that really improved their output. Later, when they bought a donkey engine from Cecil May, Kirby operated and maintained it, while his brother worked in the bush, stacking the logs so that they would be easy to pull out. Cec was the one who climbed the spar trees, as Kirby didn't like heights.

Although Margaret couldn't handle the heavy haulback lines, she was able to do most of the whistlepunk's job. "You just had to look sharp and pay attention," she said. In addition to giving signals, the whistlepunk had to top up the water in the donkey, measure the logs and coil up the steel lines. "I heard of one person who didn't [pay attention] and lost all his teeth when the coil unravelled." (That "one person" was Joe Little, who quit logging immediately after the accident and went to work in the quarries—wearing false teeth.) At the Woodheads' operation, as soon as Cecil's children were old enough, first Nora and later David took on the whistlepunk's duties.

Early in the century, mainland and Vancouver Island logging outfits began installing railways to take their timber out, but the Texada terrain was too rough and steep for locomotives, so the big railway outfits stayed away. Even when trucks became available, the early ones were not able to handle the island terrain, although by the end of the 1930s, sturdier trucks became available, and it was one of these that became the Woodheads' first vehicle. It was a White, and Margaret, who was the second woman on Texada to get her driver's licence, drove it. (Tilly Bell got the first licence.) Eventually, the Woodheads had two trucks, and they loaded both before driving them, one behind the other, down a rough, single track road to the beach, where they used a donkey engine to lower the arms that held the loads in place, allowing the logs to roll off into the water. It took about a month to assemble a boom big enough to call in even a small tug to tow it to the Fraser River and in later years to Nanaimo. Number one quality logs with no knots that were cut to a specific length brought more money, because they could be sold as "peelers" for plywood and veneer. Buyers paid the best prices for cedar and white pine, but unfortunately, the Woodhead logging sites were short on these; they had plenty of hemlock, but there was little market for it. While they waited for the boom to sell, they purchased supplies on credit from the stores in Blubber Bay, Gillies Bay and Van Anda. When the cheque came, they paid the bills and bought one bottle of booze to celebrate; anything remaining went toward groceries and other necessities.

The brothers moved their operation to Surprise Mountain[8] in later years, and in 1962 Kirby Woodhead retired—for the first time. After 1965, when the government began holding auctions of Crown timber, the brothers worked together on the bidding. Kirby retired at least twice more before finally leaving the company in the 1970s. In their thirty-five years of operation, the Woodheads had no serious accidents, though once Kirby tumbled into a hole left by a prospector. Cecil looked back, saw his brother's legs waving in the air and hauled him out, but Kirby's face was a mass of bruises. "Of course," said Margaret, who related the story, "he told everybody it was me!"

A younger brother, Phillip Woodhead (1924–1989), operated a separate logging show servicing homesteaders and private timber sales. "He wanted to be the boss, and he knew that, if he worked with Kirby and Cec, Kirby would be the boss," said Margaret Woodhead.[9] Less skilled than his brothers, Phil often had to call on them for help during the nearly thirty years he worked independently. His wife, Frieda, had been a teacher, but in those days married women were not allowed to teach, so she worked beside her husband in the bush. When the tide was high, she often worked on the boom until two in the morning. Phil and Frieda Woodhead also went brush picking and ran a farm with pigs, chickens, forty-seven Herefords and seven Jersey milk cows.

THE POST-WAR LOGGING BOOM

The 1940s saw an influx of small truck logging operations, bringing the total number of logging outfits on Texada to twenty-eight, and they employed a total of approximately 175 workers. The advent of chainsaws on Texada in 1948 stimulated even more activity.

Until 1950 there was no road access to Anderson Bay at the south end of Texada, so it was outsiders who logged it. In 1941 O.A. Buck of Nanaimo had asked Hammie Dougan of Cobble Hill to log a couple of blocks of virgin timber that he had purchased at the south end of Texada. Up to this time, Dougan had been running a family logging company, working his sons six and sometimes seven days a week with plenty of overtime and no wages. Although he gave them money for movies and for the roller skating rink, and as they grew older bought them vehicles, he didn't share financial details of the operation with them, as he didn't consider it to be any of their business. The first time his sons—Dave, Jim, Charlie and Garth—were paid wages was when they moved to Texada with their spouses in 1942, barging all of their buildings and equipment up from Ladysmith. Two of Dougan's daughters also came to Texada, but they were expected to work for free or marry and have their husbands support them.

Initially, Dougan ran the new operation using fifteen Chinese fallers who were under contract to Buck, but they left after their contracts ran out a few years later. This was fine with Dougan, as his family provided most of the manpower he required. When he couldn't get anyone to bring a pile driver to the island, he and his sons constructed their own in order to drive pilings into the bay to provide a booming ground, which was run by Jack Wray from Blubber Bay. *The Texada Queen*, a small scow-like vessel the family used for weekly grocery trips to Pender Harbour, was not always equal to the southeasters; after four changes of engine failed to improve its reliability, it became Pender Harbour's fire boat. (It is now beached at Sidney Bay in Loughborough Inlet.) In order to have alternative transportation, in 1951 the Dougans built an airstrip,[10] and Garth and Roma obtained their pilot's licences. The family ran several planes, including a Piper Tri-Pacer, a Cessna 180 with tail drag and a 185 Amphibian.

In 1952, ten years after the Dougans arrived, Bill Cox brought his family logging outfit into Anderson Bay in order to set up operations west of the Dougans' show. The Coxes then paid a fee to use the Dougan camp facilities, especially the dumping ground. At its peak in the mid-1950s, the population of Anderson Bay reached a total of fifty-five people including children. Most of them were either Dougans or Coxes, as Charlie Dougan had married Daphne Cox and Roma Dougan married Gordon Cox. A one-room school ran from 1952 to 1960. After Hammie Dougan died at Anderson Bay in 1948, his son Dave reluctantly took charge, and when Buck's original timber rights were exhausted, he purchased the rights to a further three thousand acres of Crown land.[11] Around 1964 the Dougan/Cox families moved their entire community from Anderson Bay to Jervis Inlet on the mainland, and Dave Dougan transformed the company from a small gyppo outfit into one large enough to successfully bid on government contracts.

In the 1940s, Davie Bay, halfway up the west coast of Texada where the hydro lines now cross the island, was the site of the Yank Camp, owned by Callow, Linde and Sjobloom of Oregon.[12] Callow and Linde ran it, while Sjobloom came in every payday to issue cheques, which the employees had to go to Van Anda or Powell River to cash. Only a few Texada people worked in this camp, but among them was "Horrible" Bill Roach, who drove in every day from Van Anda to work. (The nickname "Horrible" was a badge of honour given to a small man known to be a very tough fighter.) Another employee was Jocko Cawthorpe, whose job was bringing in supplies for the three or four bunkhouses and the cookhouse. Fallers from Washington State flew in by float plane and made one thousand dollars a day by cheating on their pay slips, which the bosses never checked. However, Cawthorpe learned of their deception after he, Slip Sulyma and Horrible Roach went falling for the company, because it took them a week to make the same amount. The American fallers got away with cheating, because they only stayed ten days before moving on. The company soon went broke, complaining that Texada logs were much smaller than those below the line.

After the Yank camp closed, Cawthorpe stayed on in Davie Bay to work for Andy Gibbs' smaller camp. The Gibbs brothers, Andy and Russ, had moved their logging outfit from Denman Island to Davie Bay in 1947 on an old navy landing barge,[13] a move that took them two or three weeks. Alan Corrigall came with them at a salary of $1.25 an hour, but they couldn't pay him till their logs were both in the water and sold, which took another three months. Then Corrigall got a cheque for eleven hundred dollars, a small fortune in those days. He boarded with the Gibbses for eighteen months before they were able to build a bunkhouse and hire a cook. In the spring of 1949, eighteen-year-old Claire Bushby [14] came to cook, and she married Corrigall a year later.

In 1948 hockey star Brian (Breezy) Thompson (1912–2001), and his brother Al logged Raven Bay, but a couple of years later, they moved their outfit half a mile south of Davie Bay. There they both logged and ran a sawmill. In 1960 Breezy's wife, Helen, insisted the family move to Gillies Bay, where Breezy established a sawmill. With lumber from his mill, he erected a large building at the Oasis near Paxton Road, which he began running as a Marshall Wells store. In 1969 he leased the property to the provincial government for the island's first liquor store and went to work at Texada Mines, from which he retired in 1975.

Martin Fogarascher logged the north side of Gillies Bay and built a network of roads that the owners of the iron mine were later happy to take over. Fogarascher was an Austrian violinist who had played with Vancouver orchestras, but when Hitler's invasion of Austria cut off his funds, he took up logging instead. His Timber Ventures Ltd., which owned all of the lands formerly held by the Alberta Logging Company, was bought out in the 1950s by Elmer Paton (1910–1989), Gordie Pillat and Bill Shepherd,[15] who renamed it SPP Logging. When Shepherd left, Paton bought out Pillat so that he could work on his own.[16]

Bob Jones's Van Anda Logging worked north of the old Surprise Mountain iron mine. Jones (1918–1990), who had been born in the Van Anda Hospital, was the son of Robert Lloyd Jones (1883–1970), who had been the cage man for the Marble Bay Mine. When it closed, Jones had been hired by Pacific Lime in Blubber Bay, but by the time his son Bob was old enough to get a job, quarry work was scarce. Instead, Bob Jones had turned his hand to logging in the Van Anda area using Cats and wooden spar trees. In 1948 he incorporated Van Anda Logging with three partners,

SPP Logging boomed their logs at the head of Gillies Bay, on a site used by the Alberta Logging Company. Courtesy Doug Paton

Orville Allan, Al Matson and Glover Hall, but he gradually bought the others out. Expenses were high, especially for tires. When Jones worked around Kirk Lake, he had eighteen flats in a single day between the woods and the beach. (Another operator, Cy Boys, thought he had the tire problem aced when he bought war surplus tires for his gravel trucks. Unfortunately, they were all rotten due to being left out long hours in the Prairie sun.) Many tires on Texada sported patches attached with stove bolts.

J.W. (Bill) Cuthbertson (1889–1969) was a colourful Texada logger who had followed the rodeo circuit and ridden in the first Calgary Stampede in 1912. Around the same time, he went logging in California and learned high rigging skills. He came to Texada in 1935 on a timber cruising contract, and later returned in 1944 to buy a house in Van Anda and a thousand acres of timber on the High Road. He logged there with his own company, C&C Logging.[17] As he loved big Percheron draft horses, in his first years on the island he used some of them in the woods, but in 1948–49 he brought in a Cat, a truck, a donkey and a yarder. He put his cedar logs down on the beach at low tide in order to build cribs of them and floated them out at high tide.[18] Cuthbertson retired in 1969.

In 1944 Oke Nyvall and partners, Walter Edlund and Dave Maitland, bought out Charlie Klein's outfit in Mouat Bay and finished his contract with L&K sawmills in Vancouver before establishing a quota of board feet that was the largest on Texada at the time. Maitland died of polio at the age of thirty-one in 1952, and the partnership paid out the estate. Nyvall and Edlund continued as partners, building twenty or thirty miles of road up to their work area, which ran from the Bell Road junction to Bob's Lake. Their initial crew included a hooktender, a whistlepunk, a chokerman, a donkey puncher and two fallers. Nyvall drove the company truck. They used wooden spar trees and a hayrack with a gas-powered winch to load logs, but in the mid-1950s they replaced this set-up with an NW shovel loader on wheels. A diesel-powered Skagit donkey yarded the logs into the landing, using a one-and-a-quarter-inch mainline with a three-quarter-inch haul-back and seven-eighth-inch, twenty-foot-long chokers. In the 1960s, they replaced the wooden spars with a steel one and bought first one and then a second Mack truck.

Charlie Klein had built a breakwater in Mouat Bay by partially sinking the hull of the *Princess Beatrice*, the first CPR vessel to be built at Esquimalt. Launched on September 10, 1903, the ship had been luxuriously appointed to run on the Victoria–Seattle route as well as to Alaska, but in 1928 the *Beatrice* was stripped of her machinery and used as a floating cannery before becoming part of Klein's breakwater, along with a rock-filled barge and an old sailboat. When Nyvall and Edlund needed a better breakwater for their expanded operation, Nyvall buried the boats deeper and began hauling waste rock from Texada Mines to place on top of them. However, the company stopped him when it was discovered that his trucks were damaging their roads.

Launched in 1903, the Princess Beatrice *was the first CPR ship to be built in the province, and at 193 feet long, she was one of the largest to be tackled by any British Columbia shipyard at that time.*

Determined to be a logger, Oke Nyvall turned down his first job offer of bull cook and persisted until he found a job in his chosen field.
Courtesy Bill Nyvall

He then blasted a rock bluff on his own private land to finish the job, but the rocks were not big enough, and over the years they kept sloughing off into deeper water. (In the late 1990s, Carl Hagman used bigger rock and made a more permanent breakwater.)

Oke Wilhelm Nyvall (1912–2001)[19] was born in Finland and immigrated to Canada when he was sixteen. Upon landing in Vancouver, he hired on with a railway logging outfit near Kingcome Inlet, but after travelling by boat for two days to get there, he was told he was to work as a bull cook instead of logging. He said, "No, I'm a logger," and got back on the boat. He found a logging job at Port Renfrew, but on his seventeenth birthday, he twisted his knee and had to be carried out of the bush. As there was no medical help available, in two days he was back at work, but that knee bothered him for the rest of his life. During the 1930s, whenever the woods were closed for the fire season, he would go to Alberta and work on a threshing crew. It was in Alberta that he fell in love with the fifth of the seven Israelson daughters on their family farm near Metiskow. In 1939 he got a job at Port Neville, where he was quickly promoted from high tender to high rigger to foreman with fifty men under him; he and Mabel Israelson were married the following December. On purchasing the Texada operation with his two partners in 1944, he barged his Port Neville house, complete with wife and two sons, to Mouat Bay; Mabel Nyvall described the ride as "hair-raising."

In the early days of this operation, Mabel acted as camp cook, bundling up her children in the early morning and taking them to the cookhouse, where she produced the crew's breakfast.[20] McLennan, McFeely & Prior, Ltd. of Vancouver, known up and down the coast as Mc & Mc, sent up everything from logging supplies to groceries on the Union boats, and Oke Nyvall collected them in an old Federal truck with the gas tank lodged beneath a disintegrating horsehair seat that plugged up the gas line every few miles. Driving to and from Van Anda meant stopping several times on each journey to blow out the gas line.

Loggers could not afford to be scared of heights, as they had to climb tall trees, limb them and rig heavy lines to move logs from place to place. High riggers were paid well, so when Oke Nyvall became one, he could afford to marry. Courtesy Bill Nyvall

The Nyvalls' first house did not last long. In 1948 a babysitter was hired to look after Bill Nyvall and his younger brother, Jack, while their parents were away. When it grew dark, the babysitter decided to light the coal oil lamp, and in order to see better while she refilled it, she lit a candle. Unfortunately, she spilled some oil as she was pouring it into the lamp's narrow opening, and the spilled oil was ignited when the candle fell over. There was an explosion, and young Bill, who was walking toward his bedroom, suffered burns to his face. Jack hid under the bed, but Bill pushed open the bedroom window, jumped out and ran down to the camp for help. The men raced back with him, but the house was engulfed by the time they arrived. Meanwhile, the babysitter had hauled Jack from his hiding place and taken him outside. The Macauleys, who had a radio telephone, sent the Nyvalls news of the disaster, and Cap Harrison and his wife, Winifred, took in the children until their parents returned. The Nyvall family then moved to Van Anda.

Nyvall had been using an old camp on Klein property just south of Mouat Bay for his outfit, but after the fire, he decided to build a new camp right in the Bay close to the log dump. It happened that one day he gave a lift to Albert Rairie, who was on his way to Texada Mines to apply for work as a carpenter. Nyvall hired him instead, and they drove straight out to Mouat Bay without stopping at Texada Mines. Rairie built most of the

This house was floated down from Port Neville to Mouat Bay, where its was hauled up on the beach for the Nyvall family's home. It burned to the ground in 1948 when a babysitter accidently set it on fire, almost causing the deaths of the two boys, Bill and Jack Nyvall, shown in the picture. Courtesy Bill Nyvall

new camp buildings, but Nyvall also barged in two of the houses that had been part of the wartime army base at Cassiar and Rupert in Vancouver.

In the fall of 1965, Oke Nyvall and Walter Edlund sold Texada Logging Ltd. to Prince Johannes von Thurn und Taxis of Germany, who owned one of two German companies competing for Texada's timberland. The new owners kept the name Texada Logging Ltd. The agreement also required that they retain Ernie Jago on staff, and he became the company's local manager. Jago (1932–1994) had learned the art of logging in Eric and Thure Gustafson's camp on the Deserted River in Jervis Inlet, and although he never owned his own outfit, he had mentored men up and down the coast till he came to Texada in the 1950s. He remained with Thurn und Taxis until they restructured in the mid-1970s and started using smaller machinery, which, to a man like Jago who had been "a high rigger extraordinaire," seemed like toys. He left and worked for BC Ferries until his retirement.

On Texada's rough, steep, hilly ground, using trucks was more practical than building railways. Oke Nyvall bought one of the Mack Brothers' heavy-duty vehicles.
Courtesy Bill Nyvall

One day in the late 1940s, when Carl Hagman (1911–1996)[21] was getting bored driving a taxi in Vancouver, one of his fares, a man named Bill Nicholas (brother of island historian Ben Nicholas), extolled the benefits of cutting huck brush on Texada for the Vancouver florist market. Hagman's wife, Virginia, who had lived on a High Road farm in 1922, was enthusiastic about moving back to Texada, so they packed up their two children and brought them to Davie Bay, which was the centre of huck brush cutting at the time. Although the two logging camps at the south end of the bay were winding down their activities, the Hagmans discovered a couple of dozen brush pickers living there. In those days, a good huck picker could make more money in a day than a logger. Although the cutters' primary target was evergreen huckleberry, they also gathered cedar boughs and ferns, each bunch weighing a pound and a half; fifty bunches became a bale worth eleven dollars. Diligent, organized pickers could pick two bales a day and sometimes three. Hagman bought from the pickers and marketed the bales in Vancouver; eventually, he was employing twenty-five pickers and four or five girls to make up the bales.

As there was no school at Davie Bay at that time, the Hagman family only spent summers in Davie Bay. The rest of the time they lived in Van Anda, from where they continued the huck business into the 1970s. Meanwhile, Hagman went into logging on the side, his first venture taking place on the Devaney property at the south end of Davie Bay, where he cut trees with a crosscut saw and used a second-hand tractor and a spar tree to haul them out. For a long time he worked alone, as he couldn't afford to hire help unless he paid for it with proceeds from the huck business.[22] Everything was new to him: he had to learn how to fall a tree, climb and top a standing tree, then rig it and splice cable. If anything went wrong, he had to figure out how to fix it himself.

In the early 1950s, Hagman went into partnership with Phil Woodhead, then later into a new partnership with Howie Barbour, Ernie Matson and Bill Arnett to log in the Crescent Bay area. They called themselves Sandy Island Logging, and Barbour's brothers, Dick and Ken, worked as crew. Howie Barbour (1918–1987) had worked in all the big logging camps on the coast before joining up with Ernie Matson on his horse logging show in the mid-1940s. He was a good problem solver, often resolving on-the-job problems that had defeated others, and he was equally at home dealing with derelict loggers from skid row and government bureaucrats. He is also remembered for his part in a famous baseball game between Van Anda Logging and Sandy Island Logging in the summer of 1951. It took place at Blubber Bay, which at the time had the only ball field on the island, and was played in caulked boots and no baseball gloves—though hard hats were allowed. The losing team had to fund a case of whisky for a party held in the bunkhouse opposite Gerald "Stump" Rairie's old house.[23]

In 1964, when Carl Hagman Jr. left school, father and son risked their all to buy out Cap Harrison's H&H Logging. This transaction brought them a camp, trucks and booming equipment at Pocahontas Bay. Five years later, Carl Jr. borrowed from Household Finance to buy his first chainsaw, a Pioneer 750, but it got damaged in less than a week, so he had to negotiate a second loan to replace it. The Hagmans bought their first steel spar in 1973 and began loading with a spreader-bar system using a donkey and cables with two six-foot-high tongs hanging off a fifteen-foot spreader. Although they had been using a shovel loader with a grapple since 1969, they now graduated to self-loading logging trucks, each with its own crane. Most of the Hagmans' logs went to the Fraser River to be sold on the open market. Later they sold to Coastland, a Nanaimo veneer mill that wanted smaller logs with a tight grain—of which Texada has plenty.

Alm Forest, a company owned by Maximilian Graf von Spee (1928–2009), was Thurn und Taxis's main competitor for the purchase of timberland on Texada. The company, bankrolled by an eight-hundred-year-old trust, started to buy forest land on the island in the early 1960s as the Cold War forced them to diversify their investments abroad. The twenty-five hundred hectares that make up the company's Texada Island Forest Reserve (TIFR) holdings are rumoured to comprise about 5 percent of the Graf von Spee total holdings. Executives and family members visit the island about once a year. In between, a local manager carries out their instructions. TIFR lands are identifiable by discreet signs featuring the company logo of a blood-red rooster. Both Thurn und Taxis and Alm Forest contracted with local companies for their logging operations.

In 1969 Howie Barbour's sense of humour and a colourful command of derogatives without the use of profanity came in handy when he and friends discovered that Thurn und Taxis was negotiating with the government to buy the property where the Nature Trail and the Bella Maria Campground are located in order to log it. Eventually, a swap was arranged so that Thurn und Taxis got logging rights to Lot 14 in a different area of the island, and the Texada Parks Board took responsibility for the development of the Nature Trail and the campground as part of Harwood Point Park, which since 1986 has been known as Shelter Point Park. Barbour leased the booming ground there so that his lease payments became a major part of the park's revenue prior to the Regional District taking over in 1972. He and other volunteers also did a yearly spring cleaning of the park prior to the opening of the camping season, and volunteers such as Dr. Kay Garner built the fire pits.

RECENT LOGGING DEVELOPMENTS

By the late 1960s, logging in BC had become very competitive, because the quota system that the government put into place in 1965 was based on each company's last three years' production. On Texada twenty logging companies vied with one another at auctions, where sometimes bids exceeded what was profitable. Many quota holders sold their quotas to others. Phil Woodhead did particularly well out of this situation, as each of his three logging companies received a quota, while loggers who had scoffed at him for this tax strategy had only one.

Under this new regime, local logging companies resorted to a variety of strategies to stay afloat. Elmer Paton supplemented his logging income with several other businesses that successfully kept his bank account in the black—a septic service, a trucking and gravel business and the Gulf Oil Agency. For a while, Rick Jones partnered with Walter Gussman and Doug Merrick in JMG Logging, which worked in Knight and Kingcome inlets. After they had lost enough money, the partnership was dissolved. Walter Gussman built logging roads for Bob Jones, Carl Hagman and others. At first he simply used a cat and later an excavator to flatten out the easiest route and take the stumps out, and he soon became known as "an artist with a bulldozer."[24] However, after the Ministry of Forests got into the act in the 1980s, the roads were preplanned and vetted by an engineer, and he was required to follow the pink ribbon, which was a problem, as he is partially colour blind. A layer of local fill, usually from gravel pits on site, finished the job. These roads used to be seasonal affairs, as loggers didn't work from mid-December to mid-March or in wet Junes, but he graduated to building all-season roads with layered rocks.

Walter Gussman grew up in Marble Bay and soon learned how to operate heavy machinery. He has logged up the coast but prefers to build roads on his native island, where he has a reputation for being "an artist with a bulldozer."
Heather Harbord

By the mid-1970s, only three logging companies remained: Hagman & Son Ltd., Van Anda Logging (Bob and Rick Jones), and Eric Hein, who had married Howie Barbour's daughter and taken over his company. The three outfits had a gentleman's agreement to stay in their own areas of the island. As the banks refused to lend them money, they approached the sawmills and the log brokers for financing. As machines gradually became more specialized and expensive, they had to keep their equipment working longer and needed a big enough cut to justify continuing operations. Whenever possible, they contracted out their trucking work. Steady jobs in the industry became a thing of the past.

In 1972 Bob Jones turned Van Anda Logging over to his son, Rick, and opened the Centennial Service Station of Van Anda, which he operated for the next fifteen years. (Once one of five gas stations on the island, it is now the only survivor. The others were across from the Gillies Bay Store, the Oasis, Cecil May's Repair Shop, and Al Dolman's at Shelter Point.) When Rick Jones inherited his father's logging company, it was little more than a name. However, he had earned enough money with Anvil Mines at Faro in the Yukon that he could afford to buy a skidder with a winch and crane as well as a pickup. Working with a variety of partners and having Ernie Jago as his mentor, he logged around Van Anda and the High Road and also along the west coast of the island from Cook Bay [25] north.

When the iron mine closed in 1976, Bill Nyvall returned to the logging scene, working as a faller first with Wayne Klein, who was contracting with both German companies, and then with Helmut Vossler, who bought out Klein and finished the contract. Vossler had a new Mack truck, which Nyvall bought in August 1985 to ensure his job, and then after setting up Tyra Enterprises Ltd., he continued to log under contract to Texada Logging. He also did "stump to dump" logging in his father's old area, picking up anything left from those old days, with his skidding done by Stump Rairie, the son of Albert Rairie, the carpenter who had built Oke Nyvall's Mouat Bay logging camp.

By the 1990s, Nyvall was doing everything from falling trees to transporting logs and booming them, then selling them to Terminal Sawmills in Vancouver and also to Nanaimo. In 1994 he bought a Feller Processor

Excavator 130 LCM Samsung that felled and limbed the trees, then measured and cut them to required lengths. A second machine gathered the logs into small piles and a grapple skidder took them to the landing, where they were loaded onto logging trucks. Machines and metal did everything except apply the stamp markers. These sophisticated machines proved to be a godsend when, just after he had ordered the Feller Processor, the top of a hemlock that had hung up in another tree fell on him and broke his neck. He woke up in a fetal position, unable to move, but he could feel his legs, and as he'd never heard of a quadriplegic who could do this, he figured he would be all right. He made a good recovery in hospital and was able to go back to work. In 2001 he sold the assets of his company to RAW Select Logging, a company formed by Stump Rairie and Brian Walker. They continued to do contract work for Texada Island Forest Reserve.

In recent years, Rick Jones has used his logging equipment to build roads for BC Hydro and the Ministry of Forests, develop subdivisions, landscape and install septic fields. By 2010 he had four excavators, a gravel truck and grader, two Cat skidders, two low beds, one low-bed truck, two water trucks for fire suppression and two loaders. In recent years, he discovered that keeping a machine for more than ten thousand hours reduced its safety, and he began trading his equipment in when it reached that stage. Finning finances him with better deals than he can get at the bank. "Sometimes I wonder how long I can wiggle my nose to get work," he says. Jones has learned the fine art of forming partnerships. He and Carl Hagman formed Gyrfalcon Enterprises to work on the pipeline, buy land and operate the Mouat Bay booming ground. They also plant trees, although the big problem is protecting them from the deer until the tops grow tall enough to be beyond their reach. With Brian Thompson, Jones formed Sturt Bay Enterprises to do mechanical repairs. With Carl and Stump Rairie, he formed Pac III Resources for contract logging and land acquisition. Until two years ago, Jones did everything himself, but now he often gets others to help; whenever possible, he uses local labour. Four or five years ago, he got his pilot's licence and bought a Cessna 182, using it to fly to Campbell River or Langley when he needs parts.

When Prince Johannes died in 1989, Thurn und Taxis sold all their Texada land to Doman but continued operations elsewhere under the name Texada Logging Ltd. This proved embarrassing for Texada islanders when Thurn und Taxis did some controversial logging on Saltspring Island that resulted in protests and adverse publicity. After Thurn und Taxis left, Texada Island Forest Reserve was the sole German company on the island. The company consolidated its holdings into three areas—around the iron mine, on the Mouat Plateau and along the High Road—then built roads into them and systematically installed trails off the roads on a grid of fifty-metre intervals. Bill Nyvall cleared the trails, selling the alder for pulp to cover the cost of road building. The trails are wide enough for machines to go up them to harvest individual trees. Local manager Dave Opko, who leases some of the High Road property for farming purposes, has tramped most of the land. Under the supervision of professional forester Rainier Münter, RFP of Fruitvale, Opko patrols the trails, identifies codependent trees, flags the weaker of the two and arranges for loggers to remove it.

SAWMILLS

When a number of companies started manufacturing small sawmills, Carl Hagman Jr. installed one in Van Anda to turn out a variety of building supplies. After Ron White, Walter Gussman, Ken Ryan and others followed suit in the early 1990s, Hagman graduated to a bigger machine for cutting beams and large timbers. At one time he was sending about fifteen thousand board feet of clear Douglas fir each month to Vancouver. On the return trip to the island, his truck brought back plywood and other building supplies, which he sold locally, along with cedar lumber and other species. When his export market eventually collapsed, he concentrated on supplying local needs. Stump Rairie had a competing mill.

Logging has provided a good living for two and three generations of Texada families. Those still involved in the industry have every intention of continuing to operate using the sustainable practices that have stood them in good stead.

Don Pillat inherited his father's love of logging. Over the years he collected every kind of chainsaw he could lay his hands on and has kindly donated some of them to the Van Anda Museum. Heather Harbord

Part Two: Texada's People

CHAPTER 8:

Early Settlers 1895–1919

BY 1893, AFTER PROSPECTOR HUGH KIRK went missing, there were only a handful of settlers on Texada Island. John Edwards (1847–1929), who had seen traces of whaling at Blubber Bay, claimed to have been the first European settler on the island. "Old Felix" was another, but almost nothing is known about him. Lawrence Souverin was a German bachelor who planned to farm seventy acres of swampland a mile and a half from the Puget Sound Iron Company's property and market his produce to the mining community. However, he never obtained a Crown grant for

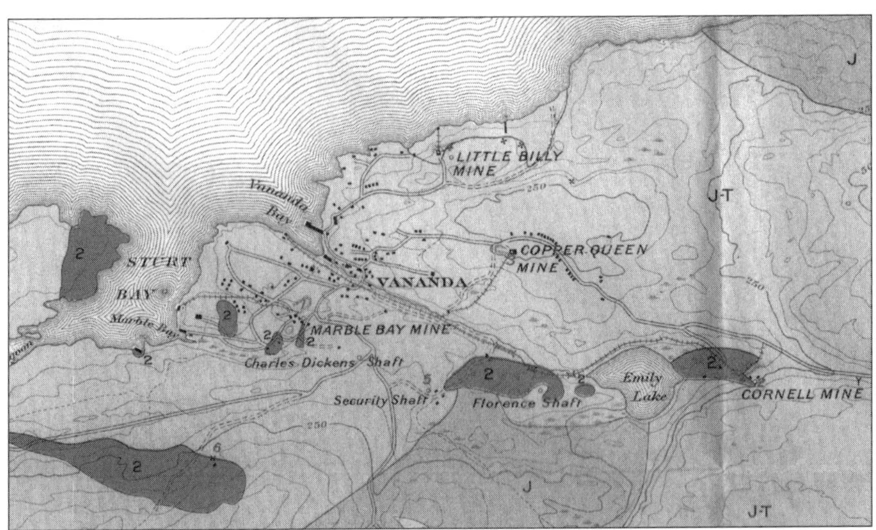

This 1908 map of the settlement and mines of northern Texada was prepared for the Geological Survey of Canada.

this land. Prospector Calvin R. Miller and his wife, Caroline, built their home around 1887 near their very profitable Golden Slipper claim. She apparently enjoyed the isolation of her little cabin with its vegetable and berry garden and its flock of a hundred hens, which fed her family and provided $150 in egg sales in a single year. It is not known when they left the island.

James Raper first came to Texada with his cousin Alfred to prospect in the 1870s. Neither actually settled on the island at that time, and James left for the United States in 1880 after his family's difficulties with A.B. Gray's dry goods company. He returned in 1893 and went to work for his cousin's Texada Gold and Silver Mining Company. In Newcastle, Washington, he had met and married Catherine Jenkins, who already had three children. Together they had another eight, five born in Washington and three in Nanaimo, but the entire family came to Texada with him. It was a rugged existence; in November 1893, Raper, his wife and seven of their children, plus his cousin Alfred and two other men, were reported overdue on an extended canoe trip, probably prospecting. They had been delayed by bad weather and finally all turned up safely.

When James Raper's job at the mine ended in 1895, he returned to Nanaimo, but he and his family came back to the island two years later to work at Alfred Raper's Victoria Mine. James Raper's daughter Annie, who was eight at the time, remembered the family's return on the *Maude*, which landed them on the iron mine beach. The family's log cabin, which James had built, was four or five miles inland between Kirk and Priest lakes. "The girls loved the dolls which their dad carved from wood for them—and never forgot the day their brothers gave the dolls measles with a hot poker."[1]

In 1898 James moved his family to Van Anda, where they planted a garden and an orchard that eventually produced the largest walnut tree of its kind in Canada. James began working for the Van Anda Copper and Gold Company. Later he became its foreman and, after it closed down, its caretaker.

According to local history, Catherine Raper was the only woman to bring her children with her to Texada at that time, although the couple's eldest child remained in Nanaimo attending school while Catherine taught the rest at home. In the summer of 1905, the family rowed across to the mainland, where Powell River is now, to picnic and pick berries to preserve for winter. Annie (Raper) McLeod recalled that "there wasn't a soul there, not even a cabin." Later the Rapers bought a gas boat and would spend three or four days up Jervis Inlet, hunting and berry picking while sleeping in tents or on boughs under the stars. The Rapers and their children became pillars of the community; their descendants continue the tradition.

Around 1891 Alfred Raper built a large log home on a Crown-granted quarter-section of land east of the iron mine on the site of what became Ideal Cement's quarry. He also planted an orchard that he enclosed with a split-rail snake fence. However, his wife, two daughters and twin sons apparently remained in the home he had built for them on Gabriola Island. In 1908 Alfred Raper, by then a Justice of the Peace, moved to Vancouver,[2] where he and his sons became involved in a printing and stationery business similar to the one the family had previously owned in Nanaimo. A series of setbacks followed.

The 1898 Henderson Directory lists Charles Bedford Rabson as a farmer at Van Anda, but Rabson seems to have been more prospector than farmer. The *Coast Miner*, interviewing him on his return from the Atlin goldfields, reported that "according to Charlie, all you have to do there is pick up a handful of earth and sort out the nuggets." They thought he had "probably told the Atlinites the same of Texada." Rabson and James Raper pre-empted Lot 36 on May 8, 1900. Although this pre-emption was "granted on the understanding that the prior rights of mineral claim holders are reserved and excepted," the two men may have been hoping that the prior claim would lapse due to lack of work and it would then fall to them.

In addition to this handful of people who actually lived on the island, there was, of course, a constant parade of prospectors looking for the minerals that would make them rich. This scene changed completely after Edward Blewett came to Texada in 1895 and established the Van Anda Copper and Gold Company, followed by John Jackson (J.J.) Palmer in May 1897 to reopen the marble quarries at Sturt Bay.

VAN ANDA AND TEXADA CITY

The first settlement on the island was created by J.J. Palmer, who brought in surveyors in May 1897 to lay out a townsite, which he called Texada City, immediately north of his Marble Bay Company property on Sturt Bay. He advertised lots for sale there at prices ranging from seventy to one hundred dollars [3] and included an added buyer's incentive: the first three hundred purchasers would receive a ticket on a draw for ownership of a five-star hotel overlooking the water. The lottery was never held, as only ten or twelve lots found buyers, but in June 1897, Victoria contractor Andrew Fairfall won the bid to build the hotel, which was to cost five thousand dollars and be completed within sixty days. Perhaps this deadline was imposed because Palmer knew of the plans made by his father-in-law, William Christie of biscuit fame, for a family trip around North America, and he hoped that the hotel would be ready in time to accommodate them. Unfortunately, when the party, including Palmer's wife and daughter, reached Victoria on August 4, 1897, the hotel was still unfinished, so they never saw Texada. However, the Marble Bay Hotel's twenty-eight furnished rooms, with all modern conveniences including water piped from Turtle Lake, were finished and open for guests by January 1898. A wharf on Sturt Bay had been completed by this date and the road to it graded.

Nothing but the finest satisfied John Jackson Palmer, who built the Marble Bay Hotel in anticipation of a visit by his wife and father-in-law.

The townsite of Van Anda was laid out later that same year, the creation of Edward Blewett, president of the Van Anda Copper and Gold Company, and secretary–treasurer Harry Whitney Treat. It was composed of 700 lots, each of them 40 by 120 feet. A party who visited the site in December 1898 reported that a school was under construction and a hotel was in the planning stage. There were homes as well, among them that of Harry and Olive (Graef) Treat. Dr. John Sebastian Helmcken of Victoria, who visited the Treat house in August 1899, described it as "a log cabin of a couple of detached rooms, very simply furnished. The mantel [is] made of pretty specimens of minerals, and on it [are] family portraits, the chief of which being that of the equally energetic, enthusiastic Mrs. Treat, who discovered the Cornell mine!"

Several street names survive from this time. Olive Street is named after Mrs. Treat. Gracemere was her parents' house in Tarrytown, New York, and Wall Street commemorated Treat's New York office address. Smelter Street was named for the smelter that operated there from 1899 to 1902. The Blewett house, where Edward Blewett and his son Ralph lived until they left the company in March 1899, was probably located on Blewett Street, which was conveniently near the company's Little Billie Mine, but no trace remains of this building.

Treat, who became company president after Blewett bowed out, donated land for a church in his company's model community and at first let the community use his own "Honeymoon Cottage" for a school whenever he and his wife were not in residence. However, the community soon pressed into double duty an old mess hall next to the company's sawmill. During the week, Alfred Raper's daughter Emily, who had previously taught on Gabriola Island where she grew up, taught twenty students there. On Sundays church services were held in the same mess hall. The first service was Anglican officiated by a Reverend Stoney, but he also had to share the building with the Presbyterians under Reverend W.H. Madill. At one of the last church services in the old mess hall before the first Texada church was dedicated on June 20, 1900, a mouse that had taken up residence in the organ made its presence known, causing the lady organist to jump onto the revolving piano stool.[4] The new church, graced with a tall white spire, stood on the hill overlooking Sawmill Cove. The thirty members[5] of the congregation opted to call it the Texada Presbyterian Church. In 1906, before Reverend Madill left after seven years of service, he persuaded the Presbyterian Church Mission Board to supply student ministers, and a number of them came.[6]

The first building to be specifically constructed as a schoolhouse was not ready for occupancy until 1904. It was midway between the settlements around the Copper Queen and Marble Bay mines and served this purpose until 1954. After-school fights for the boys were the norm. Initially, these were held in a shed beside the school but later moved down the hill to a level piece of ground in front of Buskey's cabin. Although they might start with Papists against Orangemen, after a day or two, when someone asked, "What are we fighting for?" no one knew. However, some fights were conducted according to the Marquess of Queensberry's rules, and one lad who learned them went on to become a lightweight champion.

Olive Treat watches the kettle in Honeymoon Cottage. The ore samples ornamenting the fireplace are probably bornite, the peacock ore. Several newspaper reports commented on it. Courtesy Patsy Schweitzer

Starting in 1896 and continuing for most of the next five years, the social scene in Van Anda had New York overtones, largely due to the presence of Olive Treat, who had brought trunks of the latest New York fashions with her to the island. After work the miners changed into suits and ties to promenade the streets wearing their high-buttoned shoes, boiled white shirt fronts, and bowler hats or Stetsons. The ladies, their hair elaborately coiffed, wore long dresses with wasp waists, high necklines, frills, ruffles, ribbons and lace. White high-buttoned shoes were all the rage. On Sunday afternoons, the beautiful people met on the Van Anda Hotel's spacious verandah to display themselves.[7]

When the ladies went swimming from Erickson's Beach (or discreetly on the far side of Dick Island at Gillies Bay), their bathing costumes included long stockings and high boots, and they piled their hair up on their heads. According to Annie (Raper) McLeod, who arrived in Van Anda in 1898, visitors were entertained by taking them "down the mine. You got into a big bucket, held onto the rope, and down you went." Picnics, funded by the Treats when they were in residence, were held at the lakes. Annie McLeod remembered that "Mr. and Mrs. Treat didn't live here, but they'd come up [from Seattle] and stay for two or three weeks at a time." In 1900 Harry Treat wrote to Victoria City Council to ask them to donate a pair of swans "for the decoration" of Emily Lake, where the Treats had a cabin. The matter was referred to that city's parks department, and it is not known whether the swans were ever delivered. Camp-outs were held over on the mainland and the campers entertained themselves picking huckleberries and blackberries. The men of the community often took the opportunity for leisurely hunting and prospecting expeditions to nearby inlets. Some of these people came from New York, and there was more than one Harvard graduate among them; most subsequently left the island, but their brief passage there is still bright in the memories of the descendents of the old-timers. Although this lifestyle was fairly common in Vancouver and Victoria at the time, it was a thoroughly remarkable scene to be occurring in a brand new mining settlement on the tip of the northernmost Gulf Island.

When people settled down to actually live in the communities of Van Anda and Texada City, they paid little attention to the plans that Treat and Palmer had put on paper. According to Annie McLeod, "Although two townships were laid out, everyone went back and forth between them and there was only one company store. People did send orders out of town to Woodward's but most supplies were bought locally. People were satisfied and very community minded." (Woodward's Stores, founded in Vancouver in 1892, began providing mail order service up and down the coast five years later.)

The early Van Anda/Texada City was a mixture of the wild and the sophisticated. Log shanties stood cheek by jowl beside a few well-built houses such as the Treats' second home on the west side of Columbia Street, which they called the White House. Like most old houses, it has changed hands and been renovated many times with rooms, turrets and gingerbread added, so that it is much more impressive now than in those

In letters to each other, the Treats referred to this dwelling as the White House. It was built on Columbia Street above the smelter. Over the decades, gingerbread and a turret have been added, making the original structure unrecognizable.

early days. Today it is known as "the manager's house." Not to be outdone by the Treats, J.J. Palmer built a house that is now called "the visitors' house." The white pillars on the front are somewhat reminiscent of those at John Jacob Astor's summer residence, so when Palmer celebrated its opening "with great éclat" on April 3, 1899, he christened it the Astor House. It was heated by steam from the boiler at the Marble Bay Mine.

Annie McLeod remembered Van Anda, its skyline dominated by the mine's big boiler house and hoist, as having three hotels in those days. However, although construction dates are not available, it would appear there were actually four. Bob Lyons ran the Van Anda Hotel; the Marble Bay Hotel housed the single miners—most of them from "back East, especially Ontario"—and was the scene of "wonderful dances" on Saturday nights. There was also a Texada Hotel, but all the roughneck miners, many of whom were Irish, congregated at the fourth hotel, the "Bucket of Blood," where differences were settled with fisticuffs. One of the members of the

J.J. Palmer built himself a comfortable house whose white pillars reminded the Treats of John Jacob Astor's summer house. When he opened it "with great éclat" on April 3, 1899, he called it the Astor House.

Leroy family, who owned this two-storey building, was alleged to have shot someone in the US.[8] Annie McLeod, on the other hand, recalled Van Anda as "a very respectable place . . . If you didn't work, you didn't stay, because there was nothing to do . . . Unlike many mining towns, it had no red light district."[9] In fact, for a short time there really was a house of ill repute on the shores of Emily Lake, but it only lasted until some of the wives of the community hid in the bushes and saw their husbands enter it.

Annie McLeod also recalled "a Chinese town where the ore sorters and the men who cut wood for the steam engine lived." There were actually two "Chinatowns" in Van Anda.[10] Both had about fifty inhabitants and were controlled by a "Boss Chinaman" who liaised between them and their employer. One settlement was at the south end of Emily Lake beside the Cornell Mine. Its boss, Chow Dan, astonished his countrymen by being the first to cut off his pigtail. The other settlement, presided over by John Kee, was near the north end of Emily Lake, closer to Van Anda. Kee was a popular storekeeper who sometimes appeared in church. The Chinese often got their jobs through agents such as Yip Sang, the CPR's Chinese agent in Vancouver, who supplied that company and others with labour and fresh produce. His Wing Sang Co. also forwarded remittances from workers to their families back in China and generally liaised between them.

According to journalist and historian Bruce A. McKelvie, although Harry Treat and J.J. Palmer were not known to have worked together on any other project, they did agree that having an island newspaper would foster a feeling of contentment in their adjoining communities.[11] At first the *Coast Miner*, which was initially edited by Justice of the Peace Louis J. Seymour, was printed by Jack Lawson's Vancouver print shop. Then, as the arrangement was cumbersome, just after Christmas 1899, the Van Anda Copper and Gold Company, apparently without help from the Marble Bay Company, simply bought the print shop and transported it and its owner/operator to Van Anda. Treat had seen a problem and fixed it. Palmer on his next visit probably applauded his actions. When Seymour left Texada, Lawson became editor as well as printer. In fact, he did everything from reporting to setting type. William Raper, Alfred's son, was the printer's devil or assistant, while young Bruce McKelvie sold papers on the street, where the miners often told him to keep the change from a dime.

Only two copies of the *Coast Miner* have survived: Vol. 1, No. 2, dated January 15, 1900, edited by Seymour, and the November 1, 1900, issue, edited by Lawson. The paper's life was abruptly terminated after a fracas known on the island as the "tea fight." The wife of one of the metallurgists had given a tea party for the wives of the managers, doctors and other important personages and then followed it with one for those whose husbands were less eminent. Lawson wrote a scathing attack on this attempt to establish a club of the elite. As he was cleaning up after the print run, the irate husband of the lady who had given the tea appeared. The two stepped outside for more room. Bruce McKelvie later wrote that "it was the best scrap I ever saw. Lawson had a bandaged left hand but a considerable knowledge of boxing; his opponent had courage and indignation." Spectators separated the pair before anyone was seriously hurt. The managers whose wives attended the first party were infuriated. The company closed the paper and the school moved into the vacant building.

THE UNION STEAMSHIPS AND THE CPR

On November 28, 1900, after one of his visits to the island, J.J. Palmer sent a letter to the *British Colonist* complaining about the lack of scheduled ferry service to Texada. Up to this time, although one of his partners was Captain John Irving, owner of the Canadian Pacific Navigation Company, he had not been successful in achieving this end. Finally in 1902, the Union Steamships' *Comox* began a service to Blubber Bay,[12] and soon the company's black and red funnelled ships were running six trips a week out of Vancouver, stopping both northbound and southbound at Van Anda and Blubber Bay. There was still no fixed schedule, because the ships' captains never knew ahead of time at which communities they would need to stop to unload passengers or freight. Starting the same year, the CPR began running a twice weekly service from Vancouver to Blubber Bay and Comox and back. This service was punctual and passengers' comfort was a priority, but the first CPR ship to call at Blubber Bay, the *Queen City*, had no reverse; if it missed the dock on the first try, it had to circle around and come back for a second attempt.

January 7, 1913, was a tragic day for the Union Steamships and the only day in the company's entire history when passengers lost their lives. Twenty-seven months after her launch,[13] the Union's *Cheslakee* came into Van Anda in a howling southeaster at 3:45 in the morning, discharged eight passengers and forty-five tons of freight, and then headed out into the storm for her next port of call, Westview. Fifteen minutes later, a squall broadsided her and shifted her cargo, resulting in a dangerous list to port. The helmsman turned her around in an effort to right her, but the list worsened, and when she reached the Van Anda dock again, the captain ordered everyone off the ship, which promptly sank. Two schoolteachers drowned because they stayed below to dress before leaving. A list of those on board showed that altogether seven were drowned, but not all passengers were on the list. A Mrs. Dawson, who lived at Blubber Bay, had booked passage on the *Cheslakee* for that sailing but for some unknown reason had refused to go. Her husband was furious with her but forgave her when he learned of the boat's sinking.

After a salvage team raised the ship, it was towed to Vancouver for repairs. A Van Anda man named Brandy who went with the ship later told Bill Young that the bodies of an additional eleven Chinese loggers, who had been in the ship's "bull pen," where rowdy loggers were put, had been heaved over the side off Jervis Inlet.[14] However, when Bob and Bev Blackmore researched the story for the video they made of the sinking, they discovered that the *Cheslakee* had not had a bull pen. The ship, which was subsequently lengthened and renamed the *Cheakamus*, served on coastal runs for another thirty years.

The first local service from Van Anda to the small mainland community at Myrtle Point was provided by Walter Pinnock, an English bachelor from Cornwall or Somerset, who probably arrived around 1903. (He is not listed on the 1901 census, but his name appears on the 1911 census.) He was also known as "Steamboat Bob." His boat, *Wood Nymph*, travelled at six to eight knots, powered by the driftwood he often stopped to collect from the beaches. Locals called it "Speed and Safety." Time was of no importance to Pinnock. He also used the *Wood Nymph* to perform small towing jobs but dropped everything if a load of people wanted to go to a "dawnce," as this was Pinnock's passion. All this came to an end in 1908 when a new boiler inspection act grounded his ship. Later, Ben Nicholas picked over the remains and salvaged the anchor, the starting wheel and a couple of iron propellers. Walter Pinnock then became a quarryman and in 1930 a charter member of the Van Anda Community Society. He died sometime after 1956 while on a trip to Hawaii.

THE CULTURAL LIFE OF THE COMMUNITY

During the last decade of the nineteenth century, every town in British Columbia constructed an "opera house," which really had nothing to do with opera but gave the community a combined performance and meeting space. Van Anda's opera house was located in Texada City. It was built by volunteers, and all kinds of social activities took place on its "lovely stage and beautiful dance floor." [15]

Many dances, both in the opera house and in local hotels, were organized spontaneously. A dance held in Van Anda, probably in one of the hotels, and billed as "The Bachelor's At Home," was described in the *British Colonist* of February 1, 1899. It was organized by Messieurs Planta, Russ, Eschwege and other gentlemen of the mining community. The festivities, which were attended by about fifty-five people, began about nine in the evening, and at one in the morning, the Bachelor's Club provided refreshments that "deserved the high encomiums of praise which the ladies showered upon the viands."

However, a dance held at the opera house to raise funds for the Boer War went awry when the local lads had another idea. They had saved up sixty cents—enough for one boy's admission plus ten cents for a package of red pepper. When Bruce McKelvie, who was probably one of these lads, told the tale in later life, he called this boy "George."[16] As soon as George went into the hall, he was assigned to feed wood into the stove. Just before supper was served, when the cook went for a turn on the dance floor, George emptied his package of pepper onto the hot stovetop and fled into the supper room, bolting the door behind him. He threw open the back door, and in poured a dozen boys, who cleared out all the cakes, sandwiches and pies together with a barrel of soft drinks. Ten minutes later, nothing was left and there wasn't a boy in sight. George hid in an old mine tunnel for a week.

The opera house was also used in June 1900, when James Dunsmuir canvassed for votes on Texada before being named premier of the province. He made a speech promising to build roads from the mines to the smelter and said he "would advocate a separate grant being made to the island, to be spent there in whatever way the residents thought best." He also said that "he had found it very little cheaper to hire Chinamen in the mines, and it only meant the difference of a few cents per ton."

Unfortunately, the enthusiastic volunteers who built the opera house on J.J. Palmer's Marble Bay Mine property had not troubled themselves to get legal ownership of it, and consequently, when the Marble Bay Mine was sold to Tacoma Steel in February 1902, the opera house went with it. In 1907 the company decided to close it down and donate it to the Columbia Coast Mission for a hospital, as this would ensure the provision of medical services for the company's miners.[17] And this was how Dr. J.H. MacDermot became the first resident physician on Texada. The winter of 1907–8 was hard, and conditions within the new hospital were appalling.[18] Despite a small but red-hot stove outside the door of the main ward, the temperature within the room dropped to minus 3°F (-19°Celsius). Thirteen patients shared six sheets and they had three hot-water bottles between them, one of which leaked. Pipes froze and toilets were plugged so that the doctor also became a plumber and water carrier. "It was very good for one's soul," Dr. MacDermot later reported.

With no television, internet or even cars or telephones, everyone in the community pitched in to make their own entertainment. On New Year's Day 1900, about three hundred people gathered in front of the Marble Bay Hotel to watch a tug of war in which, amidst much laughter, James Raper twisted his rope end around an ornamental tree and George Le Roy used a bystander's feet for the same purpose. This was followed by a drilling competition with a prize of twenty-five dollars won by Ed Russ and Charlie Rabson for drilling 23⅛ inches in fifteen minutes. The 1906 May Day picnic was held on the mainland across Malaspina Strait, on

The opera house was really just a community hall. After the 1907 Marble Bay strike, the owners, the Tacoma Steel Company, decided to turn it over to the Columbia Coast Mission for a hospital, which ran from 1907 to 1920.

the site of what later became the City of Powell River, where a sumptuous lunch was served under the trees. A concert that year in the schoolhouse featured a stereoptic light to show scenes of a Monte Carlo gambling saloon, the life and death of Little Eva, a poverty story from New York, the Boer war in South Africa and so on. A smoking concert, complete with cigars and hosted by the Texada Hotel, was very popular. Annie McLeod, who was a good pianist, enjoyed practising for the community concerts. "If you had a social evening, you didn't have drink," she recalled. "If men were drinking, they didn't come inside."

By 1910 the dances held on Texada had become very popular with people from the mainland communities of Stillwater and Myrtle Point. On one occasion when a group of mainlanders brought Ernie Liebenshel and his band with them, the sea was too rough when it was time to go home, so the band just kept on playing. In addition to the band's fee, a hat was passed for tips, and these more than doubled their evening's take.

The Blanchard family and their relatives the Lowthers, both members of the 7th Day Adventist faith, came to Van Anda in the early 1900s from Bishop Auckland in County Durham. The Blanchards returned to England just before World War I to be with an ailing family member. After the war, they came back to Texada where they lived in Blubber Bay. Courtesy Maurice Liebich

In summer during those pioneer years, the people from Van Anda often packed up their families and walked over the trail to the sands of Gillies Bay. One such trek was described by newspaper writer Violet Seaman, the granddaughter of James Raper. Her mother, also called Violet, had married Reverend Hugh Archibald Bain, a Presbyterian minister, who was serving in New Denver in 1911 when Seaman was born, but his calling took the family to many other places in the province. However, every summer they, like many former Texadans, returned for their vacations.

A Union Steamship brought the Bain family to Van Anda, where they stayed overnight with Violet Bain's sister, Annie McLeod. The next day, they piled their camping gear and food, blankets and clothes onto a wagon drawn by an old white horse and began the day-long, eight-mile journey to Gillies Bay. The children rode, except when they came to sandy or rocky places that were difficult for the horse. Then they had to lighten the load, walking behind it to pick up anything that fell off. In Violet Seaman's memory, the journey always took place on a hot day, but they stopped for refreshments at cool springs and lakes along the way; a favourite stop was Priest Lake, where everyone had a drink, including the horse.

The sight of the moss-covered rocks of Cranberry (or Cranby) Lake meant they had only two more miles to go, and the children raced ahead to get the first glimpse of the glorious sea, glittering before a backdrop of the white-capped mountains of Vancouver Island. "There it is! There it is!" they screamed and ran till they were out of breath. In the early years, the family pitched tents, sometimes with floors or half-walls, but later they built little cabins at the head of the bay. The James Raper family cabin had a spacious veranda and was later expanded with a lean-to behind it; in time, Violet Bain inherited it from her father, and she later gave it to her daughter. "But it was the hot beach and the sunshine and the millions of stars at night—we watched them while we sat around our bonfires—that made Gillies Bay what it was to us," Violet recalled. "And the clam digging was part of it, and the ugly red cod that tasted so good. They were happy, care-free days."[19] A photo exists of the Raper family paddling around a big rock near their cabins; that big rock has since been moved inland.[20]

TEXADA'S PIONEER FAMILIES

The 1901 census, which reported 26,133 people living in Vancouver, listed 504 on Texada Island, which by then was one of the major population centres of the coast. But this was its population peak, as copper prices fell soon afterwards, resulting in layoffs at the mines. However, it was at this point in the island's history, as the roving miners and prospectors were leaving for greener pastures, that new, long-term settlers were arriving.

One of the men who came to the island at this time was Mike Pillat (1861–1922). He and his wife, Mary (1870–1907), moved to Texada in time for the birth of their son Joe (1900–1991) on November 22, 1900. (Legend has it that Joe Pillat was the first child to be born in the Van Anda hospital, but this was not established till he was seven years old.) Back in 1880 Mike Pillat and a friend had walked from their home in the Carpathian Mountains of Austria–Hungary to Germany, where they boarded a ship bound for the USA. Mike had worked his way from mine to mine, from one end of the country to the other. In 1888 he sent for his sweetheart, Mary, who came from the same Carpathian village. The couple married and continued to follow the mines, but after coming to Texada and starting a family, Mary refused to leave, so Mike settled into a job at the Cornell Mine and pre-empted Lots 272 and 304 in the centre of the island. Clearing land was a slow job, as everything was done by hand and horses. Huge piles of brush had to be burned and stumps dug out or carefully blasted out of the ground. Although the black, peaty soil would not grow nasturtiums for Mary, it did grow huge vegetables.

The Stromberg family came to Van Anda in 1900. Born in Finland, William Stromberg (1867–1945) had sailed around the Horn and jumped ship in San Francisco. From there he made his way to Vancouver, where he became a foreman at the BC Sugar Refinery and met his wife, Emma Peterson (1880–1962). She had left Finland at the age of fifteen to live with her brother in Vancouver. Emma and William married in 1898. The year after the birth of their daughter, Edith (1899–2002), they moved to Texada, where William earned his stationary engineer's ticket. For many years, he was in charge of the powerhouse at the Copper Queen and Cornell mines and did a little prospecting on the side.

With no high school on the island, in 1915 the Stromberg children, Bill and Edith, had to go to Powell River to sit the entrance exams to King George High School in Vancouver, and they became the first boy and girl from Texada to pass. Another five years went by before the Texada school was granted superior school status, thus enabling students to take the exam in Van Anda.

Billy Uzzell arrived on Texada in April 1903. Although his name is of French origin, he appears to have grown up in Britain, so his family may have been Huguenot refugees. His search for adventure had led him to serve in the Boer War and then to travel on to Canada, but the East Coast had not impressed him, and after an encounter with a blizzard on the way to visit a brother in Manitoba, he went south to the warmth of San Francisco. There he met two miners who said that Van Anda was "a lively little camp," so he headed north and caught the Union boat. Uzzell estimated the population of the island to be about one thousand at that time. Although some were permanent residents, others were floating miners who were following the well-defined route from mine to mine across the west. Although there were many prospects all over the island, there was also a feeling that, with the exception of the Marble Bay Mine, the place was past its peak.

It happened that a visiting Anglican priest, the Reverend Miller of St. Barnabas Church in Victoria, came to Texada to hold a service about this time, but he was very discouraged at the poor turnout. Billy Uzzell volunteered to drum up more interest for his next service, so when the *Cassiar* called in at Van Anda the next Sunday evening with a boatload of off-duty loggers anticipating a good time in Vancouver, he persuaded them to stop over and come to the service. One tall man with a goatee beard had a trained tenor voice, in which he led the singing while he noticeably chewed tobacco. That was the last time Uzzell himself attended church in Van Anda.[21]

One of the workmen who came to build the Carter brothers' sawmill at the head of Van Anda Cove in 1899 was George MacKenzie McLeod (1877–1951), who stayed on to marry James Raper's daughter, Annie, and become a pillar of island society. The McLeods started their married life in the present-day Rosebank Cottage on Van Anda Cove. The building hung over the water, so when the seventeen-year-old bride had a cooking failure, she just heaved it over the side. This opportunity to experiment without repercussions served her well, as in later life her preserves, especially her pickled crabapples, were much prized by her family. Some of the McLeods' furniture was acquired when Harry Treat changed his mind about building a second cabin on Emily Lake, perhaps as a result of the Marble Bay strike. Although the bird's-eye maple furniture Treat had ordered for the cabin had already been delivered to Van Anda, he asked the newly married George McLeod to dispose of it, which he did by purchasing some of it for his own house.

Once the Carter brothers' sawmill was built, McLeod turned his hand to other jobs. In 1905 he bought Jack McRae's drugstore, which sold stationery, tobacco, candy and gifts, although prescriptions were sent to Vancouver to be filled. He also acted as town photographer, recording many community activities such as mining operations, mainland picnics,

Brothers John and Henry Carter moved their sawmill from Cumberland to Van Anda in 1899 and continued to operate it until the mid-1920s. Henry held many responsible positions in the community, including JP, mining recorder, secretary-treasurer of the Gun Club and member of the school board. His daughter, Isabel, married Reg Deighton and helped him run the store after his father, Al, died.

and the official openings of the hospital and the new church. He also supervised the construction of the road from Van Anda to Blubber Bay in 1910; this was a plank road that followed deer trails. The Blubber Bay population at that time comprised both whites and Chinese with many of the latter commuting from Limekiln Bay.

Bill Young (1888–1992), who was interviewed in 1990, remembered that "the mines were doing good" when his family came to Texada, "but for a stranger coming in with two little kids, it was tough." Young was just nine years old in 1897 when he arrived with his mother, Nellie, and sister from Cumberland. His father was a railroad engineer, but the family had broken up after diphtheria claimed the lives of three of his siblings within twenty-four hours.[22]

When George McLeod married Annie Raper in 1907, mine owner Harry Treat asked George to dispose of some fine bird's-eye maple furniture that he had purchased for a second cabin on Emily Lake. George and Annie bought it and their granddaughter, Donna Lechner, who retired to the island, still uses it today. Courtesy Gary McLeod

When the family was dropped off on the uninhabited shore of Gillies Bay, the boy had to find the trail to his aunt's ranch three miles away. Although Annie Sumner's sons, Harry and James, would not officially pre-empt their side-by-side lots 274 and 275 until 1904 and receive their Crown grants until 1907, they were already well-established farmers when the Youngs came to Texada. One or both of the Sumners also worked in the mines in the winter to earn enough to support the family. Soon after he arrived, Bill Young rode the Sumners' Jersey bull into Van Anda, stopping on the way at the Hammond farm in the interior of the island. Jack Hammond had arrived earlier the same year and built a log cabin which still stands, but he soon moved his family to Hidden Basin on Nelson Island. His adventures there were chronicled by his son, Dick Hammond, in *Tales from Hidden Basin* (Harbour Publishing, 1996) and *Haunted Waters* (Harbour Publishing, 2000).[23]

After six months the Youngs settled in Van Anda, where Bill's mother, Nellie, took in washing from the miners. With no running water or electricity, she had to rely on her son to haul water for her and cut wood for the stove. To help out, Bill caught trout in the lakes and sold them; it was illegal, but they had to eat. In 1905, when he was seventeen, Bill Young began working in the Marble Bay Mine, 671 feet down the shaft, but he reported that he "couldn't lift the rocks they expected me to lift . . . We were supposed to shovel sixteen tons of rock in eight hours, and fourteen tons was the best I could do." During the blackberry harvest, he and three friends camped out at Lang Bay on the mainland, commuting to and from work daily in a twenty-four-foot canoe with Young on the steering oar and the three others each wielding a pair of oars.[24]

After several difficult low-paying jobs, including a year of bundling shingles for $1.50 per ten-hour day, Bill Young built a gas boat, the *Comeback* (opinion is divided on whether its engine was five or eight horsepower), and beachcombed to supplement his income from a trapline. After provincial inspection regulations beached Walter Pinnock's *Wood Nymph* in 1908, Young took over his duties, glad to have found an easier way to make a living. Then in 1909, he began carrying the mail twice a week from Van Anda to Blubber Bay. In good weather he made the trip by water, but when the seas were too stormy, he hiked the trail along the rocky shore through Sturt Bay Lagoon to Eagle Bay and the Loyal Mine and then over the hill to the Texada Development Company in Blubber Bay. He had to make this trip and return before ten in the morning so that the outgoing mail could leave on the southbound Union Steamship.

As a small community was developing around the Powell River paper mill, in 1912 Young had a new boat built in Vancouver to service the Van Anda to Powell River market. The *Louvain* was a thirty-foot, twenty-passenger unit built on a "Columbia River" hull, a double-ended design popular at the time. With its two-cylinder, eighteen-horsepower gas engine, it could do six knots, regardless of load. It went into service the following year, and for the next thirty-seven years he operated it as a water taxi, tow boat, beachcomber, emergency boat and grog hauler. The fare to Powell River was twenty-five cents; the service charge on a case of beer was the same price. The *Louvain*'s two cylinders sounded as if they were barking, "Two-bits, two-bits, two bits," and soon this became the ship's nickname. With its rounded hull, it rolled a lot in rough weather, but with a full load of twenty people and a hundred cases of beer safely stowed out of sight under the seats, it was fairly stable. This kind of service was essential for a population that had no local liquor outlet. Gossips often accused Young of being a bootlegger, but he didn't need to be, as there were so many on the island already. Many times Bill Young's *Louvain* took expectant mothers or people at the end of their lives to the hospital. Once, when he was asked to bring a doctor to a patient, a gale blew up and he was reluctant to go. However, when the doctor said it was a matter of life and death, they went, but the doctor had to help bail water.

Charles John Anderson (1859–1939), who had been known in the Klondike as the Lucky Swede, came to Texada in 1912.[25] Anderson, born in Sweden in 1859, had landed in New York in 1887. Six years later, he sailed north to Alaska with a party of prospectors. His wild adventures there have been perpetuated by several writers, including Pierre Berton. However, *Adventures in Service* (McClelland & Stewart, 1929) by Reverend George Pringle,[26] who was ordained in the Yukon and knew Anderson both there and on Texada, tells how Anderson bought the Eldorado No. 29 claim from three disenchanted prospectors in the winter of 1896–97 and sold it after taking two million in gold out of it. He married a Dawson dance hall girl, but they divorced a year later. He then invested his fortune in San Francisco real estate but lost it all in the 1906 earthquake. After turning up in Van Anda in 1912, he continued to prospect and was so convinced that he would eventually make a gold find on Texada that he vowed not to shave off his "neat little whisker" until he struck it rich. For the next quarter century, the Lucky Swede lived in a cabin down by the water on the Fogh property in Blubber Bay and took his meals at Mrs. Blanchard's house nearby.[27] He never did find gold on Texada. He died in 1939 and is buried in the Van Anda cemetery.

Annie Forbes, the doctor's wife, ran the Van Anda post office from June 1, 1897, to July 15, 1899, after which Emily Raper took over. Edwin Pooke inherited the job in 1903 and three years later built a store into which he

This 1899 store was likely owned and operated under the auspices of the Van Anda Copper and Gold Company.

moved the post office; later he hired Walter Planta as postmaster. After Alfred G. Deighton bought Pooke's store, he took over as postmaster from Planta. Deighton and his brother, George, had left Ontario for Vancouver in 1887,[28] then built a rowboat to row up the coast. They landed at Myrtle Point on the mainland just south of Powell River and found jobs in adjacent logging camps. Alfred pre-empted land nearby in 1892, but after completing the necessary improvements, the brothers moved to Van Anda, where George worked in the mine[29] before returning to Myrtle Point, where he operated the Springbrook Dairy and became "king of the moonshiners." Alfred Deighton remained on Texada to purchase Pooke's store and post office,[30] keeping it open till eleven on Saturday nights so that the country people could come in after work. Records of some of the store's transactions during World War I are in the Texada Archives and read like a roll call of the early settlers—Abercrombie, Carter, Stromberg, Lowther, Raper, Jones, and Young, just to name a few.[31]

Originally a logger and a prospector, when Al Deighton settled on Texada, he bought Edwin Pooke's store and passed it on to his son, Reg, when he died. Texada used to get a lot more snow than it does now.

The Kirkness brothers were also early merchants on the island. Arriving a few days after the Boer War ended, Bill Kirkness and his brother built a general store in Van Anda. In his later years, he retired to a neat little white cottage surrounded by a colourful flower garden. A man of strong views, he was known to express them in a voice easily audible above a gale-force wind. He died in 1954.

Downtown Van Anda suffered disastrous fires in 1910, 1912 and 1917. Forty minutes and a strong west wind combined with dry conditions in June 1910 was all it took for fire to destroy the stores belonging to Al Deighton and the Kirkness brothers as well as five other buildings. With great effort, the bucket brigade managed to preserve the Texada Hotel, only to see it burn down later that year. Rebuilt as the Windsor, it succumbed to the 1912 fire, along with the new and enlarged Deighton's store, which had a community hall on the second floor, and the rebuilt Kirkness store, which had rooms for rent above it. Van Anda had its third disastrous fire in 1917, and this one destroyed the third Kirkness store, the Windsor Hotel and the Union Hall. A fourth Kirkness store was built on a new site across the road, but it too later burned. Deighton's store survived the 1917 fire, but Al Deighton decided to hand over the job of postmaster to J.S. Barnes, whose wife ran a tea room and small store out of "Honeymoon Cottage," which was between Carter's Sawmill and the smelter. An article in Marion Little's scrapbook notes that "there was a big fireplace made of ore samples from one of the mines" and identifies the Barnes' cottage as the Treats' first residence on the island.

GILLIES BAY PIONEERS

In 1897, the same year that Van Anda and Texada City had been laid out, the *British Colonist* reported that a syndicate of Vancouver and Nanaimo men planned to lay out a townsite in Gillies Bay, but this never happened, as very few people lived there at that time. However, there were trails from Gillies Bay to Van Anda and Texada City, and people could make the trip on horseback and later by wagon.

For many years there were no houses at all on the beach in Gillies Bay, as the eastern side was owned by James Raper and the western side by his son-in-law, George McLeod. Swedetown, a few miles inland in what was sometimes referred to as "Snoose Valley," was called Gillies Bay in those days and is now referred to as Upper Gillies Bay. Its post office opened in 1914 on P.H. McElroy's farm, but it was closed August 5, 1931. There was also a school, of which nothing remains but the granite boulder that propped up one corner.

The founder of Swedetown was Peter A. Staaf (1872–1954), a Swedish carpenter who came to the island in 1907. He lived in a little house by the Blubber Bay creek for a year while he worked as a framer, but the following year, he pre-empted a choice piece of land in Upper Gillies Bay. He supplemented his farm income by building houses in Van Anda and Powell River, where he was also part of the crew that erected the pulp and paper mill. However, once well established on his farm in Gillies Bay, he went home to Sweden and recruited friends to come and join him.

In April 1911, the P.A. Staaf family had just moved into their new home on the farm in Upper Gillies Bay. Settlers' homes were functional rather than fancy—at least to begin with.

Unlike other Texada settlers, these people came for the land and the farming, not the mining. Although most of the properties in this area are no longer in the hands of those first settlers, the third generation of Staafs are still living on Peter Staaf's original farm, for which he got his first Crown grant in 1909 and three more between 1923 and 1925.

P.A. Staaf's careful records in his neat copperplate handwriting detail his every financial transaction, from his work on the tramway for the Little Billie Mine to how many crates of fruit he sold to specific families. In an article he wrote for the *Agricultural Journal* in 1923, he extolled Texada's soils as "easy to work in either dry or wet season . . . while patches of open meadowland contain deep black loam." In 1912 Staaf built a wharf at Shelter Point at a cost of six thousand dollars. It was only used once before World War I started and reduced its potential traffic, but he claimed it was "considered the best wharf on the island,"[32] though the water beside it was too shallow for most large ships. A few of its pilings still remain. In 1925 he bought a brand new Ford pickup for $825. It was not the first vehicle

P.A. Staaf built a six-hundred-foot wharf at Gillies Bay for six thousand dollars, just before World War I. Unfortunately, it was hardly used, because although it was sheltered, it was in shallow water.

powered by an internal combustion engine to be brought to the island, but it was the first new one. Few other people had new cars till the 1950s.

P.A. Staaf's next-door neighbours were Christ Peterson and his Finnish wife, Mary (1888–1963), who pre-empted their land in 1911. On their rather rocky, hilly ground, they built a log cabin upwind of the barn and outhouse and planted a garden area in the flat lower field.[33] Mauve lilac bushes, Mary's favourite flower, flanked the long driveway. Christ worked in one of the Van Anda mines, travelling to work by horseback along the High Road, which was a swampy dirt track that was at times almost impassable. In the most treacherous sections, two rows of wooden planks were spaced wheel distance apart; vehicles that slipped off them sank to their axles in the mud.

One day in 1916, when the youngest of the Petersons' four children, Frederick, was still a babe in arms, Christ Peterson disappeared. He was seen heading home after his shift at the mine, but if he met with foul play, his body was never found. His wife always insisted that he would never just leave "all that work for a piece of land" of his own accord, but he had not been seen leaving the island. Many years after her husband disappeared, Mary Peterson saw a man on the street in Vancouver who closely resembled him and took him to court to prove he was her long-lost husband. Although she accurately described his body markings and blemishes, the court found the man not guilty.

After her husband disappeared, Mary Peterson had no desire to return to the strict religious parental home in Finland from which she had run away to New York and met Christ. Instead, while her children were growing up, she took in a boarder to help out with the finances and the farm work and accepted help from neighbours. In 1917 she received the Crown grant for the family farm, which by this time included a house, barn, chicken house, cellar, hog house and two and a half acres of cultivated land. Her neighbours, Vitalis Copp and Carl Wesslen, verified that these improvements had been made. In 1926 she obtained a Certificate of Indefeasible Title, which gave her full ownership of the property.

Around 1914 the Petersons had sold the lower ten- or thirteen-acre piece of their land to the Copp family, who had arrived from Sweden the previous year. For a long time, there was a dispute over payment for this property, with Christ and Mary (and later Mary alone) saying they had not been fully paid, and Vitalis Copp insisting he had paid. Vitalis (1884–1951) and Emma Christina Copp built a house that still stands beside Staaf Road. Their son, Evert (1910–1976), had been born in Sweden, but their two daughters, Nan and Sigrid, were both born on Texada. As the farm produced plenty of food and they were able to obtain wood for fuel nearby, they were never hungry or cold. The Gillies Bay District School was a pleasant mile-and-a-half walk for the children in summer, but when the snow was deep in winter, Vitalis delivered them there in a horse-drawn sleigh. However, the school closed in 1928 when the numbers fell too low to qualify for a teacher, so Sigrid had to finish her education by correspondence.

The Copps kept a cow, a horse and a pig. To preserve meat, they layered it with coarse salt in a big barrel or crock that was kept in a cool place; before using it, they had to soak it well or it was too salty to eat. They canned fruits and vegetables, dried beans, and kept other vegetables in a cool, dry root cellar, though sometimes these didn't last the winter, causing the family to scrounge. Water came from the well by the pailful; there were no pumps. On wash days, water was packed in before breakfast so that it could be heated in the boiler on the stove. Everything was done by hand with the aid of a washboard. By noon the laundry was pegged on a line outdoors and kept off the ground by a long wooden prop.

The experiences of the other farm families—the Jacobsons, Ericksons, and Peter Bun—situated along the High Road (later known as Central Road) to Van Anda were similar to that of the Copps. The houses of some were built with lumber salvaged from the Marble Bay Hotel, but all have since been demolished.

NORTH ISLAND PIONEERS

On the northwest side of the island, Willis Woodhead (1884–1961)[34] arrived in 1915 and settled his wife and family in a tiny shack overlooking Crescent Bay. A short, stocky man, he had worked as a tallyman in the English coal mines, but after he came to Canada, he took a job as a diamond setter in the Hedley mine in the BC Interior. Unfortunately, his wife, Alice, a seamstress whom he had met in Salt Lake City, had always lived in cities, and she disliked Hedley because of the large predators lurking in the bush, so after moving his family to Texada, Willis commuted the three hundred miles back to his job in Hedley to earn cash to pay the taxes on his new land.

Willis Woodhead settled his family at Crescent Bay and commuted back to his job as a diamond setter at Hedley in the BC Interior. Alice, a city girl, preferred the isolation to worrying that predators would eat her children.

Courtesy Keith and Nora Hughes

The property that the Woodheads bought in Crescent Bay had been recently Crown granted to Norman Stones, whose wife had drowned in the May 7, 1914, sinking of the *Lusitania*. With no horse and buggy, the Woodheads hiked the three miles to and from the wharf at Blubber Bay. When a milk cow arrived on the Union boat, Alice and seven-year-old Kirby gamely walked it home and learned to milk it. As a young man, Kirby bought his own herd of cows and sold milk in both Van Anda and Blubber Bay, but he never wanted to become a farmer. Willis and Alice used the farm for supplementary income and experimented with an apple orchard—which is now one of Texada's Heritage orchards—and strawberry growing to supply Woodward's and Eaton's in Vancouver.

BLUBBER BAY PIONEERS

By 1918 the centre of activity on Texada was shifting from Van Anda to Blubber Bay, where the Pacific Lime Company was going full blast surrounded by what amounted to a company town. White workers lived in streets of identical neat little clapboard houses, each with a porch and a flower and vegetable garden surrounded by a picket fence. The social scene revolved around the community hall, which was used for dances, whist drives and movies. On weekdays it became a school and on Sundays a church. Chinese workers were segregated in a two-storey bunkhouse at the south end of the bay. However, the poker games held there attracted all ethnic groups.

Blubber Bay's first long-term residents had arrived in 1917. Andrew Williamson and Jonathan Ross[35] were both from Scotland; Williamson was hired by Pacific Lime as foreman and Ross, a blacksmith by trade, became the chief steam engineer. Both remained in their jobs into the 1940s. Williamson's family, which included three daughters, lived in the house that became the Holtenwood Gallery. Ross's family did not follow him to the island until 1919, but in time his three boys, Duncan, Ken and Ian, and two daughters, Flora and Isabel, all attended the Blubber Bay School.

SOUTH ISLAND PIONEERS

The southern part of the island was a separate world from the northern end, as it was not connected by road until 1965, so the people who lived there went to Lasqueti or Pender Harbour for their supplies. George Edward Whittaker received one of the first Crown grants there in 1917.[36] Little is known about him and his family, except that his name appears on the 1916 voters list and his address is listed as Anderson Bay. Jimmy Dougan, who now lives on property at Whittaker Cove just west of Anderson Bay, has found numerous things Whittaker left behind, including an anvil and a very small woman's boot, which might have belonged to Mrs. Whittaker. (Being an imaginative person, Dougan has written a speculative story about them.[37]) In the self-published book *My Daughters' Request: Spotlight on the Yesterday of Country Folk*, author Charlie Dougan has included a picture of three of his family in front of "Fulton's 1918 house, Point Upwood." This point lies on the west side of Anderson Bay, and the Dougan family also refer to the cove below the Cox trailer as Fulton Cove,[38] so it appears there were two early settlers in that area; it is possible that Fulton—whoever he was—went to war and never came back.

Although the first service in this church was Anglican, the building was used by several denominations. When it was dedicated June 20, 1900, the thirty members of the congregation opted to call it the Texada Presbyterian Church.

CHAPTER 9:

The Lean Years 1920–1938

THIRTEEN TEXADA MEN SERVED in the First World War as army life seemed an exciting way to see the world at the government's expense. Besides, mining jobs were no longer as secure as they had been in earlier days. Six of those thirteen died: Corporal S. Brister, Private Frederick Arthur Groves, Lance Corporal Gavin Hamilton, Private Andrew Law, Private Thomas Benjamin Raper and Private Joseph Reynolds.[1] Tom Raper, who fell at Vimy Ridge, was one of James Raper's sons.

Fred Lowther and Elroy Pillat were the only two veterans to return to the island. After enduring the horrors of Ypres, the Somme and Vimy Ridge, Lowther eschewed all celebrations of war. He burned his uniform and all his medals. On Remembrance Day he would shut himself in his cabin with the radio firmly off. The screams of wounded horses still rang in his head.[2] The flu epidemic that hit the returning men and their families passed by the island except for three people who had contracted it on the mainland.

VAN ANDA'S MINES CLOSE

With the end of World War I, demand for copper fell and prices plummeted. As a result, the mines on Texada Island closed one by one, and as the pumps were switched off, the shafts filled up with water, making future reopening expensive. Robert Lloyd Jones (1883–1970), a Welshman who for the previous five years had earned a good living as a cage man at the

Marble Bay Mine, was laid off when it closed in 1919. It would be over a decade before he got regular paid work again. Roy Padgett, whose family was living in Van Anda, recalled that "the town died in a matter of days. Everyone started burning their houses down for the insurance till the insurance companies cancelled all insurance on Texada Island. Fire every day. One fellow living in Vancouver gave $50 to a guy to come up and burn his house down and the guy came up and burned down the wrong house. When the hotel went up, everyone ran into the bar and grabbed all the booze so the whole town was soused."[3]

The Padgett family moved to Paradise Valley behind Powell River where they could live off the land. Others stayed, but soon the houses around the mines began to deteriorate. Some fell down and some were torn down as Texadans began their favourite pastime of recycling and reusing. The owners of a house on Para Street left a piano in it and never came back; eventually, the house and all it contained fell off the cliff.[4] After a while there were not enough children to keep the school open. The Columbia Coast Mission closed the hospital on September 30, 1920, and Dr. Marlatt and Nurse Frampton moved to the Powell River hospital. Although the Union Steamships continued to call at the Van Anda wharf for a time, Blubber Bay became the new social centre of the island.

In 1921 the Columbia Coast Mission sent Reverend George Pringle, who had been ordained in Dawson City in 1900, to Van Anda to run a mission from there to fifty-six logging camps in the upper Georgia Strait and beyond. Pringle's first boat, the *Mina W*, had an engine "that was enough to make a saint swear"; fortunately, in 1922 it was replaced by the *Sky Pilot*, a forty-foot teak launch that came with an engineer named Price to run it. Once, after an arduous trip to Nanaimo, Pringle and Price ran the *Sky Pilot* into Tucker Bay on Lasqueti, planning to get a good night's sleep. While there, they received a desperate message from a young English couple living just south of Cook Bay: "Our little girl, Mary, has been ill for some days and seems to be getting worse." The mission boat immediately crossed Sabine Channel to get them, and seeing the ship approaching, the family put to sea in their "walnut shell" of a dinghy and rowed out to meet it. With a big sea running, it was difficult to get them on board, but

Reverend George Pringle and engineer Price used the Sky Pilot, *a forty-foot launch, to run a mission to loggers for the United Church.*

Pringle and Price finally managed it, then ensconced them on quilts, pillows and newspapers on the floor of the cabin. They were told to stay put no matter what, as it was going to be a rough crossing. The ship battled the oncoming waves for hours, plunging, rolling and corkscrewing its way around the north end of Texada. From time to time, Price looked in on the family and gave Pringle the thumbs-up. The rough ride continued across Malaspina Strait and into Powell River, where Pringle hired a taxi and went with the family to the hospital. The child recovered and her father got a job at the Powell River mill, so they abandoned their homestead.

Grace Pringle was almost as well known as her husband—or rather, her light was. Every evening at dusk, Grace lit a coal oil lamp and put it in her kitchen window, and as the Pringles' cabin overlooked the Van Anda wharf, all sizes of watercraft used her light to navigate. Reverend Pringle and his family left the island in 1928. He was so well loved, however, that long after he left Texada, many local brides and grooms journeyed to Vancouver to be married by him, and the islanders mourned with him when his son was killed in battle during World War II.

In June 1922, after William Raper, one of the twin sons of Alfred Raper, died in Vancouver, his penniless widow, Mary, brought their three children, Alfred (1914–2005), Vera and Agnes, back to live in Van Anda on the three Columbia Street lots owned by the family. There was no government social safety net in those days, but Van Anda people knew the family's circumstances and many helped them out—often financially.

Arthur Blanchard lost his job in 1923 when Carter's sawmill at the head of Van Anda Cove closed. With a large family to feed, he was reduced to repairing shoes and beachcombing, then using a rowboat to tow the logs he salvaged to the sawmill at Blubber Bay.[5] The job got easier after he was able to buy a gas launch, but he was still happy to accept a job at the mill in 1925 and move his family to Blubber Bay. After that, Pacific Lime often hired his launch to tow scow-loads of lumber to Powell River and other local destinations.

When Art Blanchard graduated from a rowboat to this gas launch, beachcombing to feed his large family was much easier. After the Pacific Lime sawmill hired him in 1925, they paid him to tow scow-loads of lumber to Powell River and elsewhere.

After losing their opera house when Tacoma Steel donated it to the Columbia Coast Mission in 1907, the people of Van Anda promised themselves that never again would they be caught out where their public buildings were concerned. In February 1930 the church property and buildings were officially registered with the United Church of Canada. In the same year, a Van Anda Community Society was incorporated to run the community hall, which was located between the creek that runs out of Emily Lake and the present-day post office. Charter members were Leonard Raper, mining recorder, and his wife, Christine; George McLeod, mining foreman; Walter Pinnock, quarryman; Mary Ann Abercrombie; Mrs. Laura E. Carter; Lottie Tait; and Edith L. Furst (née Stromberg). At their meetings, the tea in their cups was not always tea.

BLUBBER BAY

In 1923 Pacific Lime contracted with Bill McGuigan to open and run a store and pool hall in Blubber Bay. McGuigan, who came from a venerable old Vancouver family[6]—two uncles had signed the petition to incorporate the City of Vancouver and one had served as mayor in 1904—was a man with an inventive mind. In his store he displayed oranges and apples in boxes temptingly tilted against the front counter.[7] Oranges being luxury items, when young boys stole them, he charged them to their parents' accounts. One Halloween he filled small bags with weevily flour and lobbed them at shoplifters as they ran outside, thus advertising their crime by the flour clinging to their clothes. In 1925 he moved to Powell River, where he and his brother opened a grocery store. (McGuigan's grandson, Peter, later retired to the island.)

McGuigan's successor as general storekeeper in Blubber Bay was Bill Pughe, and Pacific Lime celebrated the new store's opening in 1928 with a dance to which fifty people came by gas boat from Powell River. It is possible that Pughe was the store manager who, instead of bringing in refined sugar for his customers, ordered in the cheap raw sugar that ships used for ballast. After customers such as Lois Myers complained about its dark colour, Pacific Lime's manager told the storekeeper, "Either order in what the ladies want or we'll replace you."[8] Pughe stayed until 1946.

The Liebich family arrived in Blubber Bay in 1924. Gustav Liebich was an experienced coal mine mechanic and driller who had worked in the mines of the Ruhr Valley. They left Germany in 1911, coming first to Kamloops and then to Nanaimo in 1916. Pacific Lime allowed the Liebichs and their seven children—Gus Jr., Henry, Art, Norm, Walt, Mary and Bertha—to move into a sixteen-by fourteen-foot shack on an abandoned farm on the Van Anda Road. The rent was one dollar a year, but they also had to supply white carrots for the horses that hauled the five-foot slabs of wood from the sawmill to the kilns. Luckily, they only had to do this for one year, as the horses were replaced by a motorized vehicle.

The family cleared and fenced a large vegetable garden where they grew the biggest cabbages on the island and made barrels of sauerkraut. They also dug a well six feet wide and thirty feet deep. Wages were low, so they sold excess produce to make ends meet. Eventually, they had two milking cows, two calves, two pigs and some chickens. All of the children participated in chores, such as splitting firewood, milking cows, collecting eggs, churning butter, baking bread in round lard tins and making sausages.

None of the children enjoyed lessons, but their parents made sure they worked at them. At that time the one-room Blubber Bay School had thirty-five or forty students in grades one to eight. The teacher, a Miss Tait, who was the milkman's daughter, "stayed until her nerves couldn't stand it."[9] She was followed by a Miss Hopwood, who reacted in the same manner to the children, but Velma Kipp taught from 1928 to 1931 and returned to teach again in 1935. As the Liebich boys left school, they found work locally and paid their parents room and board. This and the family's ability to grow their own food kept them afloat during the Depression years, when wages were low and job security non-existent.

The tower above the school in Blubber Bay held the bell from the CPR's *Empress of Japan*. When the ship was taken out of service in 1922, John Lockhart, who was a director of Pacific Lime as well as a director of Burrard Dry Dock, salvaged the deep-toned, richly engraved bell and sent it to Blubber Bay. On school days it rang every morning and after lunch to summon the children to class.[10] From the same source, Lockhart also obtained the ship's ninety-foot steel mast, which became a flagpole near the Blubber Bay wharf. When the halyard broke, foreman Joe Rutherford shinnied to the top to fix it.[11]

Meanwhile, the children of Jonathan Ross, chief steam engineer at Pacific Lime, were growing up in Blubber Bay. Young Duncan Ross and his friends knew every boat on the coast by its whistle, having listened to them feeling their way into Blubber Bay on foggy nights while people on shore beat pans and yelled to warn them where the rocks were. High up on the bridge, captains Bowden, Muir and Talbot were the epitome of competence and dignity and seemed like gods to the children. All the kids had their own boats as soon as they could "drive a nail and lift a few boards from the sawmill after dark," and for fifteen dollars, Jack Wray would build any size of dory without plans, "all with lumber stolen from the mill."[12]

Both Jean Weisner, daughter of Pacific Lime's superintendent, Andrew Williamson, and Duncan Ross recalled an old man named Henry Alles living in Blubber Bay during these years. He had come to Van Anda in

Duncan (second from left) and Ian (third from left) Ross pose in the front row of boys attending the Blubber Bay School in the late 1920s. Their father, Jonathan Ross, was Pacific Lime's chief steam engineer. Duncan and Ian wrote about their childhood experiences and Duncan's son, Ted, carries on the tradition. Courtesy Flora Ross Shaw

the late 1890s and taken on the job of slopping the hogs for the Marble Bay Hotel, as well as acting as general handyman. When the hotel closed in 1919, Allis moved into the former dynamite shack in Blubber Bay and began looking after Pacific Lime's pig pen and mucking out the barn and cow byre. He also looked after Sparky, the last of the horses that hauled wood for the kilns, after the others were disposed of. Alles loved children, and each Christmas Day he would hide chocolates and Japanese oranges around his house for the local children to find, but as soon as his drinking buddies showed up, he sent the children home. Once, Duncan managed to stay behind unnoticed, and horror-stricken, had watched what he thought was a man dying. He was puzzled when he saw the same man walking around later.

DAVIE BAY

In 1924 Jimmie Kitto, the nearest neighbour to the young Cook Bay couple who had sought Reverend Pringle's help, sold his Crown grant at Davie Bay to Jack (1882–1954) and Mary Ethel (1888–1976) Devaney. However, Jack Devaney soon found that pioneer life was not to his liking and returned to being a sports physiotherapist at the Western Sports Centre in Vancouver, leaving his crippled wife, three sons and four daughters on Texada. Thereafter, he visited for ten days each summer. His wife, who had suffered a stroke during the birth of their last child, could only direct operations while her two oldest sons, Jack and Pat, did most of the work; two of the daughters soon left the island to become domestic servants in the city.

In memoirs taped in 2002, Margaret (Maggie) Devaney, one of the younger daughters who was by then in her eighties,[13] told how the family had moved into the cabins of a deserted logging camp at Davie Bay, an area that had been logged seventeen years earlier, where they led a somewhat idyllic though tough existence. Monthly grocery orders sent by their father from Woodward's Department Store were delivered to False Bay on Lasqueti Island, and the family rowed the twelve miles to collect them and their mail. The children's clothing consisted of denim jeans and whatever sweatshirts their father discovered in the gymnasium's lost and found. Maggie was twelve years old before she owned a pair of shoes, and she never wore underwear until she got married.

When the Devaney family went to live at Davie Bay in 1924, Margaret (on the right) often took the trail up to the Bell farm, where her best friend Tilly lived. Tilly grew up to be the first woman on the island to get her driver's licence.

The children cleared five acres of land, taking out fifty-two stumps, and built rock walls that are still visible. They constructed goat houses and milking stands near Kitto's original cabin, where there was a spring, and then planted vegetables, roses, bulbs and fruit trees, though they never managed to keep the deer from sharing them. Fishing was also a big part of their lives, both to provide fish for their own consumption and to sell to the Japanese buyers who patrolled the coast in their well-kept packer boats. Ling cod, which they caught easily during the twenty minutes of low tide, was a favourite. For meat they shot deer. All the children learned to shoot and to be meticulous about cleaning and oiling their guns after each use. When Maggie Devaney's mother objected to a little terrier dog that the girl had acquired and told her to shoot it, she took the trail up to Benny Bell's farm, where Bell's daughter, Tilly, was her friend. Bell adopted the dog and later he told her that it was "the most wonderful little cattle dog." Jack Devaney lost interest in his daughter when she declined to let him train her to be an Olympic swimmer. "Nobody showed any affection toward each other," she said. "My mother always thought it was terrible to kiss a baby or get close to anybody because you passed germs on."

The Strombergs came to Davie Bay every summer, sailing around the island from Van Anda to a cabin they had built where the creek from the falls named after them empties into the ocean. While they were absent, they stored their dishes and pots and pans in a compartment under the floor. The Devaney children knew about this cache but never touched its contents.

One year someone else stole them, and the Strombergs, disappointed, returned to their winter home. William Stromberg had seven mineral claims starting at the beach and extending one claim wide up the hill; he called them Edith, Kate, Delora, Ethel, Bullion, Hill and Big Bluff. He did some diamond drilling on them, found bornite and optioned them to a Vancouver company in 1929, but after drilling one hole, the company abandoned the project.

THE POCAHONTAS CAPER

With all the logging and prospecting activity in the Pocahontas Bay area on the southeast side of the island during these lean years, it is interesting that no one owned up to knowing what else was going on there—one of the largest illicit stills ever to operate in BC. Early homesteaders had often installed stills on their property because all that was required was three feet of copper tubing and a pressure cooker. Most of these stills were small affairs set up for the production of whisky for private consumption, though Haddon Burditt's operation was an exception. He sold the product from his still to thirsty Powell Riverites. When the police learned about it, they came to arrest him, but he dumped the evidence in Myrtle Lake minutes before they arrived.

Haddon Burditt was an enterprising farmer who bid on the lumber from the famous Pocahontas still after it was busted. He used it to build a handsome house and may have known more about the still than he let on, as he had one of his own that he had to dispose of quickly when the police found out about it.

However, the province of British Columbia repealed its liquor prohibition law in October 1920, just as the United States enacted its own, thereby creating a large clandestine market south of the border. Liquor produced in Canada, ostensibly for the Mexican market, was rerouted to grateful American consumers. On the West Coast, most of the rum-runners, as the boats that delivered the liquor were called, were based in the southern portion of the Strait of Georgia, and for a long time customs officers did not think to look farther north for the source of the rum-runners' supplies.

The Pocahontas Bay still operated quietly for nearly ten years.[14] Apparently, an Englishman who had lost money on a land deal set it up around 1920 in the vacant buildings of an old logging camp. A year or so later, when he had recouped his losses, he sold it to three men from Vancouver, and they operated it until the RCMP discovered it in 1928. These men's identities are a mystery, but they may have been influential people, as the original court records of the police bust have conveniently gone missing. In 1994, when Texada resident Bob Blackmore researched extensively to make a video of the story, he concluded that there must also have been some local involvement, because on the day the operators fled from the police, none of the children at the Upper Gillies Bay School saw any strangers around. P.A. Staaf's granddaughter, Sylvia, said that he "and everyone [on the island] knew of the Pocahontas still." She believed her grandfather had not been involved in it, though he may have had a still of his own.

PRINCESS MARY

In 1931 the CPR put the passenger steamer *Princess Mary* on the run between Powell River and Vancouver three times a week, with multiple stops in between the two points. The ship also did one round trip to Comox each week. Built in Scotland in 1910, the *Mary* was 248 feet long and 40 feet wide but could only carry cars on deck.

GILLIES BAY BEGINS TO GROW

When Herb and Bess Johnson moved their family to Texada in July 1931, they moved into the McElroy place in Upper Gillies Bay. Although originally from England, Johnson had been a steamboat engineer on the Mackenzie River but was laid off when the Depression hit. He took his family to the Lower Mainland, where his son Leonard fell off a dock at

The Union Steamship MV Chelohsin *spent most of its service years, 1911 to 1949, on the Texada route.*

Harrison Mills and broke his back. As he was to be in a cast for eighteen months, the doctors advised the family to find a quiet place to live, and that is what brought them to Texada. Leonard had a brother and a sister, Keith and Lurene, and all three remained on Texada, where they became noted citizens.

When the family arrived on the island, no one seemed to be working. People played cards at each others' houses, only coming home in time to make breakfast. Everyone grew big vegetable gardens. If someone butchered a cow or a pig, they shared the meat with other members of the community. In summer the whole neighbourhood would go to the little lakes in the centre of the island to fish. The men and their gear went by truck and by the time the women arrived later on foot, about four hundred fish would be ready for frying. Put between slices of bread and served with coffee and donuts, they constituted lunch. In the evenings, a big bonfire was built on the beach and everyone toasted wieners, and since most people played a musical instrument of some kind in those days, they played and sang late into the night.

The Johnsons made the most of what they had. One Christmas when they had no money to buy a turkey, Herb Johnson shot a pheasant. Later they raised turkeys to sell to the chain of nine David W. Spencer department stores (generally known simply as "Spencer's stores") on the Lower Mainland. Spencer's were Woodward's stores' main competition until they were bought out by Eaton's in 1948. The Johnsons saved every cent they could and invested it in a series of farms and in several lots at Shelter Point, which eventually became a park.

Bess Johnson, who loved being outdoors and riding horses, planted gardens to attract birds everywhere she lived.[15] She and her sister had grown up in Rainy River near Kenora, Ontario, and learned to speak Ojibway. In later years, when talking to each other over telephone party lines, they spoke in Ojibway to keep their conversations private. Bess also had an argument with a census taker who insisted that she had to state her ethnic background; "Canadian" was not acceptable. "Okay," she said defiantly, "I'm an Indian," and this led to a local legend that she was indeed Ojibway. The Johnson descendants still live on the island.

The curmudgeonly teacher, Miss Fee, marched her Upper Gillies Bay students down to see this dead humpback whale. One family used the blubber to make soap, and their children were ostracized because of the smell.

In 1922, when a forty-foot humpback whale stranded itself in Gillies Bay, the curmudgeonly teacher, Miss Fee, marched her students from the Upper Gillies Bay District School in Swedetown down to the beach to see it. One of the children's families

School principal Dr. Roy Sanderson discovered the fresh air and gorgeous sands of Gillies Bay in the 1920s and brought his colleagues to enjoy this teachers' paradise. He bought up land and developed the community of Gillies Bay.
Heather Harbord

subsequently made soap out of the blubber, but the children were mortified by the strong smell that caused them to be avoided by their classmates long after the whale's remains had disappeared from the beach.

When Dr. J. Roy Sanderson (1881–1966) discovered the beauty of Gillies Bay in 1925, he was in search of a place where his asthmatic son could breathe. At first the family camped on the beach, but after two years they negotiated a deal to buy the southeast quarter of George McLeod's Section 9. Sanderson's house was the first to be built in Gillies Bay. The lumber for it was reputed to be the last load from the Carters' mill in Van Anda, and it was rafted around the island to the site, as there was still no road connecting the two bays. Sanderson liked Texada so well that he encouraged his school colleagues to rent the bunkhouses left over from the Alberta Logging Company's operations, and the place soon became known as the "Teachers' Paradise."

In 1932 the Cook family built a cabin on the south side of Gillies Bay, and every summer the family rented out their Vancouver house and came to Texada to camp there. Their daughter, Eleanor Hoeg, later described the journey via Union Steamships' vessel *Chelohsin*, which left Vancouver at six in the evening. After they passed under the Lions Gate Bridge, the children went to their stateroom to wash for "our semi-annual restaurant dinner." To a small child, the clanks and rattles in the pipes in the low-ceilinged dining room were somewhat disturbing, and the tables draped in heavy white linen tablecloths and matching napkins so large that "mine covered my whole front" were intimidating. Four courses of food were served from big silver tureens and covered dishes and eaten with "a bewildering array of cutlery." In rough weather, the waiters set rims around the tables and sprinkled the cloths with water so that the dishes stuck. Finger bowls were supplied at the end of the meal.

When they reached the Gillies Bay float between 11:30 p.m. and 1 a.m., Angus Kinney, who lived year-round in Gillies Bay, would be waiting by the freight shed in his boat to row out and bring them ashore. Although Eleanor Hoeg remembered him as "rather an old reprobate with taking ways," before they arrived each summer, he opened their cabin for them and dried it out. Occasionally, Kinney would ask Mrs. Cook if she wanted some "Gillies Bay lamb." Her response was, "Yes, and would you like to come to dinner? I'll bake a pie." Kinney would then go out and kill a deer, which he butchered meticulously and gave her a haunch. But even when he came to dinner, he still didn't wash.

While the Union Steamships' elastic schedule was fine for communities like Van Anda, which had a dock, it did cause hardship in places such as Gillies Bay, which only had a float. On one occasion, when Kinney met the Cooks as they arrived on the *Chelohsin*, the sea was so rough that the ship had to leave without unloading their food and bedding. It was four in the morning before the seas had subsided enough for the Cooks to leave the float, then as the wind swept them toward shore, the rain soaked them. As they scrambled ashore, the breakers found any remaining dry spots. Shaking with cold, they squelched their way to their cabin, where they pulled blankets from an old trunk reeking of mothballs and threw them on musty mattresses. But they didn't care; they had made it to safety. After another family waited all night on the float at Gillies Bay until the ship picked them up in the morning, Captain Bob Wilson of the *Chelohsin* arranged to radio the time of the ship's arrival at Cape Lazo to Alan Sanderson, Dr. J. Roy Sanderson's son, who was a ham radio enthusiast.

Sometimes the Cook family made the day trip from Vancouver to Van Anda on the *Venture*. The family would be on the dock at eight in the morning in hopes of being early enough to get their favourite seats. In fine weather they sat in deck chairs on the starboard side, and in wet weather on the hard benches under cover in the stern. Often the ship didn't leave the dock until mid-morning, but the family didn't mind, as it was fun to watch the freight being loaded in rope slings. When one broke, its contents would spill onto the deck, or worse, into the water. The *Venture* came up the

Inner Coast, as the Sunshine Coast was then known. After Howe Sound, it called at every bay and cove for which there were passengers. At each place a crowd of summer visitors and locals would be down on the dock or the shore to watch the action. These summer people were either "boiled lobster pink or muffled in slickers, depending on the weather," while the tanned, bareheaded permanent residents would be wearing shorts. Pith helmets were as ubiquitous as the Tilley hats of today. Freight unloading provided endless entertainment for the passengers aboard ship and the spectators on shore, especially where there was no dock. Men in rowboats had to carefully position them to receive crates of squawking chickens or squealing trussed pigs. "But seeing a terrified cow being lowered onto a raft barely six feet square really took the cake," Eleanor Hoeg reported.

Roberts Creek, Sechelt, Buccaneer Bay, Redrooffs and Pender Harbour all appeared in sunlight in Hoeg's memory, but it was always wet at Stillwater, the last stop before Van Anda. Most of the people meeting the boat at Van Anda were residents, so pith helmets were not in evidence there. Kinney's truck would be waiting to take the Cook family the rest of the way to their cabin at Gillies Bay, but although the man was reliable, his truck was not. Its radiator frequently boiled over, so they stopped at every creek and slough on the way to top up the water. It was a slow journey but they forgot it as soon as they came over the last hill and glimpsed the water.

In the 1930s, Edward Tabor Russ (1875–1957) was the only other person to winter in Gillies Bay. Russ, who had worked in mining camps all over the American southwest, had arrived in Vancouver in 1895, and after listening to a rousing speech by Edward Blewett about Texada's potential, he immediately set out for the island. On arrival he camped on the beach where Van Anda now stands, before pre-empting a quarter of Section 636 south of Swedetown. He built a house there amid a beautiful stand of Douglas firs on an old lake bottom with very rich black soil. He received his Crown grant for it in 1914. In addition to prospecting and farming, Russ also worked as a miner till silicosis reached his lungs. He married and had a son, but his wife died soon after.

Maurice Liebich remembered Russ as a grizzled old guy who lived in a sixteen- by twenty-foot cedar-shake cabin at the head of Gillies Bay.[16]

Its spotless single room contained two beds, one for Russ and the other for visitors. The cookstove and table took up most of the remaining space. Pantry shelves had been built above the stove, and spare clothes hung from the rafters. An extra heater provided comfort in winter, as the cabin's only insulation was building paper, but Russ kept everything neat and clean. Mondays were always wash days, and by ten o'clock each morning, his breakfast dishes were done and he would be sitting in his armchair, enjoying his pipe and a last cup of coffee. No one passed without stopping to say hello and have a chat, and anyone going away for a day or a month dropped off their cats, dogs or chickens for Russ to care for in their absence—and they were well looked after.

Eleanor Hoeg's memories of Russ were not as pleasant. She had thought he was "a nice old man" who kept his cottage fastidiously neat and spotless, but when she was seventeen, he suddenly grabbed and kissed her. She never went near him again and never told her parents. He died the next year.[17] Russ's cabin had been located where the recycling bins are now, but it was moved to the Poock property after he made a deal with them that he could occupy it for life, and on his death in 1957, it reverted to them. He was buried with his prospector's pick in the vivid green coffin that he'd had Bill Stromberg build for him; he called it his "hope chest." Russ's pre-emption later became known as the Bennie Bell farm after a subsequent owner.

From 1937 to 1939, Lurene Johnson (right) and Nan Copp (left) ran a summer bakery at the head of Gillies Bay. At the end of the third summer, they married each others' brothers, with Reverend Pringle officiating.

As the Gillies Bay population grew, enterprising people provided more services. In the summers of 1937 to 1939, friends Lurene Johnson and Nan Copp operated a bakery at the head of Gillies Bay and just across the road from the old school.[18] Their store was a tent with wooden sides and shelves, and they lived in the lean-to behind it. Every morning they baked ten loaves of bread, white and brown on alternate days, and sold them for ten cents each. Their lemon pies were fifty cents each. On Sundays they served hot dogs and ice cream brought up on the Union Steamship in dry ice. This was very popular, and everyone turned up for it. At the end of their third summer of baking, they boarded the Union Steamship from the float in the bay and went to Vancouver, where Reverend Pringle officiated at a double ceremony that married Lurene to Nan's brother, Evert Copp, and Nan to Lurene's brother, Keith Johnson. After Pringle announced, "You can now kiss the bride," he proceeded to kiss both brides himself. Both couples made their homes on the island. Working in the various quarries, in time Keith Johnson rose from labourer to plant manager.[19] Evert Copp worked as a logger and at other odd jobs, including building the road out to the iron mine before it reopened in 1952.[20] (Oke Nyvall also lays claim to this latter distinction.)[21]

THE BLUBBER BAY STRIKE

The Blubber Bay strike of 1938 had a profound effect on the community. Those islanders who had been even peripherally involved in it suffered. Evicted from their home on a farm that was owned by Pacific Lime, the Liebich family squeezed together enough money to buy three lots in Van Anda. Fortunately, both Gus Liebich Sr. and Jr. and the Liebichs' son-in-law, Bill Bushby, soon found work at the Beale Quarries. Kirby (1909–1986) and Cecil Woodhead (1919–1982), banned from working at Pacific Lime because of their support of the strikers, went logging.

For many years after the strike, feelings within the community ran high as many people held grudges, especially toward those who had testified against the workers at their trials.[22] "The less said about that the better," said Jean Weisner seventy years later. (At the time of the strike, she had still been a schoolgirl.) By the 1950s, though the sons of the strikers and scabs still scuffled from time to time, many adults were prepared to recognize that "every man had to feed his family."[23] However, even today, although new people have come in and diluted the situation, some strikers' descendents are reluctant to talk to those of the replacement workers who stayed on.

CHAPTER 10:

The War Years 1939–1945

VAN ANDA IN THE WAR YEARS

WHILE THE ONSET OF WAR IN SEPTEMBER 1939 took many workers away from Texada, there was also an influx of new people. Ben Nicholas (1914–2010), his wife, Jessie, and their young son arrived on Texada in 1939. Born in Cumberland in 1914, Nicholas had lost the sight in his left eye at the age of eight when a rock struck it. He had spent ten years underground amidst the gassy fumes of the No. 5 Cumberland coal mine, but during that time, he studied hard in the fields of electricity, diesel engines and first aid. His first job on Texada was at the Little Gem Mine (previously known as the Nutcracker), but in January 1940, the government closed the Little Gem, as gold was not necessary for the war effort. To sustain his family, Nicholas returned to the Cumberland mine, which had lost most of its workers to the war effort. However, a year later he was back on Texada to wire a diesel engine for Pacific Lime in Blubber Bay, and he continued to work for them for the rest of the war years.

Josef "Joe" Kempe (1908–2006) and his wife, Margaret, also arrived in 1939. They had immigrated from Germany to Saskatchewan, then came to Texada after investing two hundred dollars in the Secondee Mine, which, when discovered by Walter Planta in 1901, had been called the Marjorie Claim. However, the mine closed in February 1940 after its equipment was repossessed, and shortly afterwards, the Kempes were evicted from

Despite their Canadian citizenship, when Joe Kempe and his wife arrived from Saskatchewan in 1939, they had to report to the police in Powell River every week.

their home on Pacific Lime's property in Limekiln Bay. Fortunately, Fred Beale not only hired Kempe to work in his quarry, but because no rental houses were available, also financed Kempe's purchase of Edwin Pooke's house on Wall Street in Van Anda. Beale charged no interest, and Kempe repaid the principal out of his wages over the next five years.

As soon as war broke out with Germany, Kempe and Gus Liebich were required to go over to Powell River every week to register with the police on behalf of all family members born in Germany. But while some communities ostracized enemy aliens, neither the Kempes nor the Liebichs encountered this on Texada. This was a relief to the Liebich family, who had bad memories of being unable to get work while living in the BC Interior during World War I.

Fred Beale bought the old Pooke house on Wall Street for the Kempe family. Joe paid him back over five years, and Fred never charged a cent of interest.

For six years beginning in 1940, Kempe ran the stucco mill for Beale Quarries, which was by then owned by Balfour Guthrie Ltd. He then took a brief fling at logging, but in the fall of 1947 he returned to the quarries, this time with Stan Beale, and remained with that company even after it was sold to Ideal Cement in 1956. He retired from Ideal in 1983.

Other newcomers to Van Anda in the early war years included the Waldorf and Grayson families, who had finally given up on the Saskatchewan drought, and Mary and Al Waters, who came from Vancouver. Al Waters took over the Esso agency from Fred Lowther and Bill Young, who had been operating it for the previous twenty-five years. Bill Gussman (1892–1985) and his wife, Mary (1924–2011) anchored their fish boat, *Sea Maiden*, in Sturt Bay until, with a second child on the way, they moved ashore to a small house right next to the Marble Bay Quarry.

After store owner Al Deighton died in 1940, his son Reg and daughter-in-law, Isabel Carter, whose father, John Carter had owned the sawmill at the head of Van Anda Cove, took over the Deighton family store. Late-night Saturday openings became a thing of the past after they instituted new hours of 9:00 to 5:30 and all-day closings on Thursdays and Sundays, but the "country store" atmosphere was enhanced by the acquisition of a new bench beside the big round heater, and people sometimes sat there for hours. Although consumers of large quantities of food, such as Lester Prosser's mining camp, which fed forty-two men, bought their food wholesale from Vancouver, most Van Anda people dealt with Deighton's store, running a tab and paying as much as they could each payday, though rarely clearing it all off. (A few of those who couldn't pay skipped town.) The unpaid accounts and Reg Deighton's habit of lending people money without charging interest meant that sometimes the store was hard-pressed to meet its own bills to the wholesaler. He and his wife were careful not to overlap their stock with that in other island stores, concentrating on general groceries, vegetables and packaged meats, with a few dry goods such as towels; they left the ice cream business to Lowther and Young. Goods were barged up once a week and unloaded into the shed on the wharf. Deighton then drove down in his old truck to collect it and store it in his warehouse. The family rarely left the island because it was so difficult to find someone to look after the store.

Those who gathered at Deighton's store on boat night listened carefully for the call from the *Lady Cecilia* giving her estimated time of arrival, though often this was amended to accommodate last-minute stops. Islanders tuned in to a special frequency around 5 p.m. for the magic words: "This is Captain . . . of the *Lady Cecilia*. We're at Stillwater and we expect to be at Lang Bay at . . . , Van Anda at . . . , Blubber Bay at . . . and Westview at . . ."[1] Sometimes the ship didn't arrive until after midnight. On such nights, Fred Lowther, who had become postmaster in 1923 and remained in that job until 1948, had lots of help hauling the mail up the dock. In summer, boat nights were also ice cream nights. But by the time Bill Young and Fred Lowther had brought the barrel in which the ice cream was packed in dry ice up to their store beside the wharf, it would be beginning to melt. So Young would unpack it quickly and start scooping it into cones for the assembled children.

After the Japanese shelling attack on the Estevan lighthouse in June 1942, Texada organized its own defences under the auspices of the Powell River Air Raid Precaution (ARP) unit. Five wardens were appointed for Blubber Bay and three for Van Anda. There were none for Gillies Bay, which at that time was still a community of summer homes.

PACIFIC LIME WEATHERS THE WAR YEARS

During the war, Pacific Lime had a tough time recruiting staff, so the company took up an offer by the federal government to employ men who, for reasons of conscience or religious faith, objected to military service. The small group—probably no more than ten—who were sent to Texada were Mennonite farmers from Yarrow in the Fraser Valley, and as they had no previous quarrying experience, they were used as unskilled workers. Only one brought his family; the remainder were single men.

The shortage of professional staff during these years may have been why Quene Yip (1905–1994), a younger brother of the company's foreman, Dang Yip, got the chance to use his university training. Quene Yip was halfway through medical school in Ontario when he had realized that his ethnic background would limit his opportunities to practise as a doctor, so he graduated as a chemist instead.[2] He was also a soccer star in the 1920s and 1930s, leading the Chinese Students Soccer Team to win three league championships, including the BC Mainland Cup in 1933. (He was finally inducted into the BC Sports Hall of Fame in 1998.[3]) He and his wife, Vicki, and their family lived in Blubber Bay from 1942 to 1971, at first in a house on the edge of Chinatown, and later within the townsite. Vicki Yip was quite a force in the community, especially with the PTA, which organized school Christmas concerts and the maypole dances to celebrate the Queen's Birthday, and with the Arbutus Bay Community Club.[4] She taught classes in painting and Chinese cooking and once organized the local children for a performance of *Snow White and the Seven Dwarfs*. The Yips' three sons, Randall, Roderick and Robert, attended the local school, but their mother made sure that they remained connected to their Chinese heritage by enrolling them in Chinese correspondence school as well. All three worked at Pacific Lime in the summertime, doing everything from working on the bull gang to sampling and analyzing ore.

In addition to quarry personnel, during the war years Blubber Bay had a hard time keeping teachers. So it was that at 2:30 one morning in August 1942, after a stormy voyage, young Frieda Blasha and a collection of freight boxes were off-loaded from Union Steamships' *Chelohsin*.[5] She had been told the ship would arrive at 6:15 p.m. but the many stops along the way at logging camps and isolated cabins had pushed its arrival at Blubber Bay far into the night. Having just graduated from the Vancouver Normal School following two years at UBC—which was all her parents could afford—Frieda Blasha was now on her own. Prairie schools often only paid teachers in kind, so she hadn't wanted

Young Frieda Blasha's first experience of Blubber Bay appalled her so much that she got back on the boat and returned to Vancouver, only to be persuaded by the chairman of the school board to return. She later married on the island and never left. Heather Harbord

to go there. A job in Richmond paying $900 a year would have meant spending most of it on bus fares. The Blubber Bay job paid $1,050, so she had come to see what it had to offer.

She stood on the dock in the pitch-black night as the ship steamed away. Two small lights twinkled in the distance and then a truck rattled onto the dock. "Are you the new schoolteacher?" a man's voice asked.

"Yes."

"Climb in and I'll take you to where you're supposed to spend the night."

She climbed into the truck with the mail and the groceries and off they went. He dropped her outside a house and she knocked on the door. The man who opened it wasn't wearing a stitch of clothing. Frieda's sheltered upbringing had not prepared her for this, but she had no alternative. When the man and his wife invited her in, she accepted the bed they offered.

After breakfast a grumpy old farmer (who turned out to be Willis Woodhead, the school board secretary) arrived to escort her to the school. No one had cleared up after the Saturday night dance in the building, which doubled as the community hall. Beer bottles were upended in the ink wells and on the windowsills. Just then a ship's whistle sounded as the *Chelohsin* returned on its southward voyage. "Good bye," she told Woodhead firmly. "I'm going back to North Vancouver," and she ran back on board.

Shortly after she arrived home, BC Cement manager Rob Hamilton, who also served as head of the school board, phoned. "Won't you please come back? We need a teacher so badly. There's no one here to teach these kids. My company will guarantee your salary." She returned to Texada and actually enjoyed it from then on.

Frieda Blasha taught grades one through eight, with a few high school correspondence students sitting at the back. On the first day, some of her students asked if they could open a window, and then threw their books outside. She strapped twelve of them. The next day she strapped thirteen. "Holy hell, but that teacher can hit!" one of the offenders said, but Frieda had no more trouble. She liked teaching history and geography but also taught English and home economics. She was forced to resign when she married Phil Woodhead, the school board secretary's son, as in those days married women were not allowed to teach.

While living in Blubber Bay, Frieda Blasha became acquainted with carver Jack Leslie (1885–1968), who lived at nearby Clam Bay. He liked to entertain the teachers to tea and cookies and made each one a model ship; Blasha's was a model of the *Bounty.* Some of his ships are now on display at the Blubber Bay museum. Leslie had built his own cabin using the same hand tools and naphtha lamps he used to build his ships. He also gave impromptu history and geography lessons to the local kids when he rowed them over to Harwood Island to fish and stargaze.

Only two Texada men died in the war: Frank Russ and George Pringle Jr. Frank Russ had been coming home on leave when his ship went down in the Atlantic. Though George Pringle had left the island in 1928 with his parents, Reverend George and Grace Pringle, the people of Texada still considered him an islander.

In Blubber Bay, the company supplied workers with identical neat three-bedroom homes, each with a porch and flower and vegetable garden surrounded by a picket fence. Alternate houses were painted green or brown with Company paint.

CHAPTER 11:

The Post-War Years 1946–1960

AT 10:15 ON THE MORNING of Sunday, June 23, 1946, a 7.3 magnitude earthquake ushered in the post-war era on Texada Island. Its epicentre was in the Forbidden Plateau area of Vancouver Island, just west of Courtenay and Campbell River, so it was felt very strongly on Texada, and a tsunami struck the west coast of the island in two waves, though their crests were only six feet and three feet high. Noreen Paton, with her baby in her arms, hurried to the front door of her house across the road from the Ravenous Raven restaurant at the head of Gillies Bay, uncertain whether she should remain in the house or venture out onto the rolling landscape. Chimneys were swaying and woodpiles tumbling.[1] Out at Shelter Point, Evert Copp rushed outside with his young son, Richard, and they stood hand in hand to watch the rocks jump up and down. As they began to subside, young Richard cried, "Do it again, Dad! Do it again!"[2]

Although there were no reports of serious damage on the island, this earthquake was one of the most damaging in the history of British Columbia and demolished three-quarters of the chimneys in Cumberland, Union Bay and Courtenay on Vancouver Island. It also caused landslides and extensive damage to homes and other buildings in Comox, Port Alberni and Powell River, and lesser damage in Vancouver and the northern part of Washington State.

VAN ANDA AFTER THE WAR

When logging activity on the island picked up after the war, Cecil May (1914–1977) and his new bride, Phyllis, opened a repair shop in Van Anda, where he did a brisk business maintaining and repairing logging equipment as well as doing repairs for the quarries. His shop had enough room for two vehicles, a press, a lathe and a workbench, while outside a ramp and pit allowed him to work under vehicles. In addition, he had a shop truck equipped with a portable gas-driven welder for off-site repairs. If May couldn't make something work, he dismantled it, carefully storing the parts until his shop looked like an Aladdin's cave, with shelves full of parts reaching to the rafters. As he never threw anything out, he could always either find a necessary part or fabricate it.

A six-foot salamander heater, which burned used oil, stood in the middle of May's shop, its soot turning the walls and ceiling black, but customers crowded around it as they waited for their vehicles to be repaired. Al Matson, who chewed snoose, used to spit it into the salamander's chimney and the heater would go into orbit, dancing around the floor. Carl Hagman Jr. remembered the long waits in the dark shop while repairs were being done and complained that May seemed to spend more time talking than

Cecil May's repair shop was a social centre where messages were passed along and gossip exchanged as men waited for their vehicles. Sometimes it seemed May spent more time talking than working.

repairing. As the shop had one of the few telephones in Van Anda, it soon became a social centre from which messages were relayed and where people met. It also became the scene of a Van Anda Christmas Eve tradition. May would take the settling bowl out of someone's vehicle, give it a wipe, fill it full of rye whisky and serve it. It is reported that the first couple of drinks tasted a bit like gas but it was fine after that.

May "carried" some of his logging customers for months, as the banks wouldn't loan money to loggers. "Cec was good with young people that way," Hagman recalled.[3] Phyllis May did the books in a front office overlooking the gas pump, which Cap Harrison operated in his retirement years. May was also the BA–Gulf Oil agent; his storage tanks for gas, diesel and stove oil were located beside the Van Anda Cove wharf, where they had been moved from their original location above the boat harbour in Marble Bay. He used a tanker truck for deliveries.

In March 1947, the Van Anda Water District organized volunteers to install a new water main from Priest Lake, replacing the old one that Tacoma Steel had installed in the early 1900s. This was also the year that the local school finally had enough children to qualify for a second teacher. Three years later, the children were moved from the old building that had served as a school for nearly fifty years into a brand new one on the site of the opera house. In 1951 the newly formed Elks Club extensively renovated the old school building, which then became the venue for twice monthly dances. Music was supplied by a band organized by Carl Hagman Sr. He played the saxophone and sang while his daughter, Virginia, and Pat McKay played the piano. The band's roster also included Spence Hughes on accordion and Joe Kempe on drums; later, Bill Campbell joined with his saxophone. Sometimes when the band came back on Sunday mornings to clean up the hall, everyone started to dance again. Other musicians who played at various times up to the mid-1970s included Dave Spragge, Dennis and Ted Fox, Rol Morris, Kathy Roy and Louise Escallier.

In 1948 fifteen returned servicemen started the Texada Legion Branch #232 and received their charter on April 14, 1949. Among them were Art and Walter Liebich, Joe Little, Cliff Staaf, Bill McKay and Michael Zaikow and two Texada Island newcomers, "Mac" McNicol, the timekeeper at Van

Anda Mines, and Tony Bakker, the island's new postmaster (1949–1955). McNicol became the president and Bakker the secretary. The Legion's first home was the upper floor of a house belonging to Paddy Moran; Carl Hagman Sr. used the front of the ground floor to sort huck brush and Moran lived in the back half. Four years later, the Legion moved into new premises at the corner of Legion Road and Cadet Street. It was the only legal "watering hole" on the island; non-members could reserve seats at the post office.

In 1949 Stan Willes, an airforce veteran and professional butcher, and Dick Woods arrived on the island. Woods was an old family friend who had raised Willes after his parents died. Two years later, Willes partnered with postmaster Tony Bakker to buy a town lot on which to build his twenty- by thirty-foot Van Anda Meat Market. Later he enlarged his store and built another room onto the back of it in which his sister, Florence, opened the Fashion Room, where she sold men's and women's clothes. Bakker had the cookhouse from the defunct Little Billie Mine dragged onto his half of the lot and converted it into a post office.

The Van Anda church had been destroyed on September 16, 1942, when a brush fire got out of hand and burned it to the ground. As there had been no money to rebuild it at that time, services were transferred to the community hall. That hall was still being used for church services on February 25, 1950, when a truly Texada Island couple were married there. Alan Corrigall, a logger from Davie Bay, married Claire Bushby, daughter of Bill and Bertha Bushby, active participants in the Blubber Bay strike, and granddaughter of Gus and Bertha Liebich, who had arrived on the island in 1924. Retired minister Hugh Bain, son-in-law of early prospector James Raper, officiated. During the ceremony, Bill Bushby's homemade wines, the basis for "a very potent punch," produced "a fine aroma"[4] throughout the hall, and most of the island's population were happy to attend the banquet and dance that went on till well into the small hours. The following morning, the CPR's *Princess Mary* stopped at Blubber Bay to pick up two cars containing the happy couple and their relatives. Unvarnished advice for the newlyweds was hollered from the dock up to the ship, where it was clearly heard by all passengers and crew.

The rebuilt Van Anda church opened on August 13, 1950. The altar cloths were edged with crocheting done by Alice Burroughs, Walter Pinnock's sister, and there was an oil of "Jesus in Gethsemane" painted by R. Wood, a miner at the Little Billie Mine.[5] After a fine address by Reverend William Graham of St. John's Church, Powell River, Reverend Hugh Bain christened Mr. and Mrs. Lionel Dee's baby, David. The Dees, who had lived in a tent beside the Little Billie Mine when they first arrived, had recently moved into the house on Gracemere vacated by the Zaikows in 1949. The church was dedicated at a service held on April 29 of the following year. In July 1958, the CPR presented the church with one of their locomotive engine bells to replace the one that melted in the fire.

Since the founding of Van Anda, whenever the children wanted to play ball, they had to catch a ride to Blubber Bay or make do with street corners and backyards. However, in August 1951, Bert Thomas and Dan Lockstead took the problem to Stan Beale, owner of the Marble Bay Mine property, and pointed out the suitability of his old tailings site for a ball park. Beale took samples from various parts of the tailing piles and, finding that the ore was of fairly low grade and therefore of minimal value for re-milling, gave permission for the area to be converted into a ball field. The very next night the community held a meeting to discuss strategy, and since the local logging companies were banned from the woods due to the high fire hazard, there were plenty of volunteers ready to begin work on the job the following morning. A sixty-foot-high mountain of tailings weighing approximately 150,000 tons was pushed into a swamp and levelled. Three weekends later, seven bulldozers, four power shovels and eight trucks, all

After an accidental brush fire burned the church to the ground in 1942, it was eight long years before the island gathered together enough money to construct a new one. It opened August 13, 1950.

provided free of charge by local people[6] and businesses,[7] completed the job. Even the kids helped by heaving small rocks from the field into the swamp, and afterwards they were able to admire their handiwork while seated on top of the head frame at the Marble Bay Mine to watch the games.

NEW HOUSING FOR TEXADA

In 1951 the federal government offered the houses that had been built for wartime shipyard workers in North Vancouver for sale. Oke Nyvall bought several for his Mouat Bay logging camp and barged them north. Stan Beale, who had reopened the old Marble Bay Quarry after the war, also brought some of the houses to Van Anda for his workers. The smaller houses became the homes of Jocko Cawthorpe, George Kilroy, Charles Selin and Jack Sellentin, although most of these new owners soon made additions to them. Two of Beale's two-storey houses became the homes of Bill Gussman (beside the boat harbour) and Sid Robillard (next to the fire hall). The third went to Joe Kempe, who stored it on land beside Sturt Bay for a year while he prepared a lot for it. Back in 1947 Kempe had bought Lowther and Young's store and moved it up the hill from its location beside

One of Texada's most spectacular community efforts was the building of the Van Anda ball park. Seven bulldozers, four power shovels and eight trucks, as well as everyone in the community who could pick up a rock, flattened a sixty-foot high mountain of mine tailings.

the wharf to a lot he owned on Copper Queen Street. Now he cleared more of that lot, levelled the land and built a foundation for the house. Next, with the help of a local logger, he put skids under the house and dragged it up the hill and onto a ramp built beside the new foundation. At that point the skids broke, and the logger left after wishing him good luck. Later, with the aid of a Gilchrist jack, Kempe patiently manoeuvred the house into place. He stocked his store with everything from novelties to work clothes and candy bars, lamps, coal oil, fireworks, fishing tackle, Model T parts and gift cards. "You'd find most anything in there," said Bill Nyvall, who remembered buying bubblegum there to build up his collection of baseball cards. In the evenings, customers could ring a bell outside the store to summon Kempe or his wife from the house behind it.

In 1948 Kempe had also become caretaker for the former Astor House, built by J.J. Palmer in 1899. By that time it was known as the Beale House; later it would become known as the Ideal Staff House, though it is now simply the visitor's house. Using a machete, Kempe began creating topiary from the fir seedlings that he planted in the yard, and one of these eventually became a twenty-five-foot Christmas tree. Every year for nearly twenty-seven years, he spent two hours on a twenty-foot ladder, hanging a hundred and eighty lights on the tree, and as he threw the switch to light them, villagers sang Christmas carols and enjoyed hot chocolate and cookies. Since Joe Kempe's death in 2006, the topiary has gone wild, and no one sings the German version of "Silent Night" anymore.

Mike Zaikow, the hoist man at the Little Billie Mine, and his wife, Maria (Christensen), became forces in island life. Zaikow had contracted polio in 1952, and as he lay in his Vancouver hospital bed worrying about how his family was going to cope, he received word that the community had held a benefit dance and raised fourteen hundred dollars for his expenses. After two years in hospital, he returned to the island in a wheelchair and tried his hand at a number of jobs before buying Ben Nicholas's general insurance business in 1957. He became Texada's first licensed realtor in 1961 and later a broker. "People brought me all sorts of problems besides insurance and real estate," he said. "Any time they received a government form that they didn't understand, they brought it to me . . . to explain it to them in plain English and advise them what to do. I was there at 8:30 a.m. for those on their way to catch the ferry to Powell River, and after 4 p.m. I was there for the loggers and others whose work prevented them arriving earlier. Once I suggested a man come to see me at 7 p.m. so that both of us could have supper first. He turned up with four other guys and they all brought business."

For twenty years Mike and Maria Zaikow also staffed the volunteer firefighters' phone line. Once, when the phone rang in the middle of the night and Maria called the men out to fight the fire, Mike realized that he had sold a fire insurance policy to the property owner earlier in the day. After arson was proved, the owner, who was already wanted by the police for other crimes, spent some time in jail. At one point the Zaikows also manned the ambulance phone line as well, but it proved to be too much to handle both lines. Mike Zaikow's other volunteer activities included acting as treasurer for the Texada Cemetery Board for fifteen years and being service officer and treasurer for the Texada Legion. He was also a life member of the Elks.

Healthy and handsome Mike Zaikow, who ran the hoist at the Little Billie Mine, fell victim to polio in 1952 and came out of the hospital in a wheelchair. With the help of his indomitable wife, Maria Christensen, he went on to run a successful insurance and real estate business, as well as participating actively with the Legion, the Elks, the Credit Union and the Great Garbage Caper. Maria Zaikow

On September 18, 1956, the Texada Mine Mill Union 816 was instrumental in establishing a credit union with ten members; it was headquartered in Mike Zaikow's office. Members borrowed to buy trucks, houses and other large purchases, and all profits from the interest on the loans were returned to members in the form of interest and shares. In the early days, only one person defaulted on a loan and fled the island. He was never caught, but he never came back either.[8] When Mike Zaikow sold his property in 1972, the Texada Credit Union moved to a trailer behind

Keith Johnson's house on Priest Lake, where it was open on Monday evenings for deposits and loans. However, as no chequing services were offered, members needed to maintain an account at another financial institution; this was usually the Canadian Imperial Bank of Commerce (CIBC) in Gillies Bay, until it closed in 1988.

Fire destroyed Deighton's store on December 27, 1959. Five-year-old Debbie Orpen of Texada Hardware, next door to Deighton's, raised the alarm. Three days later, the Van Anda Volunteer Fire Department was established, and within a month thirty-two men had signed up to be part of a volunteer fire brigade. Deighton's store was subsequently rebuilt for the fourth time.

BLUBBER BAY AFTER THE WAR

With the end of the war, the conscientious objectors working at Blubber Bay went home to the Fraser Valley and were replaced by war veterans. It was also in 1946 that Art Yip married Vancouver-born Molly and brought her to Blubber Bay. Except for Quene and Art Yip and their families (foreman Dang Yip and Yuey Yip had left Blubber Bay by this time), the rest of the Chinese people on the island were still living at the eastern end of Pacific Lime's property in three bunkhouses. Conditions there had not changed very much over the years. Although Molly Yip never saw the inside of the bunkhouses, as women were banned, she was told that a variety of homemade dividers cordoned off the cubicles that were lit only by a large light bulb. Heat came from a four-gallon coal oil can in the centre of the room. The company supplied electricity, but as the bunkhouses were at the end of the line, the voltage was often very low and subject to cuts, though a roll of "primary-cut-out" fuse wire, kindly supplied by the plant electrician, helped keep the power on. Molly Yip recalled that every day at lunch and supper, each worker took home a piece of slabwood from Pacific Lime's kiln pile. In the shared cookhouse space, a cook presided over two large woks, where vegetables from the community garden were prepared along with fish from the sea.

When Vancouver-born Molly Yip married Art Yip, who worked at Pacific Lime, she had never lived in the country before. She soon got to know everyone in Blubber Bay. A constant stream of visiting relatives, including her popular sister-in-law, Vicki Yip, kept her busy cooking one meal after another.
Heather Harbord

Among the Chinese men Molly Yip remembered was a Mr. Mah, who was well liked and had lived with Art Yip before she arrived. Big Joe Woo had come directly from China, and when he died, his widow, who was much younger than he was, remained for a while in Blubber Bay with their three boys; later, she moved to Vancouver. Frieda Woodhead remembered when Old Bill, a ninety-five-year-old gardener, went home to his children in China; he hadn't been back for so long that his "children" had probably been fathered by his brother, who had remained behind. "Lame Duck," who was not lame, was the laundry man. "Old Charlie" was a gardener who helped with the cooking; he, too, was in his nineties when Molly Yip knew him.

There were about 250 people living in Blubber Bay by 1947 when Peter and Mary Kucharsky arrived there, attracted not only by the possibility of work but the hope of having their own house as well. Initially, the Kucharskys lived in Limekiln Bay, but the walk to work was too much for Peter, who had injured his leg while in the army, so they moved to a house on the beach near boat carver Jack Leslie's property in Clam Bay. As their family grew and other houses became available, the Kucharskys moved many times, ending up in one of the BC Cement houses that had been located so that they overlooked Blubber Bay. Moving was cheap, as the company provided a truck and the family had few possessions.

Most of the Pacific Lime houses had three bedrooms, and their small yards contained a woodshed and two fruit trees and were enclosed by a picket fence. As these houses had been built before most islanders had cars, garage space was limited and often not particularly convenient to the houses, but the rent was only seventeen dollars a month, and every year the company supplied each house with a gallon of paint; alternate houses were painted green and brown. Alex Fielkowich moved four times during his years at Blubber Bay, as everyone was always looking for a better house, but choice was ruled by seniority.

When a new three-classroom Blubber Bay school building was finished in 1949, fifty-six students in grades one to eleven moved in, glad not to be sharing their classrooms with the community hall any longer. It was just as well, as the previous winter the temperature had dropped so low that ink had frozen in the inkwells and the teachers refused to teach for two weeks because there were no boys big enough to handle the three-foot-long slabs of cordwood that fed the school boiler.[9] The school's official opening was delayed to the following June.[10]

To get to the school, Henry Liebich's children, Maurice and Nikki, walked through the plant. "It was an exploratory thing," recalled Maurice Liebich. "The road went under Pacific Lime's big rotary kiln or you could walk along the dock instead." He was often late for school, because he liked to watch the wooden boom on the crane that unloaded hog fuel from the barges. But as a child, he never went into the Glory Hole. "The superintendent came to the school to talk about what you could and could not do. Your father could be dismissed if you, as a kid, didn't follow the rules." After school the children rushed home, changed their clothes and went out to play, especially on the ridge between No.1 and No. 2 pits and the tunnel underneath. At 5 p.m. the whistle at the Powell River mill could be plainly heard across the water, and this was the signal for the children to run home for supper.

In September 1954, Alma Willis arrived to teach in the Blubber Bay primary school. She had been on her way from her home in England to New Zealand when she stopped off in Vancouver to visit two uncles who had emigrated before World War I. Finding it difficult to get work in Vancouver to raise the money to continue her trip, she signed up to teach on Texada. During her first year there, she shared the teacherage attached to the school with middle-school teacher Pat Charters, and the following year with Joyce Whiteley. Rent was five dollars a month. At this time, due to overcrowding at the new school, grades one to three had been moved back to the old school, but they could only use the building from nine to five on weekdays, as the rest of the time it was used as a community hall. On Friday nights, Henry Davis ran the projector to show movies, which were eagerly attended by the Chinese community. However, they did not turn up for the Saturday night dances, which attracted people from all over the island. Square dancing was extremely popular, and Blubber Bay soon had its own square dance group, the Lime Dusters. On New Year's Eve, the Lime Dusters opened the floor to everyone and also had old-time dancing, and in summer square dances were held on the tennis courts behind the hall.

Poker games were still held in the company bunkhouse. Two big tables were in constant play, with more players waiting. If the company's night watchman did his round quickly enough, turning the keys at the fire shack by the manager's house, at the bunkhouse and at several places in the plant, he had time to fit in a game before he was due to start his next round. However, it was not long before card sharps from Vancouver were attracted to the place and made a killing.[11]

The managers installed by the new owners of the quarry, Gypsum, Lime and Alabastine Canada Ltd., kept largely to themselves and demanded respect from the regular workers. They held their parties in the Blubber Bay Guild Hall, usually all male affairs called "smokers," at which cigars were enjoyed undisturbed by feminine influences, their wives having been bribed with boxes of chocolates to stay home.[12]

But Blubber Bay had its full quota of nonconformists and eccentrics. Florence (Flo) Gibson, generally known as "Gibby," and her husband, Jimmy, a former coal miner, lived in a little cottage near the present museum. Maurice Liebich remembered her as "a very large English lady with a good sense of humour who nipped at her gin all day and was very happy by evening. Her husband was small and somewhat henpecked." And Frieda Woodhead recalled that "when she gave you a piece of her mind, she didn't mince matters." Betty Kucharsky Zaikow was once locked in Gibby's house on Halloween and had to stand on a chair and sing for her life (or so it seemed). After that she confined her "trick or treating" to the Chinese bunkhouses, where she and her friends were given ginger candy and peanuts.

Another Blubber Bay character was Paddy O'Brien, a shell-shocked veteran of World War I who, whenever the moon was full, would march through town and up and down the tennis court and out onto the wharf, shouting drill commands. He was unemployed and lived in a shack on company property; when he died, the company demolished the shack.

Perhaps the most colourful of the island's characters was Elma Haapanen (1907–1995),[13] generally known as the Flying Finn. Her impact on Texada[14] began late one night with a telephone call to Ben Nicholas to tell him that there was a lady waiting at Westview to go to Blubber Bay. The lady had one suitcase and a birdcage and told him she was going to join a friend named "Kusti" at Blubber Bay. No one met her on the Blubber Bay float, and door knocking failed to reveal the "Kusti" she was looking for, until Alex Fielkowich suggested he might be the new driller, who lived across the bay at BC Cement. Door knocking there found the place where Kusti lived, but no one was home; Nicholas left the lady there, warbling happily as she settled in. But Elma Haapanen and her Kusti often had differences of opinion. After one such episode, he opened his lunch pail to discover that all it contained was a large cod's head. He went home, knocked Elma out and then called Dr. McCallum. After the doctor brought her around, she smacked him, thinking he was her attacker.[15]

An independent woman, Elma had owned a laundry in Finland and later worked as a stevedore and a miner. During World War II, she had been a bus conductor in Berlin. On Texada she was often seen cleaning up roadside beer cans and bottles. She also operated saunas at both Gillies and Blubber bays for the iron mine workers, charging them two dollars a session. Naked, she would leap among her clients with a bundle of leaves to switch them. It was a popular service.

Ben Nicholas discovered that Elma was never afraid of rough weather, as she was used to storms on the Baltic and North seas. On one occasion, when Nicholas's water taxi was behaving like a bucking bronco, eleven pairs of white knuckles gripped the rail while in the back seat Elma grinned from ear to ear and sang loudly and happily. On another occasion, when the water was too rough to dock the boat at Van Anda, he took it into Sturt Bay, backed it up to the dock stern-first, and held it there with the engine in reverse. However, the "dock" was a slippery teredo-infested

Often known as the Flying Finn, Elma Haapanen took an American tourist fishing in her twelve-foot open boat and gave him such a ride that he put her on a magazine cover. Her driving was known to be accident-prone, and islanders gave her vehicle a wide berth.

cedar log, and when Elma stepped out onto it with a case of beer in each hand, she promptly fell into the salt chuck. She came up immediately, still clutching both cases.

In 1965 she took an American tourist salmon fishing in her twelve-foot aluminum boat, along with her dog. The man caught several good-sized fish and took numerous pictures before five-foot waves turned the adventure into a little more than he had bargained for. A year later he sent her a copy of *Eight-Twelve*, a monthly magazine published by the Union National Bank of Pittsburgh. Her picture was on the cover.[16]

Everyone recognized Elma Haapanen's truck with the two yapping dogs in the back and tried to give it lots of room, as she was somewhat accident prone. Brian Gooden, one of the mine accountants, said that "she wore the dents in her car like the notches in a gunslinger's gun." She rear-ended a police car in Vancouver and castigated the officer for not turning left after he had signalled left. Elma Haapanen died in 1995 in the Finnish Manor in Burnaby. Kusti had predeceased her in 1979.[17]

GILLIES BAY AFTER THE WAR

In 1947 Dr. J. Roy Sanderson retired to the comfortable home he had built as a summer retreat on Gillies Bay and became a prominent island leader. One of the first things that he did was to persuade the federal government to replace the float that had been installed halfway between Gillies Bay and Shelter Point at which the Union Steamships had delivered passengers and freight for the previous seventeen years.

Dr. Sanderson had bought up all the land between the mine property and the bay, and when he subdivided it after he retired, he hired Elmer Paton to build the necessary roads. However, the work had to be done slowly, as Sanderson had to sell properties to fund it, so he was often behind in his payments, making things tough for the Paton family. Sanderson donated a thirty-foot-wide and fifteen-hundred-foot-long strip of land along the waterfront of his subdivision as a public footpath. It ran from the head of the bay to the foot of Balsam Street.

Although the reopening of the iron mine in 1952 profoundly changed the whole island, its greatest impact was on the settlement at Gillies Bay. Many newcomers moved to the island, mainly from the hardrock mining areas of Ontario. When miners from the same area came to the Van Anda and Marble Bay mines over half a century earlier, the men had to find their own accommodation and food. In Gillies Bay, Texada Mines took over Timber Ventures' old logging camp buildings to provide limited camp facilities. They also brought in trailers in which to house the families of supervisors. These were parked at the beginning of Sanderson Road and became known as trailer row.

Up to this time, Gillies Bay had only one street: Sanderson Road. However, the company built houses for some of its executives on Pine Street, a new road that intersected with the main highway across the island. As Sanderson's development proceeded Oak and Ash streets were constructed to branch off Sanderson Road and climb the hill, with Alder, Balsam, Cedar, Dogwood and Elm streets at right angles to them.

With the influx of miners and their families, there was suddenly a need for a school in the bay, so in the fall of 1952, Andy Gibbs floated the old Davie Bay School (which had been Jim and Gladys Devaney's first home on Texada) to Gillies Bay, and it was jacked up onto the site of the present school building. That first year, seventeen students were taught by a Mr. Wright, who boarded in one of the mine bunkhouses. He told the children that the school yard extended "as far as you can hear the bell." When the company commissary burned down, he ordered the students to stay put while he went off to fight the fire. A new commissary was immediately built on the same spot. (That original school building still exists but has been much recycled. After the new school was built in Gillies Bay, teacher Roger Gibbard bought the old one and moved it to Shelter Point Road. When Albert Atkinson bought that property, he built a new house and converted the former school into a garage, which still stands.)

Although the iron mine's financial administrator, Charles Guhne, and his wife, Elva (or Pinkie as he called her), hailed from California, they were happy to make their home on Texada and became the centre of a whirl of social activity involving picnics, bonfires and cabarets. Charles Guhne mixed with everyone from manual labourers to office staff and invited them all to parties at Christmastime. Somehow he and his wife also found time to make daily checks to see that old Fred Lowther was eating properly.

Elva Guhne, who was a fine shot, had a beautiful collection of rifles. If a crow or a kingfisher disturbed her, she would shoot it and then call Fred Lowther to deal with the remains.[18] Since the crows roost at the head of the bay where the Guhnes first lived, Lowther's services were much in demand. After the Guhnes moved to a house on Sanderson Road in 1967, she shot three of Tim Buitendyk's turkeys that had escaped from his yard, and her husband had to make peace and hush up the incident. It may have been from the proceeds of this that Buitendyk, a crusher operator, was able to buy a breeding pair of chinchillas to start his chinchilla farm, which eventually filled three long barns.

Spence Hughes, who operated the Blubber Bay store, opened a second store and a gas pump in Gillies Bay in 1956, but as the new site lacked access to electricity, he had to install an Onan generator to run the cooler and the lights. Butcher Len Diggon ran this new operation while Hughes remained in Blubber Bay; he also hired old Angus Kinney, who lived across the street, to be his watchman and to gas up the generator. After two years, Hughes sold both stores to Bill Davies and Elva Le Blanc. Davies then ran the Blubber Bay store, while Le Blanc operated the one in Gillies Bay.

On September 16, 1957, after four years of planning and construction, Texada Mines completed a new community hall and leased it to the Gillies Bay and District Community Association. Volunteer labour had cleared and levelled the land, the mine guaranteed the building expenses, and donations provided chairs, mirrors, china and cleaning items. To celebrate the completion, two hundred people viewed a movie taken of the preparation and construction of the building and then participated in an evening of bingo. One group that made good use of the new hall was the Texada Teen Town Association, which organized Friday night dances for local teenagers. Most of the music was provided by a reel-to-reel tape recorder, though sometimes a live band played. Each dance was chaperoned by two adult volunteers who were there to make sure that no liquor was served and that adult rowdies from the nearby mine stayed away.

Pinkie Guhne, the wife of the administrative manager at Texada Mines, was a fine shot and was in the habit of shooting any bird whose sound disturbed her. When she shot Tim Buitendyk's turkeys, her husband had to smooth things over.

Prior to 1958, medical facilities for the whole island were administered from a part-time clinic in the basement of the Legion Hall in Van Anda, staffed by Powell River physician Dr. Ann Lees. Ben Nicholas also provided emergency care for wounds, stitching them up without anaesthetic. Student dentists came in the summer, sometimes by sailboat, but none were willing to set up a permanent practice. However, after Dr. Donald McCallum retired to Gillies Bay in 1958, Texada Mines retained him as their medical officer. He had a tiny office in his backyard, where people dropped in for advice twenty-four hours a day, seven days a week.

In January 1960, five miners from Gillies Bay, returning from a hockey game in Powell River, took a wrong turn and their car shot into the old Glory Hole in the Blubber Bay Quarry. When they didn't show up for work, people went looking for them, but it was several days before the vehicle was spotted. Later, a crusher operator at the quarry remembered seeing a flash of light in that direction around the time the miners must have disembarked from the ferry, but he had thought nothing of it. Divers fished four bodies out of the murky depths, but failed to find the fifth.

WATER TRANSPORTATION

On May 12, 1946, a group of navy and airforce veterans started Gulf Lines Ltd., a fast daily ferry service from Vancouver for passengers and freight going to lower Coast destinations. Their ships were the *Gulf Wing*, the *Gulf Stream* (which ran aground and sank on Dinner Rock in October 1947), and the *Gulf Mariner* (later renamed the *Troubadour*), and their greater speed enabled the new company to take the mail contract away from the Union Steamship Company.

Ted Ross, grandson of Jonathan Ross, recalled travelling on Gulf Lines ships. He was five years old in 1949 when he and his father came to buy a fifty-foot lot on Gillies Bay from school principal Allan Bowles. They boarded the *Gulf Mariner* in Vancouver in the morning for the all-day trip to Van Anda, and the boy spent most of his time on the deck above the coffee shop and passenger lounge, watching the loading and unloading at the many stops. At Van Anda, after the ship sidled up to the wharf, pallets of freight were swung onto the dock, where a small forklift ran them into a warehouse. On other occasions Ross travelled on the *Gulf Wing*, which cruised at seventeen knots and could make the Vancouver to Texada run in four and a half hours if there were no other stops. However, the ship had a tendency to pitch and roll. Once Ross watched his fellow passengers eat a good lunch in the shelter of Secret Cove, then he retreated to the outer deck, where he rode out the storm in the fresh air. The situation in the lounge did not bear thinking about.

In 1951 Bill Young, who had been operating the *Louvain* between Van Anda and Powell River, chose this time to retire. He sold the *Louvain* to Ben Nicholas, who continued Young's Van Anda–Powell River passenger service. The purchase was good timing for Nicholas: Gulf Lines' fast service to Vancouver had come to an end in May of that year, forced out of business by the American company Black Ball Ferries. Islanders were now compelled to take a water taxi to Powell River and catch the bus from there to the big city.

Competition for Nicholas came from a group of Powell River men operating a fast water taxi called the *Westview Flyer*. As the *Louvain* would only do six knots, Nicholas had to decide whether to compete with the

The greater speed of the Gulf Lines ships enabled them to wrest the mail contract away from the Union Steamships. The Gulf Stream, *which later sank on Dinner Rock, and its sister ships* Gulf Mariner *and* Gulf Wing, *regularly called in at Blubber Bay and Van Anda.*

Powell River outfit or go out of business, and he chose the former. In April 1953, he ordered the *Texada Ladyslipper*, a fibreglass-over-plywood water taxi with twenty seats ahead of the engine. The following year, he ordered a sister ship, the *Texada Moccasin*. On September 15, 1953, he got a call from expectant parents living in a logging camp at Pocahontas Bay. Nicholas was reluctant to take his water taxi out, as there was a twenty-knot wind blowing, but the baby couldn't wait, so the *Texada Ladyslipper* headed for Pocahontas, where the loggers waded into chest-deep water with the woman on a stretcher and loaded her aboard. By the time the water taxi reached Grief Point, the birth was imminent. Telling the father to steer the ship, Nicholas went below and used his first-aid training to help the lady through a breach birth. Then, laying the child beside the mother, he used his two-way radio to call for an ambulance to meet them at the dock. Terry Dale Waterman had made his dramatic debut into the world.

After forty-eight years of service, Bill Young sold the Louvain *to Ben Nicholas in 1951 and a new era of ferries to Powell River began.*

In 1961 Ben Nicholas sold his water taxi business to Ralph Coomber, a Powell River fireman, and Chuck McCallum, who had grown up in Ocean Falls and Powell River, then moved to Van Anda. The partners berthed their boats in Caesar's Cove in Sturt Bay but ran them out of the Van Anda wharf. Domtar also paid them a retainer to do emergency runs out of Blubber Bay.

In April 1952, the CPR decommissioned the *Princess Mary* after twenty-one years of service on the Vancouver to Blubber Bay run. Her bell and steam whistle were acquired by the City of Powell River, and the stern end of the upper deck, which contained the smoking room, became a Victoria restaurant. The reconfigured hull became Bulk Carrier No. 2 for the Union Steamship Company, but it was lost at sea two years later. The *Mary* was replaced by the 291-foot *Princess Elaine*, which could accommodate sixty cars, loading them through a side door, but the new ship, which had been built for the Nanaimo to Vancouver run, was not really suited to the Gulf Islands run, because the hull was too deep for most of the smaller ports.

In the fall of 1953, with a road from Sechelt to Earl's Cove on the Sechelt Peninsula nearing completion, the CPR gave notice that they would be

The Texada Moccasin, *along with its sister water taxi,* Texada Ladyslipper, *were the fast-paced successors to the* Louvain.

suspending the *Princess Elaine*'s service to Blubber Bay the following year. Union Steamships had already announced that it would soon discontinue service to Van Anda. By this time there were 350 vehicles on the island, and without the CPR's *Princess Elaine*, the only means of transporting a vehicle to and from the island would be as barge freight. Foot passengers, however, could still travel by water taxi to Powell River, then go by bus via two ferries with a bone-shatteringly rough road in between them.

In order to pressure Victoria for better ferry services, on January 1, 1954, the Van Anda Community Society renamed itself the Texada Island Community Society, and on its behalf Dr. Sanderson and Cap Harrison presented a petition to the provincial government requesting car ferry service for the island. In spite of this petition, the last CPR ship left Blubber Bay on April 19, 1954, with no word from Victoria on a replacement service. However, on May 28, 1955, the Sanderson–Harrison petition finally bore fruit as Captain Bert Davis from Gabriola Island started a car ferry service between Texada and Westview using the MV *Atrevida*, which took five cars. The terms of Davis's government contract required the *Atrevida* to do fourteen runs a week between Van Anda and Blubber Bay and across to

At last, albeit only five cars at a time, people could get their vehicles on and off the island to and from Westview.

Westview and back. Unfortunately, that same year, Waterhouse Company Freight Service, which among other things shipped wholesale goods to Deighton's Store, ceased operations.

TAXI SERVICE

Walt and Vi Liebich began operating a taxi on Texada in 1952 to take advantage of the service Ben Nicholas was providing with the *Louvain*. Although there had been previous attempts to offer a taxi service, there had not been enough work for anyone to make a living at it, but as the iron mine had reopened that year, the future for a taxi company looked much brighter. For workers coming to Texada for jobs in the mine, the company paid both the water taxi and land taxi fare; passengers signed Vi Liebich's account book and she billed the company. However, workers who were fired or quit of their own accord had to pay their own way off the island. The miners also had to pay for trips to and from the hotel, and if Vi Liebich thought one of them was likely to be too drunk to pay his return fare, she collected it in advance. The Liebichs' other big source of revenue was from salesmen who rented vehicles from them. They also took delivery of a brand new truck, and often Vi would load up the back with kids and take them to ball games at Blubber Bay or to picnics at Shelter Point. One of the Liebichs' station wagons doubled as an ambulance and a hearse, but as most of the island roads were still unpaved, they traded their ambulance/hearse for a new one every three years.

ROADS

Before the road between Van Anda and Gillies Bay was built, Gillies Bay was somewhat isolated from the rest of the island, and because there was also no road connection from Gillies Bay south to Shelter Point and Mouat Bay, people from there had to travel to Van Anda via Upper Gillies Bay and the High Road. But in the late 1940s, after pressure was applied by a group led by Dr. Roy Sanderson, the government authorized a road from Gillies Bay to Shelter Point, and it was built by loggers who were off work during fire season. By 1955 there were approximately eighty miles of road on Texada, half of them belonging to the government and half to the logging companies. Blacktopping began the following year on the sections of road approaching Gillies Bay and Van Anda, but the middle section of the island's roads remained unpaved, and vehicles wanting to pass often had to back up to find a pullout spot. After a double-lane, paved highway was completed across the island in 1963, Gillies Bay and Van Anda were only fifteen minutes apart.

Better roads also made it easier for students to travel farther to school, and in 1957 construction began on a new middle school in Van Anda to serve the whole island. It was located adjacent to the existing Van Anda School and officially opened on April 14, 1958.

POWER FOR TEXADA

When the Little Billie Mine finally closed in 1953, Al Waters bought its power line system and diesel generator and installed the latter beside his existing Esso tank farm. As Van Anda Light and Power Ltd., he offered service from six in the morning until nine at night to all members of the community who were prepared to fund the necessary poles and lines to their homes. He charged twenty-five cents per kilowatt. Although really just a lighting plant, the service was extremely popular, and everyone rushed to replace their kerosene lamps, gas irons and gas washers; unfortunately, there was insufficient power to allow them to have electric cooking stoves. On one occasion, George Kilroy forgot to turn off the light in his wood shed before going to a meeting, and the generator had to work all night; in the morning, Waters threatened to cut Kilroy off if he ever did it again.

On July 11, 1955, BC Electric purchased Van Anda Light and Power Ltd. from Waters, who stayed on to maintain their equipment. A year later, the company laid eighty thousand feet of submarine cable in order to provide service to the iron mine. Four cables funnelled together at Grief Point near Powell River and emerged from the water at Van Anda to become four cables again.

TV SPAWNS A DIVE CLUB

Television came to Van Anda in 1958. As the goal was to have the community-owned and -operated Van Anda Cable TV up and running in time to watch the explosion that removed Ripple Rock from Seymour Narrows on April 14, much volunteer labour went in stringing cables from the aerial to customers in the village. (Gillies Bay and the rest of the islanders used privately owned aerials.) Subsequently, one of the most popular television series for Texada viewers was an American show called *Sea Hunt*, starring Lloyd Bridges as an ex-navy frogman who makes his living as a scuba-diving salvager. The series ran for four seasons, from 1958 to 1961. Local residents Wilf Lockstead and Keith Hughes became so addicted that they ordered make-it-yourself wetsuits, which they glued together, and Hughes bought a tank.[19] Their big opportunity came when the owner of one of the fish boats anchored in Blubber Bay complained that he had lost yet another anchor on an underwater cable that ran from Pacific Lime's load-out dock to the old BC Cement dock. Hughes and his wife, Nora, went out on the boat to see if they could help. About sixty feet down, Hughes found four anchors. He was unable to lift any of them, but as he attempted to raise them, seaweed and bubbles appeared at the surface.

"Do you think he's all right down there?" the fisherman asked Nora.

"Yes, I expect so."

"Has he done this before?"

"No, it's his first time."

After this adventure, the two men took some training in Powell River, then started the Texaquatic Club, which over the next decade became the largest diving club in the province outside of Vancouver. For years it had thirty members. (Not all of them dived; many joined so they could come to the parties, which were the best on the island.) In 1960 they also started a Compressor Society in order to purchase compressors.

When Pete Stiles arrived on the island in February 1966 for a job at Ideal Cement, he was told by his boss, Keith Johnson, that he would be going for a swim on the weekend.[20]

"You're kidding," he said.

"No, we're going out to the spar buoy in Blubber Bay," was the reply.

Taking Stiles with them, they all donned wetsuits and went for a swim. Diving, Stiles quickly learned, was a regular weekend outing on Texada. "It was a lot of fun, especially the barbecue of our catch afterwards," he said. Nora Hughes had fond memories of the cabarets put on late at night during which club members partook of the club's special nectar: "Raptures of the Deep."[21]

Around this time, the sport of night fishing gripped the community. As the quarries overlooking both Sturt Bay and Blubber Bay had loading lights that stayed on all night, fish were attracted by the thousands. As a result, on any given night there would be from fifteen to twenty-five small boats in the water, each equipped with a herring rake and a thermos of tea or something stronger. On one of these occasions, Bill Young, who was out in Blubber Bay in his canoe, got towed away by a fish. When he paddled back some time later, he had a thirty-pound salmon on board. By the early 1980s, both the salmon and the herring disappeared, and so had the sport.

Television's Sea Hunt *series brought the idea of a dive club to Texada and it caught on fast. The parties after the dives were the best on the island, and many people joined just so that they could attend them. L to R: Urbain Robillard, Wally Robillard, Keith Hughes and Wilf Lockstead.*

Before Shelter Point became a park, a small community of loggers lived there and boomed their logs on the south facing beach. In this picture, Al Dolman's Home oil tanks can be seen in the centre. Gas was sold on the honour system with buyers signing for what they had taken and paying at the end of the month, when they could.

CHAPTER 12:

The Boom Years 1961–1976

TEXADA'S SECOND BOOM STARTED IN 1962 after Texada Mines discovered a big underground ore body on the Yellow Kid claim. The decision to take the mine's operation underground meant importing contractors and increasing the workforce by several hundred men in order to build a headframe, sink the shaft, install a crusher and develop an underground network of tunnels to the ore body. Word of the job opportunities spread fast in the mining community, and soon hardrock miners, especially from Ontario, thronged to Texada. After the initial preparation work was completed, some of the new men stayed on to take permanent jobs.

Typical of those who arrived to work at the iron mine in 1962 was Albert Atkinson from Ontario, who, with his wife, Peggy, bought a house overlooking Gillies Bay and stayed for decades. Others arriving on the island at this time looked for rental houses, but these were very scarce in both Gillies Bay and Van Anda. However, there were homes for rent in Blubber Bay, because Domtar had downsized its workforce in 1961 after closing its last lime kilns. Bill Campbell and his family took advantage of the Domtar housing option. He had transferred from Whistler to the Texada branch of the Department of Highways so that he would have more time for his growing family and his music. He and his wife, Cecilia, had two children when they arrived and a third was expected shortly. At first they rented the only available house in Van Anda, a duplex "so cold that you couldn't sit with your feet on the floor." The Campbells soon followed the lead of the mine workers and rented a much more comfortable house in Blubber Bay.

GILLIES BAY

The fresh influx of iron mine workers and their families resulted in more changes in Gillies Bay. The community now had a post office, community hall, airstrip, ball field and tennis courts. There was also a tiny Canadian Imperial Bank of Commerce (CIBC) branch. All the settlement's amenities, except for the general store that was now owned by Cliff Tuckey, were on mine property. In 1963 another room was added to the Gillies Bay School portable, and when lay minister Alan Thompson arrived to work as a machinist at the mine in 1969, Texada Mines donated a building lot on Alder Street for the site of a manse. Four years later, Thompson and his wife, Shirley, acquired the stained-glass windows, ornate furnishings and pews from the community church in Bralorne, as the mine there had closed down in 1971. Volunteers installed them in the Van Anda church, which was expanded and surrounded by a two-thousand-square-foot parking lot.

Gillies Bay also continued to upgrade its services. The Department of Transport blacktopped the airstrip runway so that it could be used as a practice strip for the department's Buffalo aircraft. Texada Mines installed cable TV in the Gillies Bay bunkhouses but also made the service available to non-employees. Mine manager Arnold Walker put the service in his name to comply with CRTC regulations. A petition to the provincial government resulted in the establishment of the Gillies Bay Improvement District, a provincially funded body capable of borrowing money to improve the water system that the community rented from Texada Mines.

VAN ANDA

Despite the efforts of the Gillies Bay store owners to corral the trade of the iron mine's workers, Van Anda remained the main shopping centre on the island. There, Stan Willes' Meat Market had outgrown even its enlarged building and moved into a brand new one, the forerunner of today's Lucky Dollar Store. By 9:30 on May 7, 1964, the opening day for Willes' new store, all the buggies were taken and there was a lineup to get in. Two staff from his wholesaler, Malkins, came to help, and Willes ended the day with gross sales of twenty-five hundred dollars. For a week he never got to bed until after midnight, because it took so long to restock the shelves.[1] Although Deighton's still kept many of its loyal customers, the new store attracted the newcomers to the island, as it was now the larger store. Soon Willes was doing so well that he bought Cliff Tuckey's Gillies Bay store too, and persuaded his son-in-law, Marvin Nyl, to quit his quarry job and run it for him. After Willes died in June 1974, his widow, Beryl, continued to run the Van Anda store but summoned home their son, Rod, a commercial diver in Belize, to run the Gillies Bay store until it was sold to Ron Arnold three years later.

The increased commercial activity on the island prompted the formation of the Texada Chamber of Commerce, with Dave Webster as president. This organization took over some of the functions previously performed by the Texada Island Community Society (TICS), which continued alongside it but now concentrated on organizing social events as well as raising money for youth and sports groups. At the peak of activity in the mid-1960s, the island had four women's softball teams and five men's. The women's teams were sponsored by Imperial Lime, Hagman and Son Logging, the Blubber Bay Quarry and the iron mine; the men's were sponsored by the Elks, the Legion, Texada Mines, Ideal Cement, Fred Johnson and Jocko Cawthorpe. The Van Anda, Blubber Bay and Gillies Bay ball parks were all maintained by volunteers and used every night.

A Texada Boat Club was formed in Van Anda on May 1, 1966, and its members immediately began work on a breakwater for Sturt Bay, which up to this time had only been protected from the prevailing southeasterly storms and summer northerlies by low-lying Shark Island. Lafarge, which held the water lease there, gave it up so the new club could apply for it, and as with other island projects, the mines then contributed men, rock and equipment to build up the island. As well as the breakwater, the club built docks, a boat-launching ramp and club facilities; although battered by storms over the years, boats have remained safe here. For twelve years, Mary Gussman was the wharfinger. "Gruff but fair, Mary made sure that there were few boaters who ever escaped the transient docks without paying their fair share of moorage or forgot the rules of the Texada Boat Club."[2]

In the fall of 1966, BC Telephone laid a submarine cable connecting Grief Point on the mainland to Van Anda, and phone calls to the mainland were no longer billed as long distance. BC Hydro, which had supplanted BC Electric in 1962, installed new poles and equipment on Texada the same year. Colin Soles, the BC Hydro man in charge of maintenance for Van Anda, dug holes, fitted poles, read meters, billed customers and ran the BC Hydro office. His house phone was also the emergency phone number, so he was called out at all hours to deal with trees that had fallen on the lines during storms or that had been accidentally felled the wrong way. When he was called out at night, his Powell River supervisor, Peter Newport, went to his office to keep in touch via the radio telephone in Soles' truck. Newport then phoned Soles' wife, Phyllis, to let her know how long the job would take and that all was well. Halloween night was often a problem, because people old enough to know better dropped trees on the roads to block them, sometimes bringing down the power lines as well. The power also frequently went out on weekends, when workers at the iron mine pulled the master switch rather than take the time to shut off their machines individually. This blew holes in the cables bringing the power from the mainland, and Hydro would have to switch to another cable to solve the problem. Soles finally persuaded the mine workers to shut their machines down one at a time. Helicopters dropped hydro poles when power was required at the top of Mount Pocahontas where, in addition to BC Hydro, the Coast Guard, the RCMP, the CBC and the internet service all have towers. At the same time, hydro lines were extended along the High Road so that the farmers up there could finally have power. Soles found it a mixed blessing, because it meant a wider area to service.

THE POWELL RIVER REGIONAL DISTRICT

In 1965 Victoria established a new unit of local government called the regional district, which would deliver services to people living outside municipal areas, and two years later, Powell River became the centre for a district that included Texada and Lasqueti islands as well as the rural areas on the mainland between Saltery Bay and Desolation Sound. In 1972 the board of the new Powell River Regional District decided to approve a building code, because without it no mortgages could be issued. However, at the second reading of the new code, Osa Jones of Texada discovered that the new regulations would prevent her from building the log cabin on which she had set her heart, and she raised the alarm. On Texada, everyone from redneck miners to hippies joined her protest. Leonard Ryan took a petition from door to door, and 100 percent of the people signed it before it was sent to the board in Powell River.

At that time, the Regional District was rotating its meetings to different sites within the district, and the third reading of the new building code was scheduled for a meeting in the Stillwater Hall on the mainland. The people of Texada rented the biggest bus they could find and packed the hall, planning to stage a riot at a signal from Bill Fogarty, who was delegated to state their case. However, rioting wasn't necessary, as Fogarty was very eloquent and the directors backed down. When the next election for Regional Board directors was held, some of those in revolt, such as Don Spragge, Harold Lennox and Len Emmonds, ran for office and were elected.

CATERING TO THE ISLAND'S DRINKERS

By the beginning of the 1960s, Texada Island had developed a reputation for "the highest per capita consumption of beer in BC." However, while there were four or five bootleggers on the island, there was no liquor store, so from Friday to Sunday, the hardrock miners employed by the iron mine thronged to the Van Anda Legion. It was so popular that to secure a seat meant arriving before 6 p.m. Then in September 1960, M.G. Zorokin and Company announced plans to build a complex containing ten stores and a sixteen-room hotel in Van Anda; this number of hotel rooms would, under BC's antiquated liquor legislation, allow the owners to install a beer parlour, which was probably the main reason for their investment. The new hotel opened in 1962 without the accompanying ten stores that had been in the owners' original plans, but the beer parlour instantly became an island mecca. Bob Short's submission of the name

"Texada Arms" won the naming contest, though later, due to bar fights, some called it the "Broken Arms." In addition to its mandatory rooms and beer parlour, the hotel had a restaurant that often stayed open until two in the morning to serve Chinese food to everyone who piled into it after the beer parlour closed.

For entertainment on Friday nights, teenaged Ed Liebich and his friends watched from afar as the men went into the "Gents" side of the beer parlour and the "Ladies and Escorts" to the other. Then they waited for the fights to spill out onto the street. The miners almost always gave them a show. Even women fought, rolling around on the ground as they pulled each others' hair.[3]

As the only place to buy a case of beer was the hotel, in 1964 Jocko Cawthorpe and Danny McCormack started a delivery company, Texada Transfer. Half their business was liquor orders. They could provide a case of beer for $2.50 and charged a 50¢ delivery fee; since the hotel charged $3.55, it was cheaper to order through Texada Transfer. As McCormack worked full-time for Lafarge, Cawthorpe operated the truck, calling at the miners' bunkhouses each week for orders; as it was common to receive orders of ten cases from a single miner, the truck would be half-filled with beer on its return from Powell River. However, since most of the men worked shifts, both delivery and payment were a problem. If Cawthorpe didn't deliver, they came to his house in Van Anda, usually at two or three in the morning, banging loudly on his door and refusing to leave until he gave them their orders. To forestall this behaviour, Cawthorpe left their orders in their rooms in the bunkhouse, trusting that he'd be paid eventually. Sometimes a man would quit in the middle of a week and disappear, but weeks or months later a cheque would come from Ontario or somewhere back East for the amount owed.[4]

Thirsty islanders, especially those at the iron mine, blessed Jocko Cawthorpe's Texada Transfer service, which brought them liquor at affordable prices. Heather Harbord

The iron mine's bunkhouse No. 9 was the destination of most of the liquor orders as well as the location of poker games rivalled only by those in the Blubber Bay bunkhouse.[5] In bullshit poker, also called paycheque poker, the number on the paycheque became the poker hand, and the highest number won. All the cheques were then endorsed over to the winner.

In those days the RCMP generally came over to Texada on Fridays and Saturdays, and if they did happen to arrive at a different time, people phoned around to alert their friends. However, when the police arrived on September 5, 1965, the partners at Texada Transfer were not prepared for them to seize over a hundred cases of beer and charge both men with unlawfully keeping liquor for sale and possessing unsealed liquor. Fortunately, the charge was later dropped, as the partners were able to prove that the beer had been ordered but the purchasers had not been around at delivery time to receive it.

When a province-wide beer strike loomed in 1968, a rumour started that Jocko Cawthorpe (who had by this time bought out his partner, Danny McCormack) had stockpiled supplies. He hadn't, but the police were alerted and two undercover officers came to the house and ordered two bottles of whisky. Cawthorpe's wife, Dale, took the order and relayed it to him just before he got on the ferry. When the case went to court, the Cawthorpes were able to prove what had taken place. However, the Texada Arms Hotel *had* stockpiled beer supplies, and it had been one of the partners in the hotel enterprise who had reported them. Meanwhile, the police had seized the undelivered orders in the Cawthorpes' basement; when they got it back later, they discovered that the bottles had been stored beside a warm furnace, so the beer was skunky.

In 1969, after Breezy Thompson leased his former Marshall Wells hardware store to the BC Liquor Control board for Texada's first liquor store, Texada Transfer's business dropped overnight. However, about this time Texada Transfer won the mail contract, and the Cawthorpes went from one daily trip to Powell River to two; on their mail trip, their truck was given priority on the ferry. They often carried dangerous cargo, and though they were required to report it, no one checked the manifest in the thirty-eight years they operated the service.

THE CHANGING POPULATION

In the late 1960s, Texada's old-timers began to feel they were being invaded by hostile elements. In addition to the hard-drinking hardrock miners who had come to the island when the iron mine went underground, a ragtag crowd of long-haired newcomers had also begun to appear. They squatted in every old prospector's cabin and abandoned homestead. They sunbathed in the nude and smoked pot. "They were everywhere," said one old-timer, outrage edging her voice some forty years later. Their arrival was traumatic for islanders used to keeping up more orthodox appearances (though some were no strangers to the perils of alcohol). Socially, the two groups remained apart.

These newcomers were part of a general back-to-the-land movement that was driving people from the cities to rural areas to find a simpler lifestyle. They were questioning traditional ideas and morals and espousing alternative ways of life and thinking. "They were all running away from something they didn't believe in," said Vi Liebich. "Some came from wealthy families who paid them to stay away."

Texada was the perfect place for an "alternative community" of this kind. In the island's mild climate, vegetable gardens produced all year round, there were oysters on the beach and fish were easy to catch. One of the newcomers shot deer and shared the meat. A man named Gilles—who like many in the community lacked a last name—had been raised on the St. Lawrence River, where he had learned to build boats on the beach, a craft he continued on Texada. He inspired others with his mantra of, "When you're dealing with living things, they always turn into a surplus."[6] By this he meant that it is very difficult to produce exactly the same amount as you consume. People in the community traded, shared, bartered or sold the excess. Parties were numerous and frequent. Typically, everyone brought a potluck dish of organic food, often vegetarian or vegan, and the discussions ranged from current affairs to art, theatre, fine writing and such unconventional ideas as the conservation of non-human species and sustainability of the land. These conversations, sometimes stimulated artificially, would continue into the small hours. For entertainment, everybody listened to the CBC. Newspapers were passed eagerly from hand to hand.

Among the newcomers in this alternate community was one of the first professional artists to live on the island, Jack Marlowe Wise (1928–1996). "He had a master's degree," recalled Ted Ross, who eventually lost his wife to Wise, "and he painted miniatures the size of a postage stamp full of intricate detail and he'd build up a whole mandala of this stuff. Actually, he gave me a beautiful painting in trade for my wife . . . and eventually I sold that painting to buy an engagement ring for my second wife. He lived in a lovely old wood frame house up on the High Road, the old Jacobson farm. There wasn't much evidence of farming as he was too busy as a painter." In 1966, while still living on the island, Wise received a Canada Council grant to study with Tibetan monks in Northern India, and thereafter his paintings reflected the spiritual realm. His contribution to Canadian art and in particular to the Pacific North West School is significant. Thirty of his paintings, including the Dorje series, are in the Greater Victoria Art Gallery; his work is also found in many Canadian and American collections.

A number of these "New Age" people on the island studied Buddhism. Among them was L.W. Colomby, generally known as Bo, "a very capable and muscular young man"[7] who lived as a recluse in a shack on the beach at Cook Bay from 1969 to 1985. In between travels to the Himalayan region, he translated religious texts from Tibetan into English.

Mike and Barb Evans, along with their son, Stephen, were among the first of the Davie Bay New Age settlers to arrive. In 1968, after they moved into the defunct logging camp there, the camp's owner, Art Halley, came by, but they became friends and he allowed them to stay; as more people joined them, a little community developed there. However, after a few years at Davie Bay, the Evanses bought a used garbage truck from Powell River and Mike started a garbage service on Texada. They also bought property on Gillies Bay Road across from the present-day Kingdom Hall and began building a house, finishing the upstairs sleeping area first and leaving the downstairs open. However, they cooked in the downstairs on a propane stove that Evans had installed; on the night of May 31, 1976, after a food co-op dance, that stove started a fire, and the house burned to the ground. Only the dog survived.[8]

John Kelly came to Texada in 1959. He had left Ireland in 1954, heading for Australia, but instead had worked his way across Canada as a cabinet maker. As well as being skilled as a logger, fisher and miner, he was also "a playwright, a fighter for great issues, a man of principle."[9] He bought his first Texada property at the top of Oak Street in Gillies Bay in 1959 and built a tiny house, which he referred to as his Shangri-La, from lumber salvaged from the *Princess Beatrice,* which had formed part of the breakwater at Mouat Bay. He met Pat, who had grown up in Limerick, Ireland, in Powell River in 1968 after she took a teaching job at the Kelly Creek School south of the town. In 1970, just before their daughter, Deirdre, was born, Kelly paid eight thousand dollars for a small house perched high above Gillies Bay; it was one of two East Vancouver houses that had been barged up to Texada and skidded up the hill.[10] Their son, Owen, was born two years later. After that, Kelly worked on the Coast Guard ships, in the iron mine, and diamond drilling; one year, when he was working as night watchman on the ferry, his dog apprehended a burglar. The next time the ferry supervisor came with his paycheque, he said he should give it to the dog, as he protected the ship more than the man did.

In later years, the Kellys only lived in their Gillies Bay house during the summer months, as Pat Kelly taught in the Interior, and for three years the family lived in Pender Harbour while Kelly wrote plays on Canada Council and LIP grants. These were often performed by the Texada Rock Island Players, some of whose members were particularly good at portraying the eccentric characters about whom Kelly wrote. His comedy *Loggerheads* won an Honourable Mention at a drama festival in Parksville, where the production, though adored by the audience, was a nightmare for the producer and prompter, as lines were forgotten and ad libbed and entrances and exits confused. By the time it ended, the cast had almost rewritten the whole thing. *Loggerheads* was later produced on CBC Television.

Stan Heisholt,[11] a Burl Ives lookalike who sometimes posed as the singer in Vancouver, was part of this scene. He was a very large man who drove around in a bread van with the door open so that he could get in and out easily. He grew pot and put it in the brownies he made for the Chamber of Commerce dinners. Then he'd say, "We had such a lovely dinner last night. Everyone was so relaxed." The popular swimming hole

Heisholt Lake was supposed to be named Pero Lake, but the man who put up the sign named it for himself. Now its clear blue waters are a popular swimming hole and the venue for Jazz on the Rocks.

Heisholt Lake was named after him, although this had not been the plan; his boss, Domtar quarry manager Mike Pero, had sent Heisholt to put up a sign naming it Pero Lake, but Heisholt put his own name on the sign instead.[12]

The Ward/Tilly family were among the American immigrants who came to the island in 1970. Daughter Meg Tilly's novel *Singing Songs*, which tells the story of abuse, neglect and poverty from the point of view of a four-year-old child, is set on the San Juan Islands, but the experiences she describes actually occurred on Texada.[13] Her parents often left her and her small siblings alone for long periods of time without telling them when they would be back. She and her sister, Jennifer, became movie actors, and Meg was nominated for an Oscar for her part in *Agnes of God*.

Writer Brian Brett lived on the island for two years around 1972 and described his experiences in his book *Trauma Farm*.[14] US army veteran Dave Murphy also arrived at this time. He prospected all over the province with Van Anda's Joe Christensen, saving enough to buy land in Crescent Bay, where he developed a Canada-wide organic fertilizer business. He later became Texada's representative on the Regional District Board, but after forty years of living on the island, he said some people still thought of him as a newcomer.

In addition to the alternative community at Davie Bay, there was another called the O.G. Ranch on crown land on the outskirts of Gillies Bay. It was populated by a group of hippies who had been asked to leave Nanaimo. They remained on Texada for at least ten years.

While some of the newcomers came with funds, others made their livelihoods either legally or illegally on the island. In fact, very soon after the influx began, Texada became the site of a vibrant pot growing industry, and Texada Gold became a household name as far south as Mexico. Young people from the island travelled to the Lower Mainland to learn better marijuana growing techniques, and as pot plantations sprang up all over the island, people learned to avert their eyes when going into the bush. The local maxim became, "If you find something in the woods that doesn't belong to you, leave it alone."

The marijuana scene affected the lives of everyone on the island—though sometimes in humorous ways. In the spring of 1966, the Guides and Brownies held a bazaar in the Elks Hall, and Monica Stiles, being married to one of Ideal Cement's supervisors, felt duty bound to volunteer her services. She was assigned to serve at a table where vegetable and flowering plant seedlings were for sale. Unfortunately, some fellows in the beer parlour had placed three marijuana seedlings among the tomato plants. About three months later, public health nurse Mary Lou Paterson happened by the home of Annie McLeod, a pillar of the community and long-time church organist, and beheld a huge plant on the front steps.

"Mrs. McLeod, what are you doing with that plant?" Paterson asked.[15]

"I bought it from Monica Stiles at the bazaar!" was the reply. Mrs. McLeod had transplanted the seedling a number of times, but it grew so big that her son-in-law, Joe Little, had finally moved it into a half barrel, and there it sat on the front step for all to see. In today's prices it was probably worth five thousand dollars.

Vera Liebich had a parallel experience. Her ceramics had been priced at one dollar each at the bazaar, but they didn't sell. At the next booth, brownies were selling fast for three dollars each. She couldn't understand it.

CENTENNIAL CELEBRATIONS

In celebration of Canada's centennial year, Texada sent all of its high-school students to Montreal to see Expo. These fifty young people were away for three weeks, accompanied by several teachers and parents. Travelling by bus and ferry, they arrived in Vancouver in time to visit the Maritime Museum and the newly opened Simon Fraser University before catching the night CNR train, where they were allotted their own dining car. All went well until, at one of the stops in the Prairies, Bobby Mills failed to get back on board, and teacher Frieda Woodhead was dispatched with money to round him up; the pair of them took a taxi to the next station. In Montreal the group was billeted in a bunkhouse. After experiencing Expo, they went to Ottawa, where they toured the Parliament Buildings.

Centennial year on Texada ended with a special ceremony in the Van Anda Church. On December 10, Reverend Edward (Ted) Dinsley, who had served as a lay preacher there since 1960, became the first minister to be ordained on the island.

NEW FACES AND NEW SERVICES

On September 1, 1968, Dr. Donald McCallum, the mine doctor, died and the island was left without a physician. To attract another doctor to the island, Kaiser Aluminum built a medical clinic in Gillies Bay; it had two examining rooms, an X-ray room, a waiting room and an emergency ward for overnight patients. In April 1969, Dr. Kay Garner, who had practised obstetrics in Vancouver from 1942 to 1969, became Texada's first full-time doctor. Garner worked full-time as a general practitioner until April 1971, when Dr. Stephen Gislason took over.

Texada's first full-time doctor in modern times was Dr. Kay Garner, a former obstetrician, who arrived in 1969. She fished from her own boat, built fire pits at Shelter Point and commuted to Vancouver for the opera season. The Shelter Point Nature Trail is named after her.

Thereafter, she worked part-time until the fall of 1986. She enjoyed fishing in her own boat and doing volunteer work such as building fire pits at Shelter Point Park, and she commuted to Vancouver for the opera season. She died in 2005, and the Nature Trail at the park has been named in her honour.

Cecilia Campbell became the Blubber Bay post mistress on February 14, 1969, and remained in that job until 1999. Her first office was a small lean-to attached to the grocery store. It had split barn doors at either end to keep customers out of the work area, but the only washroom facilities were inside the store, which eventually closed. The post office then moved into a little house opposite the Holtenwood Gallery, Domtar having decided that it was cheaper to convert the house into a post office than to send someone to and from Van Anda every day with the company mail. The house not only had washroom facilities but an electric stove as well, and Campbell soon got into the habit of mixing bread dough before leaving home and bringing it to the post office. The dough rose while she did her mail chores, and by lunchtime it was ready for the oven. She also baked cookies and put some beside the wicket for her customers. At lunchtime she went home and prepared supper for her family, setting the timer on the stove to cook it. "Everything had to be on time because we lived by the ferries and the many band practices and women's ball games in the summer." She worked from 9 to 4:30 five days a week and 9 to noon on Wednesday. Texada has never had letter carriers, though today rural route delivery is contracted out.

For thirty years, Alberta-born Cecilia Campbell was the postmistress at Blubber Bay, where lucky customers sometimes got cookies with their mail.
Heather Harbord

In September 1968, the school board began busing all of Texada's grades eleven and twelve students to Powell River. On stormy days, this was a hair-raising journey. A year later the Blubber Bay school was closed for lack of students. By the fall of

1973, the board had decided to bus students to the various schools around the island in order to give each grade its own room. Kindergarten to grade two were sent to Gillies Bay, grades three and four to Blubber Bay, and grades five to ten to Van Anda.

FERRY SERVICES

In 1963, Chuck McCallum and Jim Humphries bought MV *Atrevida* from Captain Bert Davis's Texada Ferry Ltd. and took over his government contract to provide Blubber Bay–Van Anda–Westview car ferry service, which was much more popular than the passenger-only water taxis, though they carried on until BC Ferries took over in June 1969. Demand for ferry service continued to increase until the *Atrevida*, which only carried five cars, was stretched to its limit.

In 1965 pressure was applied to force the Department of Highways, which was now operating ferry services across the province, to provide a car ferry from Powell River to Comox. The result of that pressure was the *Comox Queen*, built for a Comox–Blubber Bay–Powell River run, but when the ship went into service, Blubber Bay was left out of its itinerary, much to the chagrin of local journalist Helene Orpen, whose diatribes hit the national news. (In 1977, the *Comox Queen* was re-engined and renamed *Tenaka*, and in 2011 the ship was in use on the Quadra–Cortes run.)

Early in 1969 McCallum learned that a Vancouver shipyard was building a thirty-car ferry for the Ministry of Highways and that the new ferry was to run on the Texada–Westview route. He kept track of the construction process, and about two months before the ship was likely to be in service, he requested a meeting with the Ministry. Knowing that it would be difficult to move one of the other government ferries onto that route on short notice, he explained that he would be withdrawing the *Atrevida* immediately because he had an opportunity to use it to run supplies to Yellow Point Lodge and other destinations in that area. The government, realizing he had them over a barrel, bought him out. The Ministry of Highways operated the *Atrevida* on the Texada–Westview route until the new ferry, called the *Texada Queen* (later renamed *Tachek*,) was due to begin service

Weather never stopped Gus Liebich, either when he was running the MV Atrevida *or BC Ferries'* Texada Queen.

on June 23. However, when completion was delayed, the *Comox Queen* filled in until July 26. Gus Liebich, a legendary captain of the *Atrevida*, who was never deterred by weather, became the first captain of the *Texada Queen*.[16] With a crew based on the island, the new ship did six daily round trips, expanding later to eight. Meanwhile, Vi Liebich's taxi business dried up overnight, as salesmen were now able to bring their vehicles over to the island.

AN ISLAND TRAGEDY

Although it is possible to walk between Dick Island and Shelter Point at low tide, there is a strong current running there on certain tides, and even in two feet of water it is impossible to stand against the flow. On July 18, 1974, John Zaikow was in the fast food concession at Shelter Point when he heard a vehicle horn honking madly. When he ran out to investigate, he was told that "a little boy just floated by on an inner tube and sank!" Two men went out in a rowboat and found the child's mother, Cathy Whiteman, floating face down in the water, and a short time later, the body of her son was discovered. The whole island went into shock, as Whiteman had been a popular dental assistant.

Stronger than normal spring tides caused the drowning of a mother and son between Shelter Point and Dick Island on July 18, 1974.
Heather Harbord

Since this tragedy, signs have been posted at that point warning people not to swim there.

CHAPTER 13:

The Protest Years 1977–1990

THE NEWS THAT THE IRON MINE WAS CLOSING at the end of 1976 came as a shock to the whole community, and by the time the last ore shipment left the mine for Japan in January 1977, many workers had already moved off the island. A total of 140 jobs were lost, thirty-five homes went up for sale, including seventeen owned by the company, and ninety-one children disappeared from the school roster.

As the lime quarries continued to operate, however, it wasn't the end for Texada, although some rearranging of lives was necessary. The Gillies Bay Improvement District, which already owned the local water supply, made a deal with Kaiser Aluminum, the final owner of the iron mine, to buy the company's fire hall and street lighting for a dollar each. One hundred residents then formed the Gillies Bay Community Television Association and took over the company's cable equipment for another dollar. The community also paid a dollar each for the company's medical clinic, community hall and ball field. In November of the following year, a local group that had purchased the airport from Alm Forest turned it over to the Regional District for one dollar. This group, all managers, consisted of Stan Beale (Ideal Cement), Dave Webster (Canada Cement Lafarge) and Jim Jack (Imperial Limestone). In 1978 the Regional District created a recreation commission to manage all of Texada's ball fields, the community hall, and Shelter Point Park (known as Harwood Point Park until 1986). Later, the commission also managed Marble Bay Bluff Park (established in 1984) and Erickson Beach (purchased from Canada Cement Lafarge in 1989).

Originally a single hull, the North Island Princess *has been cut and stretched in four directions, causing an early captain to refer to it as the "Playtex Princess." In a storm like this one, its catamaran structure enables it to continue running despite taking waves almost over its superstructure.* Heather Harbord

In spite of Texada's reduced population, in March 1979 BC Ferries replaced the *Texada Queen* with the larger *North Island Princess*, which could carry forty-nine cars and 150 passengers and crew. Built in 1958, the ship had been taken apart and stretched four ways in 1971 to enlarge it and convert it into a catamaran. The locals promptly shortened its name to "the NIP."

Many retirees bought the empty houses in Gillies Bay. Among them was Gary McLeod, grandson of pioneer prospector James Raper. McLeod wanted to buy the property belonging to Edith (Stromberg) Poock at the head of Gillies Bay, the family's traditional vacation spot. After Mrs. Poock's husband died, McLeod had told her that if she ever wanted to sell, he would buy the property but allow her to live there for the rest of her life. In the meantime, he bought one of the empty houses on the other side of the bay, though it was not on the waterfront. Then in 1980, she called to say that she wanted to sell, and they negotiated a deal for her to occupy the house for her remaining years. She was at this time eighty-one. The whole island knew the story, and over the next twenty-two years, whenever McLeod was asked how Mrs. Poock was doing, he would report that she was just fine. The inquirer would then generally respond, "Well, isn't that just wonderful!" His response was, "Only if you are Edith Poock." When she died at age 103 in 2002, he got possession of the house.

One of the ferry corporation's night watchmen at this time was Bob Blackmore (1930–2008), a photojournalist who had worked during the 1950s and 1960s on Calgary's *Albertan* newspaper (as it was known from 1936 to 1980). One of his freelance jobs during that period involved filming the capture of the orca "Moby Doll" off Saturna Island in July 1964; this was the first live capture of an orca on the Pacific Coast. After he settled on Texada in 1979, he bought the old Palm farm, homesteaded in 1915, in Upper Gillies Bay. Among the videos relating to Texada history that he made after moving to the island were *The Pocahontas Whisky Still, The Life and Times of Hadden [Haddon] Burditt* and *Josef Kempe, An Immigrant's Story.*

In Blubber Bay, Domtar systematically dismantled the company town. Although some of the workers wanted to buy their houses, the water and sewer lines were so intertwined that the company could not untangle the mess enough to make the houses saleable. Since many of the houses had been built soon after the quarry was first opened, it was costing the company to maintain them, so as they emptied, the company issued contracts to have them taken down and the land cleaned up. When Art Yip, one of the last of the Chinese workers at Blubber Bay, retired in 1984, the company made him sign off for his house. Meanwhile, in 1982 that venerable Van Anda institution, Deighton's store, finally closed when Reg and Isabel Deighton retired.

THE DAVIE BAY NEW AGE COMMUNITY

By the late 1970s, the permanent population of New Agers in Davie Bay had settled around the twenty-person mark, most of them the members of seven families. The majority were Canadians from the east, but there were also Americans in the settlement, although the two groups seldom intermingled. After President Carter offered amnesty to "draft dodgers" in 1977, some of these Americans returned to the US, though others headed for the Slocan Valley or the Kootenays. Davie Bay also played host to a

Attendees at Stella Mutch's Davie Bay wedding wore flowers in their hair and tie-dyed clothing. John Dafoe

steady parade of non-permanent residents from like-minded communities on the Sunshine Coast or Vancouver Island and even France. Some of these transients were into drugs and held all-night LSD, MDA and pot parties on the beach. However, these messed-up people soon went elsewhere, because living off the land in Davie Bay required some competence, and the permanent people were unwilling to allow the transients to sponge off them.

Texada's young people were attracted to the Davie Bay community. Doby Robillard[1] ran away from home to join them. John Zaikow and Christine Woolcott just visited. Woolcott remembered the Americans as well-spoken and well-educated.[2] In fact, she had never encountered people so articulate and was somewhat in awe of them. But the Canadians, who were more "hippy" than the Americans, roamed naked on the beach, and having recently taught in a strict Mennonite community, Woolcott found this was too much.

By this time the residents of Davie Bay had developed quite a sense of community, although just as in any community, there were some squabbles, most notably about the school. The Davie Bay school,[3] which operated

Jim Otis, like other builders in the New Age community at Davie Bay, used whatever materials were at hand, and liked to be close to the water. John Dafoe

from September 1979 to April 1983, was built out of recycled materials. The desks were hand-carved and included four that were designed to convert into easels for artwork. The Powell River School District paid Josée Meunier to supervise correspondence lessons for the students, and she used her considerable talents to enrich the curriculum with French, music, drama, crafts and environmental studies.

One of the permanent Canadian settlers in Davie Bay was Leonard Ryan. Having grown bored with his newspaper job in Ontario, he had arrived on Texada in his search for the perfect place to live. Not finding it after a couple of years on the island, he was about to leave when he was introduced to Davie Bay. Within five minutes he had picked out a spot on the beach to build a house with a big south-facing window from which he could watch the grey waves roll in. With great fondness, he remembers his pleasure when it snowed, because he knew no one was going to disturb him. His favourite part of the day was the evening, when he would make a cup of tea and sit in his big chair with a cosy fire at his back and watch the sunset.

To support himself, Ryan dug clams in winter and carried fertilizer into the bush for the serious marijuana growers in spring and summer. After the harvest the growers paid him in marijuana and cash, which provided money for his fall travelling and new toys such as a boat motor. He felt pretty prosperous. Then one year, due to genetic improvements in marijuana strains, there was a big jump in product quality. It was so strong that he found himself going around in a perpetual daze, so in the fall of 1981 he quit smoking, with the result that he had more energy and even more cash.

During the 1970s, much of the land around Davie Bay had been acquired by Genstar, the subdivision development arm of an enormous company originally headquartered in Belgium and now centred in Winnipeg. Having decided to log this property, the company sent a consultant to scout it by plane, and that was when they learned that there were squatters on it. However, when the company announced their logging intentions to the squatters, there was a protest, with Leonard Ryan writing articles that were presented to the Regional District, which then took them to the company and to Victoria. In the end, the company gave up their clear-cutting plans but they did log selectively, leaving the creek beds and the beachfront.

After this, Genstar leased the ground under each cabin for one dollar a year. When the company's representative, Joe Chance, arrived to collect, he was entertained at a delicious potluck supper with homemade wine. Sometimes he received the lease money in cash, but other times it was delivered in canned goods and toilet rolls. Later the leases were increased to two dollars a year.

In 1983, almost everyone moved out of the Davie Bay settlement in a single season. Afterwards, Neale Berjer, one of the settlers, told Ryan that "the Davie Bay that we so much loved had become a trap," because people had become stuck in their beautiful, comfortable rut. It was time to move on, because the world was passing them by. Genstar contracted with Rick Jones to bulldoze the squatters' houses, and today lush greenery covers the remains. However, long after the Davie Bay community dispersed, pot continued to be grown on the island. Though illegal, it had become a major cash crop for the islanders.

NEW ISLAND INITIATIVES

In April 1983, Texada's second newspaper was born, the first having been the *Coast Miner* nearly a century earlier. Sponsored by the Texada Island Community Society, the new paper started life as the *Rock Island Lines* and was printed courtesy of the Van Anda School. A year or so later, the Max Cameron Press at the Powell River High School began printing it but couldn't guarantee to do the work at a specific time. The printing was then turned over to the *Powell River News* and the name was changed to *Texada Island Lines*. It flourished under the strict supervision of graphic artist Ann Trousdell, although she reported that "Christine Woolcott was the driving force who got the *Texada Lines* going and got people to write for it. I solicited advertising and did the graphics and layout. We used to have paste-up parties when we all gathered together and decided where to put what in the next issue." All this is now done on computers. Ann left the paper in 1989 to attend the University of Victoria, but the paper kept going. For twenty-two years, Cecilia Campbell looked after the distribution of 130 off-island copies from her basement.

The Texada Sandcastle Competition was started in 1985 on the wide

Putting together an issue of the Texada Island Lines *involved paste-up parties for the volunteers.*

expanse of perfect sand at Gillies Bay. The four categories of participants were children, teens, families and adults, but the little kids were king. Bare feet and floppy hats were *de rigueur*. Young moms bloomed with their next child. Young dads repeatedly hiked up pants slipping off their backsides. Quiet, wet-footed dogs, mostly on leads, monitored the action. As the day progressed, dragons, sea stars, castles with ornate turrets and a host of other creations rose out of the sand. Residents from nearby homes, some even on walkers, toured the offerings as the tide crept in inexorably to fill the moats around the sculptures. Judging was a democratic, people's choice affair, with votes accepted from everyone. Originally a day of family fun, it grew until it sometimes attracted teams from as far away as California, but the recession finally scaled it back to mainly locals and people from Powell River.

After John Kelly's death in 1987, the Kelly house became the John Kelly Gallery and featured local artists. The Artists' Cooperative of Texada (ACT) re-roofed the house, installed a front porch and opened the first exhibition on May 28, 1989.[4] In 1991, when ACT found that running the gallery was too onerous, Pat Kelly took over that job, but the gallery closed in November 1995 after a retrospective of the work of the late Betty Warren.

The Texada Historical Society was resuscitated on September 21, 1987, and has been going strong ever since. Ben Nicholas became chairperson, Pat McKay secretary and Evelyn Spragge treasurer. Nan Johnson and anyone who cared to join her taped interviews with Texada's old-timers, and these tapes are now invaluable in defining the island's history.

In 1988, after twenty-five years of service, the Canadian Imperial Bank of Commerce (CIBC) closed their tiny Gillies Bay branch. The only other financial institution on the island was the Credit Union, but as it was staffed by volunteers and did not dispense cash, islanders had to go to Powell River for banking services. However, after the Texada Credit Union amalgamated with the Powell River one in 1991, a branch with full banking services was opened in Van Anda.

Although most of the miners had left the island in the late 1970s and many New Agers left in the early 1980s, Texada was still welcoming newcomers. Ted Soepboer, who came in 1990, had grown up on a canal barge in Holland during the Nazi occupation, but when he was twelve, his parents brought him to Toronto. As soon as he could, he struck out on his own, criss-crossing Canada fourteen times before he settled in the Kootenays, where he met his wife, Barbara. When they arrived on Texada, they hired a carpenter to build them a house on Marble Bay Road to lock-up stage, then finished it themselves using beachcombed wood. The old-growth floors and panelled walls glow warmly, and they remember where they found each piece of wood. Soepboer says that "the beaches around here are like a shopping mall." A builder of unconventional boats, he takes a shopping list of the materials he needs whenever he visits the beaches. "I can go beachcombing and find enough lumber to frame a thirty-foot boat in one week." His preferred tool is an axe "sharp enough to shave with."

PROTESTS

The days when it was acceptable to blast every corner of the island are long past, and islanders today are very particular about what goes on in their environment and quick to band together if they feel their well-being is at stake. At least eight times in the last thirty years, they have taken to the hustings and protested against projects they felt threatened their way of life.

One of the first of these protests occurred in 1980 and concerned Hydro's plan to cross the centre of the island with the Cheekeye-Dunsmuir Transmission Line. As soon as survey work and road construction for the dual transmission lines started, local activist Karl Rising-Moore, in collaboration with the Texada Island Environmental Association, staged protests to halt construction. Paula Laurie of the same organization told the *Powell River News* that she wanted a public hearing to determine the justification for building such a line. But Colin Soles, who was the BC Hydro agent on the island, said that many of the protesters came from the lower Sunshine Coast.

The fight that will always resonate in islanders' minds was the "Great Garbage Caper." In September 1982, they learned to their horror that Genstar was recommending to the Greater Vancouver Regional District (GVRD) that they dispose of their garbage in the old BC Cement

Mike Zaikow's insurance office became protest headquarters for the Great Garbage Caper.
Rolland Desilets

quarries, which were merely gouges out of the side of a hill rather than pits. The news broke when representatives from Genstar presented this concept as a job creation project to the Texada Chamber of Commerce. Although a few people welcomed the employment potential, the majority of public opinion swiftly came out against it, because garbage dumped there would have immediately leached into the ocean. In a flash the community came together, and a protest organization called Texada Action Now (TAN), under the leadership of Jocko Cawthorpe, was born. Mike Zaikow's insurance office became protest headquarters. Initially the group's members were ill-prepared to handle the media, but after being ripped apart by a CKVU interviewer, they learned fast and were soon holding effective press conferences. The federal government, in an effort to resolve the problem, ordered an environmental review by a board that included Senator Pat Carney.

TAN's next move was to send a delegation to a GVRD meeting, but instead of the bunch of hippies that the directors had expected, they were addressed by a trio of well-spoken islanders. Jim Brennan had worked on the island since 1942, first in the mines and then for Ideal Cement until he retired in 1974. He had served on both the water board and the school board. Ben Nicholas came to Texada in 1939, and after working for Pacific Lime had owned and operated the Texada–Westview water taxi service for many years. Chuck Childress had been a charter student at Simon Fraser University when he got a summer job at Texada Mines in 1965, liked the underground work better than studying, and stayed on to marry Sonia Zaikow, the daughter of Mike and Maria Zaikow. After training to become an industrial electrician, he hung out his shingle on Texada in 1982. This trio of island ambassadors hypnotized the meeting and persuaded the directors to visit the island.

For the GVRD's visit to Texada, Genstar chartered a plane for the Vancouver to Powell River flight and a bus to transport them to Texada, but the company failed to send a representative to show them around the island's quarries and convince them of the efficacy of their proposal. Chuck Childress therefore became their tour guide, taking them to see the Ideal Cement Quarry, Heisholt Lake and the Blubber Bay Quarry. When the tour ended at the Texada Legion, the directors were met by a crowd of three hundred placard-waving islanders—including students let out of school for the occasion and quarry workers who had been given a five-hour break from work to attend. Many of them banged on the bus to show their displeasure with the proposal, but eventually the delegation disembarked for a delicious salmon and oyster lunch catered by the grannies of the community. This was followed by a lively discussion, with most of the talking coming from Coquitlam Mayor Jim Tonn, who seemed to be strongly in favour of bringing the garbage to Texada. Texadans fought back, but when the group returned to Vancouver, the GVRD voted to send the garbage.

Chuck Childress learned fast how to be media savvy when he took part in the Great Garbage Caper. Heather Harbord

In the meantime, Genstar had switched its garbage dumping proposal to the shafts and tunnels of the iron mine, which were by 1982 under the jurisdiction of Pete Stiles, the manager of Ideal Cement. As the iron mine was also close enough to the ocean that the contents would have leached into it, he wrote a letter to the *Powell River News* pointing out that the whole concept would be turned down flat when the environmental review was completed. Unfortunately, this made him unpopular with the locals, who wanted the Genstar proposal to be quashed immediately without waiting for the review to be completed, and they wrongly concluded that he was not supporting them.

The ensuing municipal elections changed some of the players in the GVRD, and after Christmas, Childress and Cawthorpe went back to Vancouver. "All is not lost," Alderman May Brown of Vancouver told them. She explained that the City of Vancouver had asked the GVRD to reconsider the vote, but the message had not been received in time to be put on the agenda. However, Coquitlam Mayor Jim Tonn, who had in the meantime changed sides, exercised his prerogative as GVRD chair to include it anyway. The vote to rescind was passed. When Childress and Cawthorpe returned from Vancouver, people met them in the parking lot and swept them into a big celebration at the Legion. (A subsequent initiative got the Powell River Regional District to pass a bylaw zoning the whole of Texada as RU and specifying that garbage could only be disposed of in Lot 6.) [5]

In 1985 a group in which retired geologist John Dove was involved battled to prevent Fisheries and Oceans renewal of a clam lease on Gillies Bay. Following success in this fight, Dove became interested in recording the leg bands on the Brant geese that visit the bay on their spring northward migration.

In 1986 Texada Action Now held a public meeting after word leaked out that the Ministry of Forests had obtained a permit to spray poison on bracken fern on a twenty-eight hectare area between Pocahontas and Terrace bays.[6] As a result of the group's opposition, in the fall of 1986 Texada became the first community in the province to hold a referendum on the large-scale use of pesticides. That referendum passed and the use of such pesticides on the island was banned.[7] TAN, which had operated as a subcommittee of the Texada Island Community Society, subsequently incorporated as the residents' and ratepayers' association of Texada.

In the late 1980s, residents again protested when Inland Natural Gas proposed building a pipeline to run the length of Texada Island, with pumping stations at Anderson Bay in the south and Limekiln Bay in the north, in order to supply gas to Powell River and Vancouver Island. Some residents were opposed because the installation of the line would interfere with the environment, but others were opposed because natural gas would not be available to islanders. The company placated the latter by offering gas service to Texada as well. The line was built but natural gas service to islanders has never materialized, and this is now a sore point.

In 2007 WestPac LNG Corporation proposed a scheme to import five hundred million cubic feet of natural gas per day from Asia, the Middle East or Russia, bringing it to BC in LNG tankers as liquefied natural gas, to a re-gasification plant at Kiddie Point on the northern tip of Texada Island. The plant, which would go into operation in 2014, would be the largest facility of its kind. The project would also necessitate the construction of a twenty-kilometre-long transmission line down the centre of the island to hook up with the Cheekeye Dunsmuir Transmission Line. The proposal immediately aroused the population of the island, and Texada Action Now once again swung into action with bumper stickers that read "Texada Forever, LNG Never." In its campaign to stop the project, the committee pointed out that at present BC uses only 20 percent of the natural gas produced here; the remainder is exported to Alberta and the US. They also campaigned to let the public know about the enormous danger of LNG explosions, harm to the environment and false economic forecasts. They were soon joined in this fight by the Georgia Strait Alliance and about a dozen other groups, which formed a new group—the Alliance to Stop LNG. Fortunately, they were successful and WestPac ultimately withdrew its proposal.

In the fall of 1986, Texada became the first community in the province to hold a referendum to ban the large-scale use of pesticides. The following year, sticking to their principles, these volunteers cleared bracken away from freshly planted trees by hand.

CHAPTER 14:

The Tourism and Retiree Years 1991–2010

AS THE TWENTIETH CENTURY WOUND DOWN, Texadans faced new challenges. Well-paying jobs were scarce and living off the land had become more difficult with the demise of salmon populations. It was time to get serious about tourism.

Tourists had discovered Texada Island in the 1980s and 1990s, but in 1982, when the Texada Action Now (TAN) committee asked the Regional District to establish a park on Marble Bay, they noted that back in 1968, it had been possible for islanders to picnic at dozens of spots on the island, including Kirk and Heisholt lakes, Dick Island, Grilse Point, Mouat, Limekiln, Raven and Davie bays, Cox Lagoon, and the Sand Banks. Unfortunately, the public had no legal access to any of these places because they are privately owned. "Now is the time to set aside land so that our grandchildren will have some place to go down to the sea that makes Texada an island," a spokesman for TAN told the reporter from *Rock Island Lines*.[1]

Twenty years later, the parks problem is still to be properly addressed. The Shelter Point campground is a well-kept Texada secret. It is often packed, and many of the RVs that are parked there belong to former Texada residents coming back for holidays. An overflow campground has been established beside the Kay Garner Nature Trail. Several people operate bed and breakfasts for those without camping equipment.

This nurse tree is one of many wonders on the Kay Garner Nature Trail at Shelter Point. Others include a massive old-growth Douglas fir and native fish traps visible at low tide. Heather Harbord

ARTS AND CRAFTS

During the last twenty years, arts and crafts of all kinds have flowered on Texada. This became very apparent when the Holtenwood Gallery opened in the old Blubber Bay visitor's house beside the ferry lineup in March 1997, as half of its stock was crafted on the island. The owner, Adriana Atwood-van Holten, who had worked for the Full Moon Gallery in Powell River, had a keen eye for what would sell, and to pull in customers from the ferry lineup, she also served coffee and goodies. Since she died, first Doby Dobrostanski and then Emile Sarniac took over the gallery, expanded the menu and added more Texada artists. Not to be outdone, Neil Berjer's Manana, which is situated across the road, also serves coffee but specializes in New Age crafts and clothing, some of which are made on the island.

Current artists of note on the island include Amanda Martinson (paintings and jewellery), Doby Dobrostanski (paintings), Beadzerk (original glass beads and jewellery), Tim Atwood (stained glass), Peder Norbygaard (sculptures of fish and faces), Barb McCormack and Susan Sharkey (art quilts), Deb Dumka (felting and fibre art), and Roxanna Rasmussen (oil paintings). There are also many other painters, potters, jewellers and workers in wood and metal.

Famous for her sky series, painted every day for a year, Amanda Martinson is now combining jewellery making with alternative medicine cures. Heather Harbord

Peder Norbygaard uses local stone, including red Anderson Bay marble, for his sculptures of fish and faces. Heather Harbord

Peter McGuigan's Texada Iron Works, a welding and fabricating company with all the latest equipment, has produced fine examples of wrought iron work. Although Peter and his wife only moved to the island in September 1999, his roots are here, as his grandfather was the storekeeper in Blubber Bay in the 1920s. He has an eclectic background in management, architecture, commercial fishing, human rights and proposal writing. In February 2010, he started issuing the *Texada Gazette*, an old fashioned, letter-sized broadsheet featuring news about local government. He posts its 250 copies around the island to stimulate thought on island-related topics such as the Supreme Court action against Lehigh Hanson's proposal to quarry Davie Bay.

In June 2003, *Texada Island Lines* staff decided to bring out a new publication called *Express Lines*. Its purpose was to keep islanders informed of special events and announcements. The new publication did not print full-length articles, because *Texada Island Lines* is still published on a quarterly basis.

When Peter McGuigan is not producing fine wrought iron work, he writes the Texada Gazette, *an old-fashioned broadsheet featuring news about local issues. He posts its 250 copies around the island.*
Heather Harbord

Texada's music scene was enhanced in 2004 when the Texada Arts, Culture and Tourism Society (TACT) organized the first annual Jazz on the Rocks event. It is staged on the grassy beach area on the south side of Heisholt Lake, where the music makes the steep walls surrounding the warm green waters ring. The 2006 event included the Powell River Youth Chorus as well as various quartets and a brass fanfare by Alan Matheson and Walter Martella as the grand finale.[2] This event was last staged in 2008 but organizers say that it is only "slumbering" and will arise again.

Diversity, held at Shingle Beach Campground in July for a limited capacity crowd, is a weekend of creative culture with artists, composers, bands, performers and participants from the island and across the continent. Yoga, dance, cosmic clowning, African drumming, creative dreaming, and aerial silk acrobatics were among the features in 2011. The event has been going since 2002.

From time to time, Texada has had its own chorus. The Texada Singers, founded in 1991 by Richard Olfert, continued after he left under the baton of Nikki Weber of Sechelt. Although she moved back there in 1997, she has returned with her Sechelt group to give concerts several times since then. In 1996 singer/songwriter Kristine Oudot put out a CD, *Texada Tides*, featuring her own poetry and those of a couple of other Texada residents. Though she grew up on the Prairies, she has fallen in love with the Coast.

On December 5, 2001, the Texada Island Museum opened in one of the houses owned by Ash Grove Cement, after volunteers had "hammered, scraped, cleaned and painted." An outdoor display features logging equipment used on the island. A second museum was opened in the old

Van Anda School building to house the Texada Archives and additional displays including many historic pictures. Norm MacLean became the first Texada archivist and was succeeded by Doug Paton in 2006.

OUTDOOR RECREATION

Every Saturday since the early 1990s, the Texada Trekkers have explored the many trails on the island, from the tide pools of Limekiln Bay to the spectacular views from Surprise and Pocahontas mountains. Glen Downing used his bulldozer to construct a nine-hole golf course on Crescent Bay Road, with carefully calculated tree hazards left in place. Softball continues to be a popular game. The raffle prizes for the ladies team in 2010 were typical of the island: a load of gravel from Imperial Limestone, a one-hundred-dollar BC Ferry pass, and fifty-dollar credits at the Lucky Dollar store and Centennial Service gas station in Van Anda.

FLYING TIME

Over the years, the Gillies Bay airstrip has seen many carriers come and go. Queen Charlotte Airlines, Powell Air, Air West, Pacific Coastal, Aquilla and KD Air have all serviced Texada at one time, but as soon as small coastal airlines become profitable, larger ones often swallow them up, sometimes leaving Texada without service. In 1996 local pilots launched a fly-in to raise funds for the Texada Island Search and Rescue. In 2008 the Texada Island Community Service organized the first "Spacecamp" for air cadets but also opened it to any other interested students. They all received a week of instruction in areas such as navigation and fire prevention. The event was so popular that it has continued to the present. In 2010 pilots flew in from as far away as the Yukon, camped beside their planes and socialized before returning home. KD Air offered fifteen-minute sightseeing excursions over the island.

POLICING THE ISLAND

Texada's sub-police storage unit outgrew its rented quarters in 1995 and police moved their equipment into a new metal-clad storage building at the head of Gillies Bay. Around three in the morning, not long after it was built and occupied, a loud metal screech rent the air, waking the neighbours.

"Must be raccoons in the shed," one of the neighbours muttered before burrowing back under the covers.

Then car and truck lights winked from behind the trees at the police station.

"The police must be working overtime," his wife said, and she too went back to sleep. Three hours later, she got up and, as usual, took her coffee outside to enjoy while she looked at the ocean and the birds. But as she turned around, she saw a large, gaping, triangular hole in the metal police shed. It looked exactly like someone had opened it with a can opener and bent the metal back.

Although it was only 6:30 a.m., the woman phoned the police and someone in Comox answered.

"We've got a shed over there?" the officer asked.

"Yes, you do, and it's been broken into."

When local officers arrived half an hour later, there was no trace of the marijuana that a helicopter had brought in after a big drug bust the previous day. The owners had repossessed their treasure. Since then, steel bars have been installed to reinforce the shed, though the crinkles in the metal are still visible. A chain-link fence provides further protection.

EDUCATION AND RELIGION

School-aged children are fast becoming a rarity on Texada. Fewer than twenty children in grades one to six continue to be bused to the one remaining school in Van Anda. Forty-three students in grades seven to twelve ride the ferry to Powell River, leaving home at 6:30 in the morning and, if they participate in after-school activities, often not getting home until after nine at night. When they proved unruly aboard the

North Island Princess one day, the captain invoked his powers under the Law of the Sea and banned them from his ship. Parents were incensed and the RCMP were green with envy, but the captain stood firm. After several days, he relented and the students have behaved themselves since that time. To save their children from this onerous commute, some parents who work for Texada Quarries have moved to Powell River and commute back to the island, either staying with elderly parents on the island during the week or living in trailers near the gas station.

The church in Van Anda is no longer the only place of worship on the island. On May 15 and 16, 1993, the Texada Kingdom Hall was constructed by about six hundred volunteers. While some worked on the building, others landscaped, made food, ran boat and bus shuttles and controlled traffic. At the end of the second day, the Texada Congregation of Jehovah's Witnesses had their own place beside the highway halfway between Gillies Bay and Van Anda.[3]

CHANGING TIMES, CHANGING TECHNOLOGY

In 2002 BC Ferries took over the dock at Blubber Bay and closed the float at which passing yachts had tied up safely in the past. The corporation explained that this action was due to liability concerns.[4] As in all BC Ferries lots, passengers and vehicles now face their long waits strongly fenced in. In high summer, with two to four hours between ships, it would make sense to give people access to the water for a swim.

Modern technology and a dedicated radio tower made it possible in 2007 for the Credit Union staff on Texada to perform the loans support work for the entire First Credit Union, including its branches at Powell River and Bowen Island. This created several permanent jobs on the island. The following year, the Credit Union moved into a brand new building in Van Anda at the intersection of the roads to Gillies Bay and the ferry.

Texada Island culture has changed. It has become an island of retired people, with a few internet businesses and carpenters and artists thrown in. Whereas in the 1960s people came here just to work and they retired elsewhere, now the population is retired and a lot older. There is even talk of the need for a retirement home. But at present, if people have major health problems that are beyond the scope of the clinic, which is not open on weekends, they must move to the mainland or Vancouver Island to be closer to a hospital. Those who remain take their chances.

Dragons rise out of the sand at the Gillies Bay Sandcastle Competition. Judging is a democratic, people's choice affair, with votes solicited and accepted from everyone present. Judges can tour the offerings as the tide creeps in to fill the moats around the sculptures. Heather Harbord

Texada Bibliography

Akrigg, G.P.V. and Helen Akrigg. *British Columbia Place Names.* Victoria: Sono Nis, 1986.

Barman, Jean. *The Remarkable Adventures of Portuguese Joe Silvey.* Madeira Park, BC: Harbour Publishing, 2004.

Barman, Jean. *Stanley Park's Secret: The Forgotten Families of Whoi Whoi, Kanaka Ranch and Brockton Point.* Maderia Park, BC: Harbour Publishing, 2005.

Beale, Fred. Letter to his son, Stan, dated May 15, 1958.

Brewer, William M. *Report on the Copper–Gold–Silver ore deposits on Vancouver and adjacent islands* in BC Department of Mines Annual Report, 1916, K304–360.

Brewer, William M. *Report on the occurrences of iron-ore deposits on Vancouver and Texada Islands, BC* in BC Department of Mines Annual Report, 1916, K274–303.

Brinton, Stewart. "Old Fred." Unpublished manuscript dated 2006, Texada Archives.

British Columbia. Royal Commission on the Acquisition of Texada Island, 1874. Papers relating to the appointment and proceedings.

Consedine, Robert L. "Multi-plant quarry supplies premium quality stone to West Coast markets," *Canadian Aggregates and Roadbuilding Contractor*, March 1996, Vol. 10, No. 2.

Corrigall, Alan. *Looking Backwards.* Self-published, n.d. (1997).

Devaney-Taylor, Margaret. Memoirs: 06.31.19. Six tapes and a transcript, Texada Archives.

Dolmage, Victor. "The Marble Bay Mine, Texada Island, British Columbia." *Economic Geology,* September 1921, Vol. 16.

Dougan, Charlie. *My Daughters' Request: Spotlight on the Yesterday of Country Folk.* Self-published. n.d.

Downie, William. *Explorations in Jarvis* [*sic*] *Inlet, Desolation Sound, BC.* March 19, 1859. London: Royal Geographical Society, 1861.

Francis, Daniel, ed. *Encyclopedia of British Columbia*. Madeira Park, BC: Harbour Publishing, 2000.

Gough, Barry M. *Gunboat Frontier; British Maritime Authority and Northwest Coast Indians 1846–1890.* Vancouver: UBC Press, 1984.

Hadley, Michael. *God's Little Ships: A History of the Columbia Coast Mission*. Madeira Park, BC: Harbour Publishing, 1995.

Hagelund, W.A. *Whalers No More.* Madeira Park, BC: Harbour Publishing, 1987.

Hammond, Joanne. "Archaeological dig reveals clues." *Powell River Peak,* December 23, 2008.

"Harry Trim" anonymous newspaper article, perhaps from the *Vancouver Province,* probably based on an interview with him sometime before his death in 1922. Obtained from Marlene Trim.

Harris, Cole. "Voices of Disaster: Smallpox around the Strait of Georgia in 1782. *Ethnohistory* 41:4 (fall 1994).

Heap, Nicholas I. *Archival Investigations of DkSd 8 Vancouver Island natural Gas Pipeline, Limekiln Bay, Texada Island.* Brentwood Bay: I.R. Wilson Consultants Ltd., n.d. (1990).

Homfray, Robert. "A winter journey in 1891." The *Province* 1,43:613–617. December 22, 1894.

Hyatt, Allison. *Flower Child Logger: The Condensed life story of David Esmond Dougan.* Self-published, 2010.

Johnson, Bob. *A Better Life: Norm Liebich's autobiography and account of his family, beginning in Germany in 1881.* Self-published, 2007.

Keenleyside, Vi Seaman. *They Also Came: A book of tribute to missionary women of the West Coast as researched and recalled by the author.* Self-published, 1987.

Kennedy, Dorothy and Randy Bouchard. *Sliammon Life, Sliammon Lands.* Vancouver: Talon Books, 1983.

Lamb, W. Kaye, ed. *George Vancouver: A Voyage of Discovery to the North Pacific Ocean and Round the World, 1791–1795.* London: Hakluyt Society, 1984.

Lambert, Barbara. *Chalkdust and Outhouses: West Coast Schools 1893–1950.* Self-published, 2000.

Martinson, Amanda. *A Field Guide to the Rocks and Minerals of Texada Island, British Columbia.* Victoria: First Choice Books, 2009.

May, Cecil et al. *Texada.* Texada Centennial Committee, 1960.

Maylor, Robert. *Blubber Bay, BC.* Handwritten Grade IV school assignment illustrated with black and white photographs, n.d. in Texada Island Historical Society Archives.

McConnell, R.G. *Texada Island.* Ottawa: Geological Survey Memoir 58, 1914.

McDowell, Jim. *José Narváez; The Forgotten Explorer Including His Narrative of a Voyage on the Northwest Coast in 1788.* Spokane: Arthur H. Clark, 1998.

McLeod, Annie. Tape of an interview by CBC's Imbert Orchard, June 20, 1965. BC Archives Tape T0957:0001.

Munro, William F. *Diary of the Christie Party's Trip to the Pacific Coast.* Toronto: C.M. Ellis, 1897.

Parnaby, Andy. *We'll Hang All Policemen from a Sour Apple Tree.* M.A. Thesis, SFU, 1995.

Pedersen, Sandie. "My Great Grandparents." Genealogical report compiled June 2009.

Peterson, Jan. *Black Diamond City: Nanaimo, the Victorian Era.* Surrey: Heritage House, 2002.

Pringle, George C.F. *Adventures in Service.* Toronto: McClelland & Stewart, 1929.

Pringle, George C.F. *In Great Waters: The Story of the United Church Marine Missions.* Toronto: Board of Home Missions of the United Church of Canada, 1928.

Reksten, Terry. *The Dunsmuir Saga.* Vancouver: Douglas & McIntyre, 1991.

Rushton, Gerald. *Echoes of the Whistle: An Illustrated History of the Union Steamship Company.* Vancouver: Douglas & McIntyre, 1980.

Rushton, Gerald. *Whistle up the Inlet.* North Vancouver: J.J. Douglas, 1974.

Scott, Andrew. *The Encyclopedia of Raincoast Place Names.* Madeira Park, BC: Harbour Publishing, 2009.

Southern, Karen. *The Nelson Island Story.* Surrey, BC: Hancock House, 1987.

Staaf, Elmer. Interview with Elmer Staaf by Nan Johnson, taped March 23, 1988. Texada Heritage Society.

Texada Heritage Society Archives Video. A Visit with Edith Poock, Nan Johnson, Sigurd Olson, Lurene Copp, Joe and Marion Little, Glennie McLeod, October 26, 2002.

Texada Heritage Society Archives Video. An Interview with Reg and Selma Kelly, 1988.

Texada Heritage Society Archives Video: An interview with Vera Raper, 1988.

Texada Heritage Society Archives Video. An Interview with Elmer Staaf, March 23, 1988.

Texada Heritage Society Archives Video. An Interview with Joe Kempe, 1988.

Texada Heritage Society Archives Video. The Marshall School Junction cairn, October 1999.

Thompson, G.W. *Boats, Bucksaws and Blisters: Pioneer Tales of the Powell River Area.* Powell River, BC: Powell River Heritage Research Association, 1990.

Thompson, G.W. *Once Upon a Stump: Times and Tales of Powell River Pioneers.* Powell River, BC: Powell River Heritage Research Association, 1993.

Thompson, Bill. *Texada Island.* Powell River, BC: Powell River Heritage Research Association, 1997.

Tilly, Meg. *Singing Songs.* New York: Dutton, 1994.

Turner, Robert S. *The Pacific Princesses: An Illustrated History of Canadian Pacific Railway's Princess Fleet on the Northwest Coast.* Victoria: Sono Nis Press, 1977.

Turner, Robert D. *Those Beautiful Coastal Liners.* Victoria: Sono Nis Press, 2001.

Young, Bill. "Life around Texada Island and Powell River." Arn Olsen interview with Bill Young, recorded May 25, 1973. BC Archives. T11381:0001 of AAAB1521.

Wagner, Henry R. *Spanish Explorations in the Strait of Juan de Fuca.* Santa Ana, CA: Fine Arts Press, 1933.

Walbran, Capt. John T. *British Columbia Coast Names, 1592–1906.* J.J. Douglas, 1971.

Wishlaw, Robert and Howard White. "Pioneers in Paradise: Roy Padgett." *Raincoast Chronicles First Five.* Madeira Park, BC: Harbour Publishing, 1976.

Notes

Introduction

1. BC Department of Mines, Annual Report, 1909, p. K25

Chapter One: Natural History and First Nations

1. Devaney-Taylor, Margaret. Memoirs: 06.31.19. Six tapes and a transcript, held by the Texada Archives.

2. Harris, Cole. "Voices of Disaster: Smallpox around the Strait of Georgia in 1782." *Ethnohistory* 41:4 (fall 1994).

3. Harris, Cole. *The Resettlement of British Columbia: Essays on Colonialism and Geographical Change.* Vancouver, UBC Press, 2000, p.8

4. Harris, Cole. "Voices of Disaster". Note 112, p. 626.

Chapter Two: Exploration and Early Visitors

1. Homfray, Robert. "A Winter Journey in 1891." *The Province*, 1,43:613-617. December 22, 1894.

2. *Daily Standard*, August 18, 1872.

3. Letter from W.A. Hagelund, author of *Whalers No More*, to Teedee Gentile of the Powell River Museum, dated October 6, 1995.

Chapter Three: The Iron Mines

1. British Columbia. Royal Commission on the Acquisition of Texada Island, 1874. Papers relating to the appointment and proceedings.

2. Seaman, Violet. "Black Jack McLeod," Texada Narrative No. 5, *Powell River News*, August 7, 1946, p. 4.

3. BC Department of Mines Annual Report, 1897, p. 564.

4. Interview with Ben Nicholas, November 4, 2009.

Chapter Four: Gold Fever

1. *British Colonist*, December 6, 1898, p. 6.

2. Thompson, Bill. Texada Island. Powell River, Powell River Heritage Research Association, 1997, p. 527.

3. *Nanaimo Free Press*, October 6, 1880.

4. *Nanaimo Free Press*, April 24, 1889.

5. Brewer, William M. *Report on the Copper–Gold–Silver ore deposits on Vancouver and adjacent islands*, in BC Department of Mines Annual Report, 1916, K306. Brewer obtained this information from W.H. Lee, who was on Texada in 1874 and again from 1883 to 1922.

6. *Nanaimo Free Press*, March 18, 1889.

7. *British Colonist*, April 26, 1889, p. 4.

8. *British Colonist*, February 17, 1889, p. 4.

9. *British Colonist*, February 18, 1889, p. 4.

10. Brewer. *Report on the Copper–Gold–Silver ore deposits*, p. 357. Although Brewer says it was discovered in 1903, Planta made his discovery in 1901. See BC Department of Mines Annual Report 1901, p. 1111.

Chapter Five: Gold and Copper Mines

1. *British Colonist*, December 6, 1898, p. 6. James Raper was not present when this discussion took place. If he had been there, perhaps Alfred would have said both of them discovered it, since the contemporary account in *The Weekly News* of August 16, 1893, says it was discovered by James, who seems to have been the only Raper on the island at the time of this reporter's visit.

2. BC Department of Mines Annual Report, 1896, p. 562.

3. Broderick, Henry. *The "HB" Story, Henry Broderick relates Seattle's Yesterdays with some other thoughts by the way*. Seattle: Frank McCaffrey Publishers, 1969.

4. Hines, Neal O. *Denny's Knoll: A History of the Metropolitan Tract of the University of Washington*. Seattle: University of Washington Press, 1980, p. 114–15.

5. *British Colonist*, December 6, 1898, p. 6.

6. BC Department of Mines Annual Report, 1899, p. 801. Brewer's visit was made February 8–12, 1900, but it was included in the 1899 report.

7. BC Departmentof Mines Annual Report, 1899, p. 803.

8. *British Colonist*, August 8, 1899, p. 7.

9. Ibid.

10. Dr. John Sebastian Helmcken (1824–1920) was born in England. He came to BC in 1850 as the Hudson's Bay Company surgeon and stayed to become Speaker of the House from 1856 to 1871. His house on Elliott Street in Victoria is open to the public as a museum.

11. Patsy Schweitzer, granddaughter of Harry W. Treat.

12. Seaman, Violet. "Van Anda Boasted a Real Smelter." *Powell River News*, October 9, 1946, p. 5.

13. McLeod, Annie. Tape of an interview by CBC's Imbert Orchard, June 20, 1965. BC Archives Tape T0957:0001.

14. Reksten, Terry. *The Dunsmuir Saga*. Vancouver: Douglas & McIntyre, 1991, p. 88.

15. BC Department of Mines Annual Report, 1901, p. 1103.

16. Thompson, Bill. Texada Island. Powell River, Powell River Heritage Research Association, 1997, p. 238

17. Ibid.

18. *British Colonist*, April 9, 1908, p. 11.

19. Interview with Jane and Terry Waterman, August 4, 2010.

20. Letter from Fred Beale to his son, Stan, dated May 15, 1958. This was reprinted in *Texada Island Lines*, No. 87, Summer 2005.

21. Thompson, Bill. Texada Island. Powell River, Powell River Heritage Research Association, 1997, p. 110 "Van Anda Destined to Become One of BC's Biggest Gold Mines," in the *Powell River News*, September 21, 1944.

22. On April 5, 1958, this same Victor Dolmage pushed the plunger that blew up Ripple Rock.

23. Thompson, Bill. Texada Island. Powell River, Powell River Heritage Research Association, 1997, p. 416 quoting Jim Brennan, "Texada Looking Backwards," in *Texada Island Lines*, No. 5, Summer 1984.

24. At this stage, the Little Billie was basically a zinc mine. Interview with Pete Stiles, March 4, 2009.

Chapter Six: Marble and Lime

1. *British Colonist*, April 17, 1877, p. 2.

2. *British Colonist*, June 25, 1878, p. 3.

3. Heap, Nicholas I. *Archival Investigations of DkSd 8 Vancouver Island Natural Gas Pipeline, Limekiln Bay, Texada Island*. Brentwood Bay: I.R. Wilson Consultants Ltd. (1990), p. 5.

4. Vancouver District Land Registry Office Document 54180, July 24, 1895.

5. Munro, William F. *Diary of the Christie Party's Trip to the Pacific Coast*, 1897, p. 5.

6. BC Department of Mines Annual Report, 1913, K288.

7. Nicholas, Ben. "Blubber Bay—The Way it Was!"[2] *Texada Island Lines* No. 7, Winter 1984.

8. Maylor, Robert. "Blubber Bay, BC." Handwritten grade four school assignment illustrated with black and white photographs, n.d., in Texada Island Heritage Society Archives.

9. Sometimes Williamson's year of arrival is quoted as 1919, but his daughter, Jean Weisner, lists it as 1917 in her letter to the editor of *Texada Island Lines*, No. 91, Summer 2006. She confirmed this date when I interviewed her October 9, 2008.

10. *BC Lumber Worker*, October 4, 1938. A copy of this hard-to-find document is in the Texada Archives.

11. George's grandson, Gary McLeod, confirmed the two-thousand-dollar figure. Other properties changed hands in the early twentieth century for similar amounts.

12. Johnson, Bob. *A Better Life: Norm Liebich's autobiography and account of his family, beginning in Germany in 1881*. Self-published, 2007, p. 83.

13. Ibid. p. 85.

14. Interview with Alex Fielkowich, April 7, 2010.

15. Interview with Vi Liebich, May 10, 2010.

16. Nicholas. "Blubber Bay." NB: Based on the 1972 voters' list, the correct spelling is Heisholt, not Heischolt as given in this article or Hiesholt as in MINFILE. The name is often misspelled.

17. Stan wanted to call it Beale Bay, but apparently it isn't big enough. To be a bay, there has to be enough room for a boat to have a two-hundred-foot anchor swing.

18. MINFILE 092F 479 Blubber Bay.

19. Interviews with Ed Liebich, March 25, 2010, and Pete Stiles, September 29, 2010.

Chapter Seven: Logging

1. BC Archives. BC Forest Services Timber Licences GR3100, December 18, 1899, W.L. Tait 916; January 1902, W.L. Tait 1203; December 18, 1902, W.L. Tait 1721; January 23, 1904, W.L. Tait 3162.

2. Mason, Elda Copley. *Lasqueti Island: History and Memory.* Lantzville: Byron Mason (c. 1976, National Library), p. 125.

3. "Joseph Eric Little 1916–2004," *Texada Island Lines,* No. 83, Summer 2004.

4. Deighton Store account book in Texada Archives. The N.E. Point Logging Account was dated 1917, and R. Little, Matt Little and Ike Little's names are connected to it.

5. Thompson, Bill. *Texada Island.* Powell River: Powell River Heritage Research Association, 1997, p. 370.

6. Telephone interview with Horace Harrison Jr., August 19, 2010.

7. Interview with Vi Liebich, May 10, 2010.

8. Interview with Nora and Keith Hughes, December 5, 2008.

9. Interview with Margaret Woodhead, September 8, 2010.

10. Hyatt, Allison. *Flower Child Logger.* Self-published, 2010, p. 40.

11. Telephone interview with Dave Dougan, June 10, 2010.

12. Interview with Jocko and Dale Cawthorpe and Chuck Childress, March 10, 2010.

13. Corrigall, Alan. *Looking Backwards*. Self-published, n.d. (1997), p. 69.

14. Claire was the daughter of Bill and Bertha Bushby, who were active participants in the Blubber Bay strike.

15. On the 1956 Gillies Bay Voters List, he is Alfred Shepherd, but Don Pillat said August 25, 2010, that he was known as Bill Shepherd.

16. Interview with Doug and Hughette Paton, September 30, 2009.

17. "J.W. Cuthbertson" newspaper clipping supplied by his son, Bob Cuthbertson.

18. Interview with Pat and Bob Cuthbertson, June 7, 2010.

19. "Oke Wilhelm Nyvall, November 17, 1912–July 26, 2001," *Texada Island Lines*, No. 71, Fall 2001.

20. Ross, Ted. "The Bill Nyvall Story Part II with Memories of Texada Log." *Texada Island Lines*, No. 92, Winter 2007, p. 11.

21. Interview with Carl Hagman Jr., October 21, 2009.

22. "Carl Gustave Hagman, November 6, 1911–June 1, 1996," *Texada Island Lines*, No. 53, Summer 1996.

23. Barbour, Ken. "Texada's Great Ball Game," *Texada Island Lines*, No. 25, 1989.

24. Telephone conversation with Fay Johnson, September 1, 2009.

25. This bay was named for Ezra Stephens Cook (1854–1912), who bought Lot 19 there on April 6, 1889.

Chapter Eight: Early Settlers 1895–1919

1. Seaman, Violet article, "Jim Raper, Keen Island Miner." *Powell River News*, November 6, 1946, p. 6.

2. *Henderson Directories* under City of Vancouver. Edmund and William Raper appear in 1906. They and Raper Bros. Stationery at 734 Westminster Ave. appear in 1907. In 1908 Alfred Raper, Prospector, together with his wife, Edmund and William Raper, are all living at 1815 Westminster Ave., and Raper Bros. is still at 734 Westminster Ave.

3. *British Colonist* June 6, 1897, p. 6 (but in the story in *British Colonist* May 15, 1897, p. 6, it said they were $75–$150).

4. McKelvie, Bruce. "Old Texada Days," *Province* magazine section, October 23, 1943, p. 5.

5. Sigsworth, Virginia. "Texada Island Church History," *Texada Island Lines*, No. 48, Spring 1995.

6. Seaman, Vi. "The Little White Church." Texada Narrative #24. *Powell River News*, July 23, 1947.

7. Seaman, Violet. "Gay Nineties' Big Days," *Powell River News*, October 16, 1946, p. 4 and "Island's Social Life Was Lusty and Loud," *Powell River News*, October 23, 1946, p. 10.

8. Young, William. Tape of an interview by CBC's Imbert Orchard, June 20, 1965. BC Archives Tape T090958:0001.

9. McLeod, Annie. Tape of an interview by CBC's Imbert Orchard, June 20, 1965. BC Archives Tape T0957:0001.

10. McKelvie, Bruce. "Colourful Early BC Name Disappears: Twin Cities of Texada and Van Anda are Merged." *Vancouver Province* magazine section, October 16, 1963; Nicholas, Ben. "In Search of Antique Bottles," *Texada Island Lines*, No. 95, Winter 2008.

11. B.A. McKelvie. "The social graces doomed this paper." *Vancouver Province*, October 10, 1959, p. 44, in the Story of the Week column.

12. Rushton, Gerald. *Whistle up the Inlet*. North Vancouver: J.J. Douglas, 1974, p. 43.

13. Ibid., pg. 67.

14. *The Cheslakee Story*. In an interview with Ben Nicholas, Mr. and Mrs. Young of Van Anda provide an alternative account of the sinking of the SS *Cheslakee* at Van Anda on January 7, 1913. The official records state that seven people lost their lives in the sinking. However, Mr. Young maintains that eleven additional men were drowned and never reported. These men were allegedly loggers who were locked in the ship's "bull pen." Powell River Television, 1987. BC Archives V1987:17/0001.

15. McLeod, Annie. Tape of an interview by CBC's Imbert Orchard, June 20, 1965. BC Archives Tape T0957:0001.

16. McKelvie, B.A. "Colourful Early BC Name Disappears; Twin Cities of Texada and Van Anda are Merged." *Province* magazine section, October 16, 1943.

17. Hadley, Michael. *God's Little Ships: A History of the Columbia Coast Mission.* Madeira Park, BC: Harbour Publishing, 1995, p. 32.

18. MacDermot, J.H. "The Early Medical History of the BC Coast." *The Bulletin* [of the Vancouver Medical Association], 1935: 3-13. Quoted in Hadley, Michael. *God's Little Ships: A History of the Columbia Coast Mission.* Madeira Park, BC: Harbour Publishing, 1995, p. 150.

19. Seaman, Violet. "Off to Gillies Bay." *Powell River News*, September 3, 1947, p. 10.

20. Interview with Donna Lechner, October 6, 2010.

21. Thompson, G.W. *Once Upon a Stump: Times and Tales of Powell River Pioneers.* Powell River, BC: Powell River Heritage Research Association, 1993, p. 93, quoting a series of articles from the *Powell River News* beginning February 10, 1954.

22. "Fascinating Centenarians," *Texada Island Lines*, No. 31, Winter 1990.

23. Southern, Karen. *The Nelson Island Story.* Surrey, BC: Hancock House, 1987, p. 29.

24. Nicholas, Ben. "The Evolution of Texada's Marine Transportation," *Texada Island Lines*, No. 29, Summer 1990.

25. Anderson, G.P. "Correction." *Northwest Digest*, May 1953. G.P. Anderson was Charlie Anderson's nephew.

26. Pringle, George C.F. *Adventures in Service.* Toronto: McClelland & Stewart, 1929, pp. 39–49.

27. Interview with Maurice Liebich, Mrs. Blanchard's grandson, September 9, 2009.

28. Thompson, G.W. *Boats, Bucksaws and Blisters: Pioneer Tales of the Powell River Area.* Powell River: Powell River Heritage Research Association, 1990, p. 160.

29. Thompson, Bill. *Texada Island.* Powell River: Powell River Heritage Research Association, 1997, p. 103, quoting the *Powell River News* from March 7, 1940.

30. "Mural Part One," *Texada Island Lines*, No. 56, Spring 1997. This information probably came from Edith Stromberg, who once took piano lessons from Mr. Pooke's wife prior to 1910.

31. "Deighton's Store Records Go to Heritage Archives." *Texada Island Lines*, No. 43, Winter 1993. Nicholas, Ben. "Golden Memories," *Texada Island Lines*, No. 27, Winter 1989.

32. Staaf, P.A. "Texada Island, Gulf of Georgia." *Agricultural Journal*, July 1923.

33. Pedersen, Sandie. "My Great Grandparents." Genealogical report compiled June 2009.

34. Interview with Nora and Keith Hughes, December 5, 2008.

35. Interview with Ted Ross, March 15, 2010.

36. George Edward Whittaker's Crown grant B14350 is dated May 18, 1917. Mason, Elda Copley. *Lasqueti Island: History and Memory.* Lantzville: Byron Mason, c. 1976. p. 58 mentions a visit to the "Whitacker" [*sic*] family by Elda Copley's family about 1916. The row across from Rouse Bay on Lasqueti was so rough that they had to stay overnight. No information is given about the Whittakers.

37. Dougan, Jimmy. "Whittaker's Journey," *Texada Island Lines*, No. 88, Fall 2005. The editorial preface to this article refers as a source to a book called Edith Copley Mason's Lasqueti Days. This is not on the National Library's mandatory deposit list, but may mean Elda Copley Mason's book *Lasqueti Island: History and Memory.* Lantzville: Byron Mason (c. 1976).

38. Hyatt, Allison. *Flower Child Logger: The Condensed Life Story of David Esmond Dougan*. Self-published, 2010, p. 68.

Chapter Nine: The Lean Years 1920–1939

1. Ross, Ted. "The fallen, whom we remember," *Texada Island Lines*, No. 71, Summer 2001. Sandie Pedersen obtained these from the Commonwealth War Graves Commission.

2. Brinton, Stewart. "Old Fred." Unpublished manuscript dated 2006, Texada Archives.

3. Wishlaw, Robert and White, Howard. "Pioneers in Paradise: Roy Padgett." *Raincoast Chronicles First Five*. Madeira Park, BC: Harbour Publishing, 1976, p. 262.

4. Interview with Maurice and Irene Liebich, November 11, 2009. They heard Vera Liebich (1920–2002) tell the story.

5. Hopgood, Evelyn, "Remembering the Blanchard Family," *Texada Island Lines*, 42, Fall 1993. This article says the Blanchard family moved to Blubber Bay in 1925, so Carter's sawmill must have closed before this.

6. Interview with Peter McGuigan, May 12, 2010.

7. Ross, Duncan. "Blubber Bay Consumerism Circa 1925," *Texada Island Lines* 35, Winter 1991.

8. Interview with Dave and Lynn Myers, May 13, 2009.

9. Johnson, Bob. *A Better Life: Norm Liebich's Autobiography and Account of His Family, Beginning in Germany in 1881*. Self-published, 2007, p. 51.

10. Hacking, Norman. "Maritime Museum Gains Empress Bell." Unidentified and undated newspaper clipping supplied by Gord Coupland.

11. Interview with Randall Yip, October 9, 2008.

12. Ross, Duncan. "Childhood Reminiscences," *Texada Island Lines* 35, Winter 1991, p. 7.

13. Devaney-Taylor, Margaret. Memoirs: 03.31.19. Six tapes held by the Texada Archives on a restricted basis.

14. Brinton, Stewart. "The Pocahontas Caper," *Raincoast Chronicles, Six/Ten Collectors' Edition*, Madeira Park, BC: Harbour Publishing, 1983, pp. 246–47.

15. Inkster, Tom H. "Texada Island Endures," *BC Historical News* Vol. 22, No. 3, Summer 1989.

16. George McKee. "Dwellers in hidden coast corners: Ed Russ," *Texada Island Lines*, No. 29, Summer 1990.

17. Telephone interview with Eleanor Hoeg, February 19, 2010.

18. Texada Archives Video: A Visit with Edith Poock, Nan Johnson, Sigurd Olson, Lurene Copp, Joe and Marion Little, Glennie McLeod. October 26, 2002. Also a written version in *Texada Island Lines*, Summer 1985, quoted by Thompson, p. 99.

19. "Keith Johnson, October 1, 1911–February 3, 1999," *Texada Island Lines*, No. 64, Spring 1999.

20. Interview with Janet Lipus, August 11, 2010.

21. Ross, Ted. "The Bill Nyvall Story Part II with Memories of Texada Log." *Texada Island Lines*, No. 92, Winter 2007.

22. Interview with Frieda Woodhead, May 19, 2010.

23. Interview with Nora and Keith Hughes, December 5, 2008.

Chapter 10: The War Years 1939–1945

1. Interview with Vi Liebich, May 10, 2010.

2. Interview with Randall Yip, October 9, 2008

3. Yip, Robert. "Former Texada Resident Quene Yip Inducted into the BC Sports Hall of Fame," *Texada Island Lines*, No. 62, Fall 1998.

4. Interview with Maurice and Irene Liebich, April 7, 2010.

5. Interview with Frieda Blasha Woodhead, May 19, 2010.

Chapter Eleven: The Post-War Years 1946–1960

1. "Texada Trivia." *Texada Island Lines*, No. 8, Spring 1985, p. 2.

2. Interview with Janet Copp Lipus, August 11, 2010.

3. Interview with Carl Hagman, August 25, 2010.

4. Corrigall, Alan. *Looking Backwards*. Self-published, n.d. (1997), p. 36.

5. Telephone conversation with Maria Zaikow, July 23, 2010.

6. Carl Hagman, Mike Harrison, Bob Jones and Art Liebich were among those operating the equipment, according to my interviews with Rick Jones and Art Liebich.

7. According to the *Powell River News*, September 6, 1951, these were: Van Anda Logging, Iron Bark Logging, Sandy Island Logging, Marshall's Logging, Dukers, Beale's Quarries, Stanley Beale Limestone, Imperial Oil, Al Waters, Home Oil and the merchants of Van Anda.

8. Interview with Billie and Jim Johnson, August 18, 2010.

9. Lambert, Barbara. *Chalkdust and Outhouses: West Coast Schools 1893–1950.* Self-published, 2000, p. 259.

10. Interview with Ted Ross, March 15, 2010.

11. Interview with Frieda Woodhead, May 19, 2010.

12. Interview with Maurice and Irene Liebich, April 7, 2010.

13. Kelly, Pat. "Elma Haapanen, an Unforgettable Character," *Texada Island Lines*, No. 51, Winter 1995.

14. Nicholas, Ben. "Farewell: A Fond Farewell to Elma Haapanen," *Texada Island Lines*, No. 25, Summer 1989.

15. Interview with Pete Stiles, August 12, 2010.

16. Clipping from Glennith McLeod's scrapbook, Texada Archives.

17. "Elma Haapanen, 1907–1995," *Texada Island Lines* No. 50, Fall 1995.

18. Interview with Doug Paton, October 21, 2009.

19. Interview with Keith Hughes, August 25, 2010.

20. Interview with Pete Stiles, mining engineer, March 5, 2009.

21. Hughes, Nora A. "Rock Island Players—Remember?" *Texada Island Lines* No. 35, Winter 1991.

Chapter Twelve: The Boom Years 1961–1976

1. Interview with Beryl and Gord Coupland and Beryl's daughter, Cheryl Nyl, June 7, 2010.

2. Grieco, Gary. "Texada Boat Club – Past and Present," *Texada Island Lines*, Winter 2004.

3. Interview with Frieda Woodhead, May 19, 2010.

4. Interview with Jocko and Dale Cawthorpe and Chuck Childress, March 10, 2010.

5. Interview with Skip Waldorf and his daughters, Mary Anne and Tami, April 14, 2010.

6. Interview with Leonard Ryan.

7. Ibid.

8. Interview with John Zaikow, March 2, 2010.

9. "In Memorium." *Texada Island Lines* No. 17, Summer 1987. Grieco, Gary. "Texada Boat Club – Past and Present," *Texada Island Lines*, Winter 2004.

10. Interview with Ted Ross, March 15, 2010.

11. The spelling of this name causes much controversy. The Texada Archives has a book that belonged to Stan and the name inside it is spelled: HEISHOLT.

12. Interview with Pete Stiles, November 25, 2009.

13. Tilly, Meg. *Singing Songs*. New York: Dutton, 1994.

14. Email, September 14, 2010 from Brian Brett, author of *Trauma Farm*. Vancouver: Greystone Books, 2009, pp. 57–58 and 116.

15. Interview with Pete Stiles, mining engineer, March 5, 2009.

16. "Gustav Herman Liebich, November 5, 1911–November 23, 1998," *Texada Island Lines* No. 63, Winter 1998.

Chapter Thirteen: The Protest Years 1977–1990

1. Dale Robillard, nicknamed Doby.

2. Interview with Christine Woolcott and Leonard Ryan, July 5, 2010.

3. Meunier, Josée. "Memories of Davie Bay, Texada Island 1979–1983," in Lambert, Barbara, *Chalkdust and Outhouses: West Coast Schools 1893–1950*. Self-published, 2000.

4. "The John Kelly Gallery," *Texada Island Lines* No. 25, Summer 1989.

5. Interview with John Zaikow, March 2, 2010.

6. "First in BC," *Texada Island Lines*, No. 14, Fall 1986.

7. Nicholas, Ben. "It's Wake-up Time, Texada," *Texada Island Lines*, No. 60, Spring 1998.

Chapter Fourteen: The Tourism and Retiree Years 1991–2010

1. *Rock Island Lines*, July 1983, p. 1.

2. "Jazz on the Rocks," *Texada Island Lines* No. 91, Summer 2006. See also www.jazzontherocks.org

3. "Texada Island Quick-Build," *Texada Island Lines* No. 41, Summer 1993.

4. Email from Capt. Jack Renton, BC Ferries, February 25, 2009.

Photographs are indicated in **bold**.